James Harrison Wilson

China

Travels and investigations in the middle kingdom. Vol. 1

James Harrison Wilson

China
Travels and investigations in the middle kingdom. Vol. 1

ISBN/EAN: 9783337135812

Printed in Europe, USA, Canada, Australia, Japan

Cover: Foto ©Andreas Hilbeck / pixelio.de

More available books at **www.hansebooks.com**

TRAVELS AND INVESTIGATIONS IN THE "MIDDLE KINGDOM"

A STUDY OF
ITS CIVILIZATION AND POSSIBILITIES

WITH A GLANCE AT JAPAN

BY

JAMES HARRISON WILSON
LATE MAJOR-GENERAL UNITED STATES VOLUNTEERS, AND
BREVET MAJOR-GENERAL UNITED STATES ARMY

SECOND EDITION

NEW YORK
D. APPLETON AND COMPANY
1894

TO
COLONEL LEGRAND B. CANNON,
OF NEW YORK,

A LOYAL CITIZEN, A GOOD SOLDIER, AND A TRUE FRIEND,

THE FOLLOWING PAGES ARE INSCRIBED,

WITH THE AFFECTIONATE REGARDS OF

THE AUTHOR.

PREFACE TO THE SECOND EDITION.

The war now in progress between China and Japan seems to justify a second edition of this work. It is quite as true now in all essential particulars as it was when it was written. The young Emperor, the aged Viceroy, and the progressive Liu Ming-Chu'an, are each a few years older; the Seventh Prince and the Marquis Tseng have died, but China and its institutions, its government and its people have undergone no perceptible change.

The Empress-Dowager is perhaps still the most powerful personage in the empire, and will doubtless exert the full influence of her vigorous mind upon the course of events and upon the government of her nephew; but the government itself is yet without an adequate revenue or fiscal system, an adequate army or navy, an adequate civil or military administration, or adequate means of transport for the successful conduct of war by sea or land. It has discharged its most efficient foreign officers, and, while it has some troops armed with modern firearms and some fine foreign-built men-of-war, it is but poorly prepared to withstand the vigorous advance of a well-disciplined and well-commanded modern army or navy.

The railroad from Tientsin and Tongku (near Taku) to the Kaiping coal-mines has been extended through the coal fields, in the direction of Manchuria, to Shan-hai-Quan, the point on the Gulf of Pechihli from which the Great Wall takes its start. The entire length of this road is about two hundred miles. Its most important service is to carry coal to the Chinese fleet and merchant steamers, but as it is nowhere more than two days' march, and in many places less than a single day's march, from the sea, it offers an additional objective of great importance to an invading army.

The resources of the Chinese Empire, and of the nineteen provincial governments of China Proper, in men, are almost illimitable; but without modern organization, a military chest, the means of transport, and even of any high degree of patriotism, it will be difficult, if not almost impossible, for them to utilize these resources in time to prevent national disgrace and humiliation.

Special attention is called to the character and services of the Viceroy Li, to the memorials of Liu Ming-Chu'an (now the commanding general of the Chinese forces in the field), and of Tso-Tsung-Tang in regard to the introduction of railroads; also to the machinery of the Government at Peking, and to its fiscal system, as set forth in the following pages.

On the other hand, while China has stood still for the last decade, Japan, with a modernized government, under the control of able statesmen; a compact and thoroughly disciplined army, fully armed and equipped according to the best European practice; an excellent navy, with a full complement of modern ironclads and gunboats of the best English and German types, provided with the best high-power guns, and manned by thoroughly educated officers and well-trained men, has moved forward with rapid strides, and seems to be ready at every point for an active aggressive war.

The struggle is an interesting one. It has its origin primarily in the claim of China to suzerainty over Corea, complicated by the further fact that Japan is separated from that country by a strait only about seventy miles wide, across which the Japanese have gone in great numbers for the purpose of trading. The Corean Government and its officials are corrupt and oppressive, and have become more so of late; the people of the southern provinces have rebelled, and were threatening to march upon the capital. A spirit of lawlessness has spread throughout the country; many acts of violence have been committed against foreigners, and specially against the Japanese. The King's troops naturally sympathized with the rebels, and this in turn had paralyzed the Government.

At this juncture the Chinese minister, who is really regarded by his government as a Resident at Seoul, succeeded in inducing the King to ask for the assistance of Chinese troops, whereupon several thousand were sent into the country. These were followed by others shortly, and as this was regarded by Japan not only as a violation of the treaty existing between the two countries, but as adding to the outrages already inflicted upon her citizens by the Coreans, she proceeded at once, and without formal notice, with a fleet of twenty-eight transports and war-ships, ten thousand soldiers of all arms, three thousand coolies, and all the necessary *matériel* of war, to effect a landing upon the coast, and to march to Seoul, the capital, which is now completely under her domination.

What the relative rights of the combatants, the course of events, and the results of the struggle may be, the future alone can reveal, but it is believed that the facts set forth in the following pages will materially help the reader to form a correct estimate of the condition of the two countries, the habits of their people, and their aptitude and readiness for war.

In view of the fact that the two great rival Asiatic powers, Russia and England, are profoundly interested in the conflict, and that the present Government of China is one of conquest, threatened at all times by rebellion within, it is not impossible that the war now in progress may lead to important and far-reaching changes in the condition of Eastern Asia.

WILMINGTON, DELAWARE, *August* 16, 1894.

PREFACE TO THE FIRST EDITION.

OWING to the universal depression in trade for the last five years, China has strongly attracted the attention of the whole world, and especially of England, Germany, France, and the United States, as the only great country yet remaining to be provided with railroads. In the spring of 1885 I turned my attention in that direction; but, when I sought to obtain specific information as to the actual condition of affairs in respect to railroads and other modern improvements, and the readiness of the Chinese Government and people for their introduction, I could learn nothing whatever upon which it seemed to be safe to base calculations or draw conclusions. After conferring with a few friends in New York, who had also been impressed with the same general fact, and were looking about to discover new fields for American skill, enterprise, and capital, and who also found themselves utterly unable to get trustworthy information, I resolved for our common benefit to visit the countries beyond the Pacific, and see for myself whether they were ready for railroads, whether, if built, railroads would probably pay, and also whether the construction and management of them could be secured for Americans, under such terms and conditions, as promised fair returns for the skill and capital employed, and the risk involved.

I saw no other means of satisfactorily solving the questions which presented themselves. The correspondence of our diplomatic and consular agents was silent on those points, or unattainable; and, even if it had not been, it could not have been expected to contain anything more than the most general statement of facts. Hitherto our diplomatic agents, with a few exceptions, in Oriental countries at least, had imitated the traditionary diplomatic policy of Europe, and ignored such questions, avoiding as far as possible all official notice and discussion of commerce, manufactures, and the multitude of industries and public undertakings usually carried on by associated capital and labor, and which constitute the chief feature of what we call modern progress. An occasional traveler of a more practical turn of mind, or here and there a still more occasional newspaper correspondent, had called attention to the absence of railroads, collieries, furnaces, and rolling-mills in China, so that the general fact became known; but neither diplomatist, traveler, nor correspondent had yet furnished to the public any information, worthy of the name, bearing on the great question herein alluded to.

Turn which way I might, I could get no adequate account of the real situation in China. I therefore left New York for San Francisco on the 8th of September, 1885, and sailed thence for Yokohama and Shanghai on the 19th of the same month, by the Pacific Mail Company's steamship City of Peking, Captain Berry commanding. I had, of course, provided myself with a letter of credit, and such letters of introduction to diplomatic and consular agents, and to American merchants residing in the treaty ports, as I could obtain in the short time left me after I had made up my mind to go. The voyage to Yokohama lasted twenty-two days, and to Shanghai eight days more.

Without any definite information or prearranged plan, I hoped my travels and investigations would not require more than five or six months at the outside, and, as winter was approaching, I hurried forward to Tientsin, the port of Peking and of Northern China, but specially important as the principal residence of Li Hung-Chang, First Grand Secretary of the Empire, Viceroy of Chihli (the metropolitan province), and, since the suppression of the Taiping rebellion, one of the most conspicuous and influential men in China. Having been received by him with every mark of distinction, and after several conferences, during which he imparted his views fully and frankly to me, at his personal request I made journies to Taku, Kaiping, Peking, the Great Wall, and finally to the Yellow River and beyond, for the purpose of inspecting its embankments, and also of examining the Grand Canal and the country adjacent to them. During this last-mentioned journey, which was made in midwinter, I traveled over fifteen hundred miles on horseback, through the provinces of Chihli, Honan, and Shantung. I visited Kaifung-fu, the capital of Honan, and Chinan-fu, the capital of Shantung; and also Kü-fu, celebrated as the home and burial-place of Confucius. I climbed Taishan, the sacred mountain of China, and passed through many important towns and cities.

On my return to Tientsin I had several interviews with the Viceroy Li and other high Chinese officials, again visited Peking for two weeks, and, finally, almost immediately after the ice broke up in the Pei-ho and navigation was resumed, I sailed for Shanghai. From this place I made a trip up the Yang-tse-kiang, during which I visited Chinkiang and Nanking, and had an interview with Tseng Quo-Chu'an, the venerable and distinguished Viceroy of the Kiang provinces. Returning to Shanghai, I sailed for Japan, touching again at Nagasaki and Simonoseki, and landing at Kobe. From the latter place I went by rail to Osaka and Kioto, where I remained for several days. Resuming my journey, I went by rail to Otsu, at the eastern end of Lake Biwa, crossed by steamer to Nagahama and took the railroad again thence to Sekigahara. Here I employed *jinrikishas*,* or man-power carriages, and continued my travels by the Nakasendo, or the road of the central mountains to Yokogawa and Sakimoto, where I again took rail for Tokio and Yokohama.

Having spent the whole of May, the loveliest month of the year, in traveling through the most beautiful country in the world, I returned to Shanghai, and at the invitation of Liu Ming-Chu'an, the energetic and capable Governor-General of Formosa, I visited that island and spent a week in traveling over its northern end, examining its rivers and harbors, and studying its resources. While there I received an invitation by telegraph to revisit the Viceroy Li, and accordingly re-embarked on the Chinese steam-transport Way Lee, Captain Danielsen commanding, for Shanghai, where I transferred to an English steamer for Tientsin. I remained at the last-mentioned place for two weeks, and then set out for home by the way of Shanghai, Nagasaki, Kobe, Yokohama, and San Francisco. I arrived at New York with-

* Invented by an American missionary.

out accident or unusual delay; but, instead of having been gone only six months, as I had hoped, my absence had extended to within three weeks of a year.

Although my travels had carried me over nearly thirty thousand miles by sea and land, and had taken me to many places out of the usual path of travelers, I doubt if they would of themselves justify another book on China and Japan; but in view of the important personages I met, the information I obtained, and the class of questions which principally engaged my attention, it seems to me that I am warranted in submitting the following pages to the public, and in requesting its indulgent consideration of the same. In this my friends and correspondents at home have expressed their concurrence, and must bear with me the responsibility for any disappointment which they or the public may suffer at my hands.

It is suggested furthermore that, notwithstanding the great number of books on China, there is at this time room for another, which should briefly tell what China and the Chinese were before foreign influences had materially changed them, what foreigners have done for or forced them to do, and what remains for foreigners to do, with the prospect of their doing it. In other words, it should make progress in China its burden and text, and in the narrative which follows I have kept that text constantly in mind, and aimed to give the reader the materials for forming an intelligent opinion in reference to it. If any one wishes to obtain a more comprehensive account of China and the Chinese, within the limits of a single work, he can not possibly do better than to study carefully and diligently the latest edition of the "Middle Kingdom," by S. Wells Williams, for many years a leading missionary, and at various times secretary of legation and *chargé d'affaires* for the United States at Peking. These volumes are the adopted standard authority of all foreigners and foreign legations in China, and are an enduring monument to the profound learning and the great application of their author. I have drawn freely upon them, and hereby acknowledge my indebtedness to them.

The history of the Chinese Government and the dynasties which have controlled it is for the greater part an arid waste of intrigue, anarchy, and violence, varied with an almost endless series of internal and external wars. Here and there a great soldier or an honest and capable ruler emerges from the chaos and confusion, and governs the country wisely and well. He may be a Mongolian border-man, like the great Genghis or his son Kublai Khan; a native Chinaman, like Hung-Wu; or a Manchu Tartar, like Tienming, the founder of the present dynasty; but the great rulers of China can be counted on the fingers of one hand, while the essence of their history can be told in a few short chapters. But a full and faithful account of dynasties and rulers, whether good or bad, can be found in Boulger's "China," to which I refer the reader who has the time and inclination to devote to the subject.

There are besides many interesting books of travel, describing with greater or less detail the various parts of the country. At the head of this list stands the story of Marco Polo, edited by Colonel Yule, but candor compels me to say of even this remarkable narrative that the editor's notes are much more interesting and instructive than the text to which they refer. I wish to acknowledge here my indebtedness

PREFACE TO THE FIRST EDITION.   xv

to both Boulger and Yule, and also to Wilson's "Life of Gordon," and various other works of minor importance bearing upon the history of the Taiping rebellion. I am satisfied, however, that no proper account has yet been written of that important period of modern Chinese history, unless it is contained in the forthcoming "Life of Li Hung-Chang," by William N. Pethick, Esq., United States Vice-consul at Tientsin, to whom I am especially indebted for information upon every topic connected with China and the Chinese. His long residence in China and his intimate association with Li Hung-Chang, to whom he has also filled the position of secretary for many years, naturally make him an acknowledged authority, at least with Americans, on all Chinese questions. He is, besides, an accomplished scholar of Chinese literature, and both speaks and writes the language with great facility. I am also indebted to Dr. W. A. P. Martin, President of the Tung-Wen College at Peking, and author of the "Hanlin Papers," for much valuable information.

To Colonel Charles Denby, our able and distinguished minister at Peking, I am specially indebted for introductions and presentations, as well as for information and assistance which could not have been obtained from any other source, and without which my mission would have come to a speedy close. It must be as gratifying to every American citizen, without reference to party, to know that his country has never been more ably or creditably represented in China than it is now, as it is for me to make this statement. Not only the minister and his family, but his secretaries, Mr. W. W. Rockhill, Mr. Charles Denby, Jr., and Mr. F. D. Cheshire, are in every way worthy representatives of the country, and it is a source of unalloyed satisfaction to me to be able to speak of them, conscientiously as I do, in terms of unqualified praise and respect.

Finally, I am under many obligations for information and assistance to the American house of Russell & Co., and its able and enterprising partners and agencies in all the treaty ports as well as in Formosa, and especially to C. Vincent Smith, Esq., the senior partner at Shanghai; also to E. J. Smithers, Esq., acting consul-general at Shanghai; to George T. Bromley, Esq., consul at Tientsin; Richard B. Hubbard, Esq., our minister to Tokio; to Henry W. Denison and Durham W. Stevens, Esqs., advisers to the Japanese Foreign Office; and to Thomas and John Walsh, Esqs., of Messrs. Walsh, Hall & Co., Yokohama.

STOCKFORD, *near* WILMINGTON, DELAWARE, *March* 12, 1887.

NOTE.—The best general map of China is Keith Johnson's, in one or four sheets. That of Baron Richthofen is best for geology and topography.

CONTENTS.

CHAPTER I.

First visit to Japan—Genuine progress of the Japanese—Inland Sea—Return to Japan—The Nakasendo—Tokio—Received by the Emperor—The palace—The ministers and attendants—The Emperor — Ceremonials — The emancipation of the Emperor from the domination of the Tycoon—Tiffin at Uyeno Park—Dinner-party in Japanese style—Country-place and duck-pond—Gaishas—Wrestlers and wrestling—Saki and health-drinking—Kissing an innovation—Excursions—The progress and civilization of the Japanese genuine—The government and ministry—The governing class—Schools and colleges—Railroads—The prosperity of the people—Art and artisans—The original conservatism of the Japanese—The progressive movement—The Satsuma rebellion—The triumph of the progressive party—Acknowledgment of Japanese autonomy by the American Government—Treaty revision—No field for American railway-builders—Demand for American products—Delightful country for the traveler 1

CHAPTER II.

Voyage through the Inland Sea—Mouth of the Yang-tse-kiang—The Wusung River—Shanghai—Foreign and Chinese city contrasted—Chinese civilization—Ward and the Taiping rebellion—Li Hung-Chang and Tseng Quo-Fan—Future importance of Shanghai 19

CHAPTER III.

Area of China—Reached its greatest extent under Kublai Khan—Almost as great under the late Regent—China's isolated position—Approach of railroads toward western border—Communi-

xviii *CONTENTS.*

PAGE

cation by steamships—Civilization different from any other—
Origin of names of country—Provinces—Climate—Surface—
Hwang-ho, or Yellow River—Delta, or Great Plain—Inundations
—Embankments—Change of river-bed 26

CHAPTER IV.

The Yang-tse-kiang—Its navigation—Its various names—Its tributaries—Its floods—Canals and creeks in the delta—Area of its water-shed—The Chukiang or Pearl River—The Min—The Peiho and its tributaries—The Peh-tang—The New-Chwang and the Ta-wen-ho 40

CHAPTER V.

The surface of the country—Sinian Mountain system—The highlands and hill country—Origin of the loëss terraces—The outlying dependencies—Corea, Manchuria, Mongolia, Ili, Turkistan, and Thibet—The Great Plain or delta—Coal, iron, and other minerals—The Kaiping coal-mines and railroad—The first locomotive built in China—The coal-mines of Formosa and Shansi—Coal transported in wheelbarrows—The development of coal and iron receiving Government attention—Foreign experts required—Conservatism of the Government 48

CHAPTER VI.

Population of China—No complete census ever taken—The country not overcrowded—Influence of famines, rebellions, pestilence, and floods—Reproduction normal and active—Population probably greater than ever before—Country capable of supporting three times as many inhabitants—Origin of the Chinese race—Physical characteristics—Compression of feet—Manchus do not practice the custom—Its origin—Failure to practice it looked upon as evidence of abject poverty and distress—Food of the Chinese people—Domestic animals 63

CHAPTER VII.

The houses of the Chinese—The clothing—The great public works—The walled cities—The only crystallized and accumulated labor of the Chinese—The effect of depopulation—The com-

CONTENTS. xix

mon people everywhere poor—No system of popular education —No conception of or vocabulary for science—Diversity of dialects—The classical or literary language of the country— The greater wall of China—Chinese civilization—The characteristics of the race—Arrested development—Future progress . 75

CHAPTER VIII.

Voyage from Shanghai to Tientsin—China Merchants' Steam Navigation Company—American house of Russell and Company put the first steamboats on the Yang-tse—Sold them to the China Merchants' Company—Coast of Shan-tung—Chee-foo—Naval station at Port Arthur badly located—The northern fleet— Board of Admiralty—Command of the northern fleet—Need of educated officers—The Taku forts and dock-yard—"Heaven-sent barriers"—Chinese troops drilled by foreign officers in English—Chinese army badly organized, armed, and administered —The Pei-ho—Villages on its banks—Grave-mounds, and burial of the dead—Fung-shuy or geomancy—Difficulty of laying out railroads without removal of graves—How that can be managed . 85

CHAPTER IX.

Races at Tientsin—Chinese band playing American airs—No social intercourse between Chinese and foreigners—Removal of grave-mounds to make way for the race-course—Political and commercial importance of Tientsin — The foreign settlement — Foreign gunboats—The Viceroy Li Hung-Chang—His American secretary—First call upon the Viceroy—His official residence or Yamen—Subjects discussed—Railroads and canals—Intelligence and interest displayed by the Viceroy—Ceremony of leave-taking—"Setting the watch" 101

CHAPTER X.

Li Hung-Chang—His public career—Influence of Generals Ward and Gordon—English misconception of their character—The career of Burgevine—The influence of the war threatened with Russia—Gordon revisited China — The introduction of telegraphs—Messages sent in English, or cipher—Memorial of Liu Ming-Chu'an on the introduction of railways—Referred to Li

Hung-Chang and Lin K'un-Yi—The memorial of Li Hung-Chang and Lin K'un-Yi—Tso Tsung-Tang's dying memorial on the same subject—No official action yet taken thereupon—The essence of progress and the death-knell of conservatism . . 118

CHAPTER XI.

Visit to Peking—The unspeakably filthy city of the world—Its origin and characteristics—No suburbs or villas—Streets not paved—The foreign legations and society—Non-intercourse between court and diplomatic corps—The young Emperor—The Empress-Dowager—Her unlimited power—The censors—The Emperor worships at the tomb of his ancestors—The influences which control him—He can hardly become a conservative—The difficulties of his situation—Unprepared for a foreign war . 160

CHAPTER XII.

The Emperor an absolute monarch—The Government patriarchal in form—Liberty unknown—Slavery exists—No hereditary nobility except the imperial clan and heads of the families of Confucius and Koxinga—The literati are the office-holders—The Imperial Government—The Grand Secretariat—The General Council—The " Peking Gazette "—The Six Great Boards—The Tsung-li Yamen—The Censorate or all-examining court—The minor courts and boards—The functions f the great boards—Power greatly divided and distributed—The provincial governments—All officers selected by public examination—Defects of the system—Li Hung-Chang's position somewhat like that of the British Premier—Foreign ministers not yet received by the Emperor or Empress-Dowager—Much of the foreign business done by provincial governors—The central Government isolated and inaccessible—Difficulty of communicating or transacting business with it 179

CHAPTER XIII.

The eyes of the world now turned toward China as a field for investment in public undertakings—Its financial system—No statistics except those of the maritime customs—The revenues collected by " farmers "—The growth of the system—The

CONTENTS. xxi

PAGE

sources of the imperial Chinese revenue—The land-tax—The salt monopoly—The likin, or internal transit tax—Miscellaneous taxes—Maritime customs duties—Summary—Comparison of Chinese and British Indian revenues—Estimates made by various persons—No correct account can be given of the expenditures of the Chinese Government—Approximate estimate —The funded debt—Fear of the Chinese Government to negotiate foreign loans—Its obligations good and negotiable for $100,000,000—The Chinese slow to lend to their Government —No statistics of private wealth—Thought to be capable of raising $100,000,000, if properly secured—Necessity of measures to promote confidence 200

CHAPTER XIV.

Visit to the Great Wall—Decay of the ancient road through the Nankou Pass—Mongolian caravans—Origin, uses, and description of the wall—The return to Nankou—The ride to the Ming tombs—Description of the inclosures and buildings—The Avenue of Statuary—The return to Peking 215

CHAPTER XV.

The Kai-ping coal-mines and railway—The first locomotive-engine built in China—Extension of the railway to Lutai—The Kai-ping coal-measures—Output of the mines 226

CHAPTER XVI.

Trip to the Yellow River—"China's Sorrow"—Organization of the party—The route—The roads—The winter climate—The inns and inn-keepers—The old towns—The Grand Canal and its embankments—The sluices—Impracticability of keeping the canal open by Chinese methods—Necessity for a railway—The Yellow River and its embankments—Worship of the river-god —Change of channel at Lung-mun-Kou in 1853—Views of Dr. Williams and Ney Elias—Error of Abbé Huc—Probable cause of change—Embankments can be maintained—The river can be regulated and controlled by the resources of modern engineering—Railways can be built and maintained in the delta . 233

CHAPTER XVII.

Visit to the city of Kai-fung-fu—The immense number of wheelbarrows on the road—The curiosity of the citizens—Difficulty of securing an inn—Inn-yard invaded by the mob—Visit of the officials from the yamen—Mob finally driven out—Respectable merchant compelled to crawl out under the gate—Call of two young officials from the governor's yamen—Tung-ming district—Approach to the Shantung hills—Cross the Grand Canal at Chi-ning-Chou—Visit to Kü-fu, the home and burial-place of Confucius—The "Ever-Sacred Duke" and his descendants—The Grand Pavilion and grounds—The avenue—The Confucian cemetery—The tomb of the sage—Burning of the Confucian residence—Singular superstition in regard to it—Visit to Taishan, the sacred mountain of China—Ascent of the mountain—Beautiful scenery — Temples and shrines — Return to the Grand Canal and journey to Chi-nan-fu—American Presbyterian mission—But few Christian converts—Superiority of technical instruction—Influence of war, commerce, and the missionaries—The city of Chi-nan-fu—The Yellow River again—Navigable from Chinan-fu to the sea—Chinese are ignorant of science in the work of controlling the floods—Journey back to Tientsin—Old embankments—The country—Mission at Pang-Chia-Chwang—Case of first convert—Chinese New-Year—Ancestral worship—New-Year's dinner—Lost in a dust-storm—Dreariness of the Great Plain—Not over-populated—Condition of the people—The Yellow River can be crossed by railroads—Return to Peking—Received by the Tsung-li Yamen 256

CHAPTER XVIII.

Visit to Formosa—Description of the island—The inhabitants—The savages—Mountain-ranges—Camphor-wood—Eastern coast—Lack of harbors—Port of Kelung—Tamsui—City of Twatutia—The governor's yamen—Chang-hwa, the future capital—Valleys of the Tamsui—Tea-plantations—Tea-culture—Energetic operations of Governor-General Liu Ming-Ch'uan—Foreigners in Formosa—Mats and opium-smoking—Houses in Formosa—Prevalent diseases—Domestic animals—Climate—Future value of Formosa 295

CONTENTS. xxiii

CHAPTER XIX.

PAGE

Chinese system of education—Confined to classics, jurisprudence, and history—Influence upon the governing class and common people—The arrest of development—How China is to be prepared for the higher civilization—Substitution of Western sciences for the dry husks of their worn-out philosophy—The earliest communication with the Chinese by the Portuguese—The Spaniards—The French—The Russians—The English—The East India Company—The Americans—The Chinese authorities have from the first sought to restrain trade—The period of small ships—The first Protestant missionaries—The attitude of the Chinese officials in reference to trade—The hong-merchants—Lord Napier's refusal to confer with them—Action of the English merchants—The discussion at Peking—The opium-traffic—The Emperor's efforts to suppress it—Captain Elliot—The destruction of the opium—The Opium War—The conclusion of peace—the Chinese concessions—The settlement of Hong-Kong—The influence of the war . . . 308

CHAPTER XX.

History of the Taiping rebellion again adverted to—The operation of the treaties—The rapid increase of trade—The establishment of the maritime customs under foreign management—The influence of Canton and the Cantonese—The affair of the Chinese lorcha Arrow—The first and only difficulty with Americans—Demands of England, Russia, France, and the United States upon the Peking Government—The Emperor and court greatly alarmed—The practice and doctrine of co-operation—The allied fleets proceed to the Pei-ho—Negotiation—Signature of the treaties—Principal concessions—The affairs of the Taku forts—The British repulse—Return of the allies—Capture of the forts and the advance to Peking—Treaties ratified and exchanged—Death of the Emperor Hien-fung—The regency—The influences surrounding the present Emperor—The necessity for Western education 331

CHAPTER XXI.

The rights of missionaries in China—The Tientsin massacre—The French and Russians indemnified—The influence of the missionaries generally minimized—Ancestral worship and superstition—The practice of fung-shuy—The conversatism of the governing class—The censors—Chinese statesmen are progressing—The establishment of the Tung-wen College—The Burlingame mission—The Chinese students in America—Their recall—The Emperor all-powerful—Railways wanted by leading statesmen—Difficulties to be overcome—Probable solution of the question—The duty of our own Government—Impossible to predict when China will move—Surrounded by great perils —Russia's menacing position—The British Indian Empire— Their permanent interests—But little danger from Germany and France—The Chinese may perceive their real danger— Not a warlike people—Their true policy—The victories of peace 346

Djaring Nor

CHINA:
A STUDY OF ITS CIVILIZATION AND PROGRESS.

CHAPTER I.

First visit to Japan—Genuine progress of the Japanese—Inland Sea—Return to Japan—The Nakasendo—Tokio—Received by the Emperor—The palace—The ministers and attendants—The Emperor—Ceremonials—The emancipation of the Emperor from the domination of the Tycoon—Tiffin at Uyeno Park—Dinner-party in Japanese style—Country-place and duck-pond—Gaishas—Wrestlers and wrestling—Saki and health-drinking—Kissing an innovation—Excursions—The progress and civilization of the Japanese genuine—The government and ministry—The governing class—Schools and colleges—Railroads—The prosperity of the people—Art and artisans—The original conservatism of the Japanese—The progressive movement—The Satusuma rebellion—The triumph of the progressive party—Acknowledgment of Japanese autonomy by the American Government—Treaty revision—No field for American railway-builders—Demand for American products—Delightful country for the traveler.

I SHALL not detain the reader with a detailed account of Japan or its interesting features, for they have been carefully described by many travelers ; but I can not forbear recording my testimony in support of the genuine progress made by the Japanese people in all that pertains to modern civilization. During my first trip to that lovely and interesting country I hurriedly visited Yokohama, Tokio, Kobe, and Osaka, and sailed through the far-famed Inland Sea, which is certainly the most beautiful body of water and surrounded by the most enchanting scenery in the world.

Air, land, and sea were instinct with life and beauty on that never-to-be-forgotten voyage, and all conspired to fill my soul with sensations which were as novel as they were entrancing. On my return to Japan, eight months later, I found the natural charm of the country heightened by the appearance of spring in all the glory of flowers and verdure, and all the delight of sweet perfumes and brilliant sunshine. Leaving my ship at Kobe, I made the journey by rail through Osaka and Kioto to Lake Biwa, which I crossed by steamer to Nagahama, where I took rail for the terminus at Sekigahara, twenty miles away. At this place I employed *jinrikshas* and continued my journey by the Nakasendo, or central mountain route, overland one hundred and fifty miles, through scenery of ever-varying beauty, to Yokogawa, where I again took the railroad for Takisake and Tokio. I spent nearly two weeks at the seat of government, during which I called upon Governor Hubbard, the American minister, the diplomatic representatives of the other foreign governments, and also upon the ministers and dignitaries of the Japanese Government.

As a special mark of favor and consideration, I was also granted an audience by the Emperor, and was presented to him by Governor Hubbard, in company with Mr. William H. Parker, our minister resident, and consul-general to Corea, and their respective secretaries, Mr. Mansfield and Mr. Travers. The chamberlain had designated eleven o'clock as the hour for the reception, and we arrived at the palace at the appointed time. As required by the rules of etiquette, the ministers and their secretaries were clad in evening-dress, and I in the full uniform of a major-general. We were received by the under-officials of the household at the outer door of the palace, a low and extensive wooden building of Japanese architecture, but furnished inside in mixed European and Japanese styles. The floor of the first room into which we were shown, and indeed of all the rooms and halls through which we passed, were covered with English Brussels carpets of neat designs, the windows were hung with Nottingham lace curtains, some glazed and some being filled with transparent paper, but mostly with glass. European tables, chairs, bureaus, mirrors, and toilet articles were found in their appropriate places, while Japanese screens and bronzes constituted, as might have been expected, the principal but by no means profuse decorations and ornaments of the various rooms. Having deposited our hats in the antechamber, we were escorted by officials in European livery through several long halls, at each turning of which we were saluted by a sentry, also clad in European uniform.

On arriving at the outer reception or waiting room, we were joined by Count Ito, the Japanese prime minister, by Count Enouye, Minister for Foreign Affairs, and by the grand chamberlain, a viscount of the old nobility, and several high officers of the household. The ministers were clad in Prince Albert coats, and trousers of lighter-colored materials, but all the officers of the household wore handsome cut-away coats, of the finest broadcloth, richly but modestly decorated with gold braid and gilt buttons. All of these gentlemen are exceedingly well-bred and courteous in manner and bearing, and several of them, including the two ministers, are men of distinguished presence. They all speak English perfectly, except one or two who speak French, and it would be difficult to find at any European court a set of high officials who bear themselves with greater ease and simplicity, or who appear to better advantage.

After waiting a few minutes, which were spent in agreeable conversation, the chamberlain announced that "His Majesty the Emperor" (they do not call him Mikado or Tenno, in speaking of him to foreigners, but always the Emperor) was ready to receive us. Passing out into a broad hall, the side of which is composed of paper windows, and through folding-doors, which were opened by servants in livery, we found ourselves in the audience-chamber, a plainly furnished but elegant room of low ceiling, and forty or fifty feet long, by about thirty wide. The Emperor, clad in a plain and not very neatly fitting hussar's uniform, was standing at the farther end, with his dress-sword hanging by his side and his cap in hand. The prime minister took position by his right side at once, and the Minister for Foreign Affairs at his left. The American minister, with Mr. Parker on his right, myself on his left, abreast, and the secretaries behind, advanced slowly to within a few feet of His Majesty, all stopping three times to bow, and this was done with as much regularity and grace as possible without a previous rehearsal. As soon as we came to the final halt, the chamberlain announced the American minister, whereupon the latter in a few but exceedingly well-chosen words presented Mr. Parker, myself, and the secretaries in turn. His remarks were translated by the prime minister into Japanese, for His Majesty speaks no English. The latter at once, in a low and hesitating voice, asked us in turn how long we had been in the country, and how long we should stay. He also wished us a pleasant time, and a safe journey to our respective destinations, all of which was translated as before by the prime minister. Governor Hubbard then thanked His Majesty for the kind reception of his countrymen, and expressed the most cordial wishes for the welfare and happiness of His Majesty and the Japanese people. Immediately afterward we retired, walking backward, and pausing three times as before to bow.

The Emperor is of medium size, with heavy and

swarthy features, and an awkward figure, and does not appear to exhibit extraordinary ability in any direction, so far as I have heard, or could see in such a ceremony as I have just described. He seemed to be ill at ease, if not bored, by what he was going through. He did not, however, require any prompting, and it is said is well informed, and takes an active and intelligent interest in the business of the government and of the empire. He is also said to be heartily in sympathy with the progressive movement which has characterized the later years of his reign. And this is quite natural, as it has rescued him from the conservative domination of the Tycoon, a sort of usurping mayor of the palace, and put him in direct control of his empire and in contact with its leading men. Formerly he was never seen by any but the Tycoon and the members of his own household, and was treated in some degree as a mysterious state prisoner rather than as an emperor. Now he is the actual head of the government, surrounded by a responsible ministry, and in daily contact with the affairs of state. It is said that he likes to throw off the cares and dignity of his high position, and, like good Haroun-al-Raschid, wander about informally and in disguise for his own information and amusement. At all events, he does this occasionally, but when missed is speedily looked after, and returns quietly to his appropriate station and duties.

After the reception, I changed my uniform for citizen's dress, and in company with Governor Hubbard, took breakfast, or *tiffin*, as it is called in China and Japan, with Admiral Enomotto, at Uyeno Park. Count Oyama, Secretary of State for War, and several of the under-secretaries, were also present. The meal was prepared and served in the best French style, and was made particularly interesting by the intelligence, refinement, and good taste of the host, who was educated in Holland, speaks

English perfectly, and as a naval officer has visited nearly all foreign countries. He is a statesman of marked ability and great influence, and as Minister of State for Communications, has special charge of railroads and steamship lines, so far as they are dealt with and controlled by the Government.

After tiffin, I drove to the residence of a private Japanese gentleman of great wealth, who had invited me to an entertainment strictly in the Japanese style. I arrived at his house at three o'clock, and was received by his servants at the vestibule. They indicated to me that I was expected to take off my shoes before entering the inner rooms, and this I did at once, but, as the Japanese slippers are kept upon the foot by a band passing between the big toe and the one next to it, and over the instep, and as foreign socks are not made with a separate compartment like the Japanese for the big toe, I could not wear the slippers which were offered, and was compelled to go in in my sock-feet.

After passing through several rooms, all floored with beautiful straw mats, soft and yielding to the feet, and scrupulously clean, I came to the principal room of the house, at the entrance of which I was met by my host, who welcomed me in excellent English. He had learned it at school in Connecticut, and had been compelled to keep it up in connection with the business of the steamship company, which his elder brother had established. He showed me at once to a silken cushion on the floor, and, seating himself by my side, made himself very agreeable and by his genuine politeness and hospitality put me entirely at my ease.

After the usual civilities, and the arrival of another guest whom he had invited to meet me, his carriage, drawn by an exceedingly stylish pair of blood-bay, half-bred horses, with driver and footman in foreign livery, made its appearance. Inviting us to accompany him, we were driven to the outskirts of the city to his country-place, which is planted with a great assortment of American and native forest-trees, in the midst of which he is building a beautiful house designed by American architects. Near by, but beyond a piece of wood, in a quiet corner of the estate, which is something over a hundred acres in extent, we came to a duck-pond, which, upon inspection, proved to be very interesting, and may contain a lesson for the proprietors of islands on our Southern coast, visited by wild fowl.

The pond is of irregular shape, and covers five or six acres. It is surrounded by an embankment or parapet six or seven feet high, sodded and planted with young trees. At intervals of forty or fifty feet, small canals, about five feet wide at the water surface, lead out from the pond. They leave the margin on a curved line, so that a duck which is swimming about can not see into the canal, the inner sides of which are quite steep. These canals are bordered by an embankment high enough to conceal a man stooping down behind it, and are terminated by a screen at the outer end, and this screen, which is made of poles or bamboo, is pierced by peep-holes, and also by a bamboo pipe, down which grain may be poured. At the proper season the pond is studded with decoys, and baited with grain. A man takes his place behind each screen, and is accompanied by two assistants, each of whom is armed with a fowler's net. No shooting or shouting is allowed about the pond, and, when the wild ducks fly over, they are lured to alight, and go to feeding at once. Hunting about for food and finding it more plentiful near the little canals which they follow till well up toward the screens, where they find it in still greater abundance, as soon as the canal has enough birds in it to satisfy the screen-man, he sends his assistants out on either side, behind the embankments, to scoop up the birds with their nets as they rise from the surface of the water. Over six thousand ducks were taken in that way from the pond last winter. I could not suppress the thought that this method of capturing wild-fowl is unsportsmanlike, but it is certainly effective, where the arrangements and conditions are favorable.

Returning to the house of our host in the city, the real entertainment began. Taking off our boots, we again seated ourselves on the silk cushions spread out on the floor. Our host's wife, a dignified but modest, sweet-looking lady, clad in a rich but subdued native costume, and two bright little boys, came in. The latter prostrated themselves in a very pretty manner before their papa, and then took their seats on silk cushions near their mamma. Almost immediately afterward, six or eight *gaishas*, or dancing and singing girls, elegantly and gayly clad, and each carrying a *samizen*—a stringed instrument something like a banjo—made their appearance and seated themselves with the family and guests on the floor. Tea was at once brought in. All one side of the room consisted of sliding windows covered with translucent paper, and these were pushed back, so as to reveal a beautiful, well-kept lawn, in the middle of which was a fourteen-foot ring of clean white sand, with all the necessary arrangements for a wrestling-match.

In a few minutes a gang of fourteen brawny wrestlers, entirely nude, except for loin-cloths and strong leather belts, marched in and took their places negligently about the ring. All of them except one or two, were quite fat, and most of them were nearly six feet high, and weighed over two hundred pounds. At a signal given by one of their number, acting as umpire, two of them stepped into the ring, and, after the usual feints and manœuvres for position and advantage, rose from their first crouching position, and seized each other shoulder and elbow, or by the belt, and then went at it with all their might to see which could throw the other or push him out of the ring. The matches were conducted with great caution and deliberation for half an hour or so. Odati San and Saruna San, the two great champions of the empire, and a number of rising younger men, were on the ground, and took part in the struggles, which abounded in surprising feats of skill and muscular strength, and lasted for about an hour and a half. After the regular matches were over, and the champions had with due deliberation shown their superiority over all comers, each successful wrestler was in turn compelled to maintain his position against the others one at a time, till he was thrown, and then the new victor had to go through the same ordeal. This gave rise to a most exciting series of struggles, following each other with great rapidity, and calling forth from the spectators, foreign as well as native, the most enthusiastic applause.

The hostess and her servants, as well as the children and the gaishas, seemed to be as much interested in the sport as the host and his guests, and were surprisingly quick to detect the fine points in the wrestling of their favorites. The exhibition was wound up by a series of exercises such as are taken by the wrestlers while they are in training. The one most practiced seemed to be for one of the younger and lighter men to ask an older and heavier one to lend him his breast, and then seizing the obliging fellow by the elbows, would throw himself head first, with all the strength of his arms, back, and neck, against the breast he had borrowed. The noise of the blows which followed each other with surprising rapidity, could be heard a hundred yards away. It seemed as though they would pound the breath out of the man who received them, but, instead of doing that, they soon exhausted the one who was delivering them, and then the big fellow, with wide-stretched legs, standing like a rock, and watching for his opportunity, with a dexterous jerk and a sudden twist, would break the grip of his antagonist and toss him out of the ring flat on his back, as though he were a bag of India-rubber. Notwithstanding the fatness of the men, it was evident they were in excellent condition, and had not only great strength and skill, but great staying powers. Their jollity and good nature were particularly noticeable. Not one of them lost his temper, though they were all very roughly handled. It is evident that the champions, who are great favorites at home, are very much superior to the wrestlers who have gone abroad, and from their great weight, strength, and skill, would probably prove a match for the best foreign wrestlers.

At the conclusion of the wrestling, the windows were closed, lights brought in, and dinner served. It consisted of a great number of little dishes, of fowl, fish, rice, and other vegetables, the most of which were very good, and all of which were perfectly prepared. They were spread out on the mats, around each guest, and within easy reach. No particular order is observed in eating them, though they are not all brought in at once, but after a dish makes its appearance it is not sent away till the feast is over. Each guest has his own dishes exclusively, and is attended by a gaisha, whose business it is to see that he wants for nothing. She passes whatever he requires, and it is her special duty to see that his little porcelain cup is kept well filled with saki, a light sort of wine, distilled from rice, and not very unlike weak sherry. During the pauses of the dinner the gaishas, separately or all together, sing and play accompaniments on their samizens. Or, if the guests become tired of music, the gaishas entertain such as can understand them by chatting and telling stories. They also play little games, and generally do their best to make the party gay and lively. These girls are selected for their beauty and wit, and are specially educated for this calling, which is an honorable one.

A Japanese lady of rank (adhering to the old customs of the country) is never seen by strangers, and is not expected to entertain her husband's guests. She sees that his house is properly ordered, and that her own servants properly prepare and serve the feast, but the task of entertaining the company devolves upon the gaishas, who are hired for the occasion. In doing this she comes and goes as she thinks necessary, but does not take a seat among the guests. It is, however, customary for her, as well as for the host, to drink a cup of saki with each of her guests, and especially with the most distinguished one. In doing this she kneels with gravity and dignity in front of the guest she intends to honor, and, after bowing almost to the floor, she reaches for his porcelain cup which he passes to her, after first carefully rinsing it in a bowl of clean water furnished for that purpose. She then turns to the gaisha, who fills it with saki; then, looking at the guest and bowing again as profoundly as before, she drains the cup and passes it back to him. After pausing for a moment, she rises and returns to a seat near her husband, and then custom requires that the guest thus honored shall in turn visit and kneel before her, and with the same ceremony drink her health from her own cup.

Toward the end of the dinner, which lasted for three hours, the three principal wrestlers were brought in and served with as much ceremony as though they had been distinguished guests. They were beautifully clad in fresh garments, and had evidently just come from the bath. After they had got well into their meal, which they seemed to relish highly, and the guests had nearly finished, the gaishas and several of the guests began a game of forfeits, of which the Japanese are quite fond. It is played by couples, each member of which breaks a chopstick into three pieces, and then conceals one, two, or three pieces, or none, as the case may be, in the hand. Each player thrusts his hand forward and asks how many, when both guess how many pieces are concealed in the two hands of the couple. Of course, there may be all the way from none to six pieces. If neither player guesses correctly, the hands are again concealed behind the back or up the flowing sleeve, and then thrust forward with the old question, and both make new guesses. This is kept up till one of the players guesses the right number, and the other is declared to be the loser. The latter pays the forfeit by drinking a cup of saki. An amusing variation of the game, now coming into vogue, is to substitute kisses for saki, and this was done with one of the foreign guests at the express command of the hostess, who told the youngest and most winsome of the gaishas that if she continued to play, and did not care to drink, she must kiss ; and, as kissing is a foreign innovation upon Japanese customs, her payment and acceptance of the forfeits were very amusing to both natives and foreigners. Her coyness and awkwardness combined were irresistible, and each exhibition of them was received with peals of laughter.

The wrestlers saw that there was a good deal of fun going on with the foreigners, and, not to be left out, they went visiting also ; but, as they were very big fellows, the foreigners declined to play with them unless they would omit the kissing, and drink three measures of saki for each forfeit. They accepted this new innovation with great glee, and seemed to like it immensely. Altogether, the evening was a novel and pleasant one ; the fun was kept up till ten o'clock, at which hour the foreigners had to return to Yokohama. The host, hostess, and little boys were charming in their unaffected simplicity; and, as all but the host and the foreigners were clad in Japanese costumes, spoke the Japanese language, and behaved themselves strictly in accordance with Japanese etiquette, the entertainment was a bit out of real Japanese life long to be remembered by those who took part in it.

I spent nearly two months, altogether, in Japan, during which I visited most of the places of interest, and especially Nikko, Chiusenji, Nantaisan, and the mountain country in the neighboring region. I inspected the farms, workshops, tea-curing warehouses, silk-shops, and attended fairs and public exhibitions of all sorts; and generally had an excellent opportunity to see the inside of the country, and to study its people and government just as they are.

After the most careful consideration, I feel it to be my duty to dissent from the carping, fault-finding disposition which has prompted more than one traveler to say that Japan has progressed too rapidly, that she has adopted the manners and customs of foreigners without understanding them, and has organized armies, laid out fortifications, and built ships of war, without needing or knowing how to use them. The truth is quite different from all this. The civilization of the Japanese is genuine, and the progress they have made is as real as it is surprising.

Their government is in theory an absolute monarchy, with a strong tendency toward liberal and constitutional forms. As might naturally be supposed, the imperial family, claiming an unbroken descent and continuous occupancy of the throne from 200 years B. C. is in some degree effete; but the actual government is in the hands of the ministers of state, and they are an unusually clever set of men, most of whom, as well as nearly all of their assistants, have been educated in Europe or America. They do not generally belong to the old nobility, but to that class which has managed the business of the old nobility as well as of the country for several hundred years. They are strong, vigorous, and capable, and seem to possess as much patriotism and practical business sense as the statesmen of the most progressive countries.

Judging from the manifold external evidences, and from information derived from gentlemen long resident in the country and more or less intimately connected with its public affairs, I can not doubt that the ministers are conducting the Japanese government with as much wisdom, honesty, and fidelity as are to be found elsewhere. They are progressive, yet at the same time cautious and conservative. They have established education on a solid basis throughout the empire. The school-house, with all the appliances of modern instruction, is seen in every town and village; while colleges and universities have been founded in sufficient numbers to furnish a higher education to such as require it. Lawyers, doctors, and engineers, educated both at home and abroad, are found in all the principal cities. Peace and plenty abound, and happiness prevails.

About four hundred miles of railroad have been constructed, from Kobe, Yokohama, and Suruga the principal seaports, to the interior, mostly under English guidance, and while an American can not help regretting that they were not built to the standard instead of to the three-feet six-inch gauge, and with all the modern improvements instead of the antiquated and awkward details which characterize English railroad practice, they are solidly constructed and generally well managed. But few foreigners are now employed about them, and it is quite certain that such future extensions as may be made of the railway system will not only be made under the control of native engineers and contractors, but will cost, under like conditions, far less per mile than the roads now in existence.

The people in every part of the empire are in a fairly prosperous condition, and, although far from rich at present, it can not be doubted will become richer in buildings, and comforts of every sort, with every year that passes over them. The arts which have specially characterized them are said by some to be on the decline, but this statement does not seem to rest on any sufficient observation or study of the facts, and I strongly doubt its truth. It is evident that Japanese life has undergone a great change. The cost of living is perhaps greater than it used to be, but the artisan is not only more comfortable and better educated than in the old days, but happier and freer, while the results of his handicraft, somewhat modified, perhaps, by foreign ideas and influences, find a readier and a better market now than at any time in the past. Whatever is genuinely good and true in Japanese art may be looked for hereafter, I do not doubt, with as much confidence as ever.

Humanity is essentially the same in all countries, and may be expected to progress in Japan, as well as in America, toward a higher and a better civilization. At the time of Commodore Perry's visit, in 1854, there was no country in the world more averse to foreigners or more bitterly opposed to foreign arts and civilization than the Japanese. They were satisfied with themselves, and regarded their own arts and civilization as the best in the world. They wanted no intercourse with other nations, and did all in their power to resist foreign encroachments upon their own exclusiveness and reserve, but the foreign powers would not be turned away. Their steamships and men-of-war could not be withstood. Their diplomacy and their arms broke down the barriers to trade, and, with trade, new ideas and a new civilization invaded the Japanese Islands. These were followed by a new impulse among the governing class. A progressive party sprang up. The conservatives became alarmed, and strove with all their might to resist the march of modern progress. A war broke out between the contending parties, and, after the expenditure of much blood and treasure, ended, as all such wars have ended in modern times—the conservatives were beaten, and progress became the watchword of the day. So far, nothing but good has resulted. The nation has surrendered its exclusiveness, laid aside its old customs and prejudices, and taken on a higher civilization. It has been more or less under diplomatic tutelage to the older powers, who have co-operated with each other in carrying out a policy of commercial aggression, and in exercising extra-territorial control over their own citizens residing in Japan.

For many years the representative of the United States, under instructions from Washington, has declined to co-operate with the representatives of other powers, and upon more than one occasion has recognized the absolute autonomy and independence of the Japanese Empire. As our Government was the first in modern times to open diplomatic intercourse, and to insist upon the establishment of commercial relations with the Japanese, it has also been the first to recognize them as a civilized people with a Government of the highest rank, possessing all the attributes, and entitled to exercise all the privileges of complete sovereignty. A convention of duly accredited representatives from all the treaty powers is now in session at Tokio, for the purpose of revising the treaties on the basis of such recognition, and it is understood that all the powers are agreed in admitting the substantial justice of the Japanese demands. It is now an open secret that the practice of co-operation between the treaty powers will be abandoned, and that, in lieu of consular courts and extraterritorial control over foreigners, a system of Japanese courts presided over by foreign judges will be substituted. The whole country will be thrown open to foreigners, with the privilege of owning property and residing and trading wherever they please. As a matter of necessity, a higher tariff on foreign imports will be levied and collected, but as the present rate is an ad-valorem assessment of only five per cent on all classes of merchandise, a material advance may be made on many articles without seriously crippling foreign commerce. Petroleum constitutes the principal item of import from the United States, and it is conceded by those engaged in the trade that a tax at least two and a half times greater than that now in force can be levied without detriment to their interests.*

From careful investigation I am persuaded that there is no great field in Japan for the employment of American engineers and contractors on railway-work, but American manufacturers of bridges, locomotives, and cars should control that market against the rest of the world. It is also probable that American architects and contractors for harbor-works may find profitable employment in Japan if they are properly represented; and it is certain that, as the Japanese advance in civilization and wealth, they will require a greater assortment of our products and manufactures, and will send us more and more of their own. They are exceedingly friendly to us, and, so far as the commercial conditions prevailing from time to time will permit, they will gladly extend their trade with us.

There is no country under the sun in which the trav-

---

* Since the foregoing was written the convention has dissolved, and treaty revision seems to be indefinitely postponed.

eler can enjoy himself with more unalloyed satisfaction and delight. The climate is salubrious, the scenery beautiful and ever varying, the people cleanly, hospitable, and genuinely polite to strangers; and these, together with the mingling of the old and the new civilizations, are such as to fill the foreigner with more novel and exhilarating sensations than he can possibly experience in any other country. For the young and vigorous, three months will be sufficient in which to make the trip from New York *via* San Francisco to Japan and back, and allow five or six weeks for inland travel; but, for such as have the time, whether young or old, six months will not prove to be too much. The sail through the Inland Sea is alone worth the trouble and expense of the voyage from America, and to such as visit China it constitutes a most charming break in the tedium of life on shipboard.

CHAPTER II.

Voyage through the Inland Sea—Mouth of the Yang-tse-kiang—The Wusung River—Shanghai—Foreign and Chinese city contrasted—Chinese civilization—Ward and the Taiping rebellion—Li Hung-Chang and Tseng Quo-Fan—Future importance of Shanghai.

THE voyage from Yokohama through the Inland Sea, and across the Yellow Sea to Shanghai, including the stops at Kobe, Simonoseki, and Nagasaki, requires about a week ; but, as the steamers belonging to the Nippon Yusen Kaisha (Japanese Mail Steamship Company) are new and exceedingly well-officered and found, and as the scenery fills one with an ever-varying sense of delight, the time passes only too rapidly, especially if the weather is fine, as is frequently the case.

The approach to the mouth of the stately Yang-tse-kiang is indicated many miles at sea by the yellow, muddy water which is poured out in such ceaseless abundance by that magnificent river. The first land which the expectant traveler catches sight of is Gutzlaff, a rocky island rising sheer and bare from the water, and surmounted by a lighthouse, erected and maintained by the Imperial Chinese Maritime Customs. This light is about forty miles from the mainland, which looms upon the sight in a low, flat, unbroken outline, in two or three hours after the light is left behind. As the ship enters the broad and muddy estuary, the shore grows more distinct, but as it rises only a few feet above the water, and is fringed by reeds and low straggling willows along the margin, a feeling of disappointment overcomes the voyager, and this remains with him during all his journeyings throughout the delta plains, however extensive they may be.

The first signs of settlement and occupation are met with at the entrance to the Wusung River, where there is a large village and strong and extensive though rudely constructed earthworks, mounting many heavy guns of European make.

Shanghai, the principal seaport and commercial entrepot of China, is situated on a great bend of the Wusung, twelve miles from its confluence with the Yang-tse. It is divided into the Chinese and foreign cities, the former of which is said to contain a population of a million souls, and the latter less than eight thousand, not counting native servants and retainers.

Nowhere else in the world can Chinese and foreign civilization be more easily compared and contrasted. Here they are seen side by side, separated only by an old city wall of burned brick, built in the middle ages, pierced with gates, surmounted by turrets and crenelated parapets, and surrounded by moats seething with fever and filth. On one side are struggling and sordid multitudes, living in low, tumble-down, and decaying mud or half-burned brick huts. The streets are teeming with dust, dirt, or slush, as the case may be, and crowded day and night with a ceaseless flow of indigent, but, so far as one can see, contented human beings, all busily engaged in the sordid struggle of life. There is nothing neat, or well built, or permanent. Everything seems stricken by decrepitude and decay, and it is the same everywhere else in China. Nothing except city walls and river embankments is solid, or strong, or durable, and nothing seems ever to have been repaired or cleaned. Whatever is worn out or worthless is thrown into the street along with the offal of the household. Stagnant water stands in ponds and pools, until lapped up by the sun or blown away by drying winds. It is all inconceivably squalid and offensive to foreign eyes and nostrils, and fills the foreign soul with a sentiment of unutterable disgust.

The river-front is lined with junks in countless numbers, and the surface of the water is covered with sampans and house-boats passing to and fro.

On the hither side of the wall is a small, compact, and well-selected population of Europeans and Americans, surrounded by every luxury and comfort, and possessing all the elements of the highest civilization and refinement. They are well clad, well mounted, and well housed. Their warehouses, shops, banks, and residences would do credit to New York or Paris. Their streets are well paved and beautifully kept. Cleanliness, order, and propriety prevail, and everything shows that they have come to stay. They have clubs, race-courses, tennis-grounds, gardens, theatres, libraries, and churches. They ride across-country, have dinner and dancing parties, and generally have carried with them to that remote riverside the industry, the thrift, and the enterprise, as well as the luxuries and the elegancies, of a higher and a better civilization. And, what is more to the purpose, they have paid for all their luxuries and comforts with the money they have earned out of the business of the country in which they have cast their lot.

The river in front of the foreign city is filled with stately sail and steamships from every port in the world; its shores are furnished with docks, foundries, and ship-yards; and nothing more aptly illustrates the difference between foreign and Chinese civilization than the contrast between the iron steamship of to-day and the wooden junk which constitutes now, as it did a thousand years ago, the Chinaman's sole means of navigating the sea. In the foreign settlement all is bustle, enterprise, and progress. In the native city all is sloth, squalor, and arrested development. The foreigner lives in the present and looks to the future, and is full of vigor and hope; the Chinaman lives in the present, and looks only to the past, and is satisfied if only his daily wants are supplied. He seems to the casual observer to have no aspiration, and to care for nothing but himself. With him everything is settled and fixed, and the thought of change fills him with apprehension. But farther on I shall endeavor to show that appearances are deceptive, and that the Chinaman, after all, is subject to the same natural laws and has the same wants as other members of the human race, and differs from the others solely by virtue of the isolation under which his civilization was evolved, and by the circumstances under which it now exists. John Stuart Mill once wrote that no one could properly say what is natural to woman till she has been long enough emancipated to show her true instinct and character; and the same may be quite as truthfully predicated of the Chinaman. He is bound and hedged in now, as in the past, by a settled and inelastic system of civilization which came down from and is sanctified by antiquity. It regulates and controls every thought and action, from birth to death, and he can no more change it of his own volition than a stone can overcome or annihilate its own weight. And yet change has made its appearance, and nowhere in a more attractive form than at Shanghai, and it will continue to exert itself till China has resumed her natural process of development, and has taken on a higher and a better civilization. Progress has planted her foot firmly on the banks of the Wusung, and, from her safe abiding-place in the foreign city, is sure, slowly but inevitably, to invade and overcome the whole vast empire.

As Shanghai is situated near the mouth of the Yang-tse-kiang, the great river which divides the country east and west into nearly equal parts, and is navigable for steamships of the largest tonnage over a thousand miles, and for steamboats of good size to the heart of the western provinces, it is probable that it will always remain, as it is now, the chief commercial city of the empire. It has been within the recent past the center of progressive ideas and influences, and so may be expected to remain indefinitely in the future. It was here that the Taiping rebellion, to which I will refer more fully hereafter, received its first serious check at the hands of the foreign merchants, who, on the approach of danger, organized a company of foreign soldiers for their own protection, and put it under the command of Ward, an American sailor. This company afterward became the nucleus of the Ever-Victorious Army which, under the leadership, organization, and impulse given it by Ward, became the most potential factor in suppressing the rebellion and restoring peace and quiet to the empire. The moral and political purpose which lay behind it came from the foreign merchants, who in turn influenced the diplomatic agents of their respective governments, and ultimately controlled their naval and military forces.

The rebellion broke out in 1850, and continued with varying success till 1864. It swept over nearly two thirds of the empire, and is said to have resulted in the death of ten million Chinamen. As Hungtse-Chuen, the leader of the rebellion, claimed to be a Christian, and actually practiced a vague and uncertain sort of Christianity somewhat like Mormonism, his progress was viewed at first by the foreigners with favor. They knew that the Imperial Government was intolerant and illiberal, and felt that any change must be for the better. It was not till the rebels invaded the region round about Shanghai, and actually threatened that place, that the foreign merchants discovered the falsity of Hung-tse-Chuen's Christianity, and the corruption of his government, and became convinced of the superiority of the existing government at Peking over any that might be established by the rebels on its ruins. Having made this discovery, they no longer hesitated to lend their countenance and influence to the imperial cause. The war for the suppression of the rebellion took on new vigor, and it was during this, its closing stage, that the imperial commanders Li Hung-Chang and Tseng Quo-Fan, father of the Marquis Tseng, until recently the Chinese ambassador to Europe, were thrown constantly in contact with foreigners, and especially with Gordon, who had succeeded Ward in command of the Ever-Victorious Army. And it was the contact with foreigners, and the demonstration of the superiority of foreign arms and organization in actual warfare, which, followed up as it was by years of intimate acquaintance with foreign consuls, ministers, commissioners, merchants, and men of business, that have made Li Hung-Chang, now holding the position of First Grand Secretary of the Empire, Viceroy of Chihli (the metropolitan province), and Northern Superintendent of Trade, besides many other dignities and honors, the foremost and most progressive statesman and probably the most powerful subject of the Chinese throne.

The primacy and importance of Shanghai as a base of political and progressive ideas, as well as of commerce, should therefore be kept constantly in view by those who would understand the probable course of the newer civilization in China. However great its influence has been in the past, it may be confidently expected to become even greater hereafter. It is of course difficult to foretell the future with accuracy; but if Shanghai were situated on the Yang-tse itself, instead of twelve miles away from it, and somewhat farther from the sea than it is, it would certainly become the future political capital of the empire, as well as its commercial emporium. And notwithstanding its somewhat eccentric position, and the obvious fact that the old capital of the Ming dynasty, and perhaps other places farther up the Yang-tse, are better situated for defense, it is entirely possible that some future revolution, if not the operation of purely commercial influences, may cause it to be selected as the seat of government of a native dynasty and of an awakened and progressive empire. But, whatever may be its future, will be due, directly or indirectly, to the guiding impulse given it by the eight thousand souls of the imperial white race residing in the foreign settlement, rather than to the brute force of the toiling millions of Turanians swarming within the crumbling walls of the Chinese city.

CHAPTER III.

Area of China—Reached its greatest extent under Kublai Khan—Almost as great under the late Regent—China's isolated position—Approach of railroads toward western border—Communication by steamships—Civilization different from any other—Origin of names of country—Provinces—Climate—Surface—Hwang-ho, or Yellow River—Delta, or Great Plain—Inundations—Embankments—Change of river-bed.

IN order that a definite conception may be had of China, as it was and is, it should be borne in mind that with the exception of Russia, it is the largest empire that has ever existed. It occupies nearly the whole of Eastern and Southeastern Asia, and lies in a regular, compact, and unbroken mass of conterminous subdivisions and outlying territories. It is composed of the original eighteen provinces corresponding to our States, and constituting what is generally described by geographers as China Proper, but sometimes as the "Middle Kingdom," together with the outlying and encircling possessions of Manchuria, Inner and Outer Mongolia, Ili, or Chinese Turkistan, Koko-Nor, and Thibet. The Government claims suzerainty over and receives tribute more or less regularly from Corea, and also from Anam, Siam, Burmah, and part of the Loochoo Islands, and it has recently erected the beautiful and extensive Island of Formosa, or Taiwan, hitherto attached to the province of Fo-Kien, into a separate province with its own governor-general who, like those of the other provinces, is appointed directly from Peking.

AREA OF CHINESE EMPIRE.

Including Formosa, it really has nineteen provinces, constituting the body of an empire the outer boundaries of which inclose one third of the Continent of Asia, or an area of at least 5,000,000 square miles. In view of the present condition of geographical knowledge, it is not possible to estimate this enormous extent of territory accurately, but, according to Balbi, it is equal to 5,126,000 square miles, while Berghaus gives it at about 5,600,000, or nearly one tenth of the habitable globe. The nineteen provinces, covering an area of about 1,800,000 square miles, are all densely populated by the Chinese, but the outlying dependencies which are of far greater extent, are mostly arid, elevated table-lands, occupied generally by nomadic and pastoral tribes commonly known as Tartars, thinly scattered over an almost illimitable succession of plain, desert, and mountain country.

The empire attained its greatest extent about the year 1290 A. D., under Kublai Khan, the son of Genghis, the great conquering Tartar chieftain, and at that time reached from the borders of the sea westward to and beyond that vague and impassable region in Central Asia impressively designated as the "roof of the world." Portions of these border-lands of varying width, and extending from British India, across the descending slopes of Thibet and Sungaria to the Desert of Gobi, the valley of the Amur, and along the latter to the Sea of Okhotsk, have at times been wrested from the control of the Chinese emperors. In the middle ages these desert wastes were the home of the conquering Tartars and Manchus, and were either maintained in their independence, or became a part of the Chinese Empire because their chieftains became Chinese emperors. In later years, the French on the south, the English on the south and west, and the Russians on the northwest and north, have been pressing forward with ever-increasing persistency, subjugating the dependencies and tribes who were doubtful in their loyalty, occupying disputed territory, and restraining the Chinese authority within definite limits. Siam, Anam, and Burmah, have been entirely detached; Turkistan has been divided, and vast tracts in Outer Mongolia and Manchuria have been permanently occupied by the advancing Europeans. The dependence of Corea upon the Peking Government has also been threatened, and yet the integrity of the empire has not been materially disturbed. Under the comparatively wise and vigorous administration of the late Empress Regent, the throne has been strengthened, peace established throughout the country, and the sway of the central power extended to the remotest tribes and dependencies. The limits of the empire are better defined than ever before, and, notwithstanding the encroachments from without, the imperial authority is probably stronger and more widely respected now than at any time since the reign of Kublai Khan.

Although a country of such vast extent, China has always been nearly as completely isolated as an unknown island. Surrounded as it is on the land-side by deserts and trackless wastes, hundreds and at places almost thousands of miles wide, no certain or regular communication between it and Europe could be had either for commerce or intelligence. From the dawn of history down to the beginning of this century, only one great traveler, Marco Polo, ever succeeded in crossing Asia and reaching China, or in giving to the world an intelligible account of what he saw, and even he found it necessary, after eighteen years of wandering, to return to Venice, his native city, by sea. An occasional merchant may have preceded him or followed in his tracks, but they were so few and far between that they produced no impression whatever upon the Chinese or their civilization.

The utter impassability of the steppes and wastes

lying between Southeastern Europe and the thickly-settled portions of China, except by the appliances of modern travel, or by the nomadic and semi-barbarous hordes which occupied them, will be still better understood when it is remembered that a line drawn from a point on the sea near the mouth of the Amur River, west-southwest across Asia, to the west coast of Africa and the Atlantic Ocean, lies everywhere, throughout its ten thousand miles of extent, in an arid and inhospitable desert region. It crosses no considerable country of high civilization unless Egypt and the valley of the Euphrates be excepted, or which has ever had a high civilization, or which has ever exerted a dominating influence upon the civilization of any other country. This vast trackless region has effectually separated the civilizations of all Southern and Eastern Asia from those of Europe, from the earliest days of the historic period down almost to the present time. Railways are now being pushed out from Russia; Merv and Tashkend are already or soon will be in daily communication with Moscow, St. Petersburg, Berlin, and Paris, and the civilization of those places will surely make its way overland into the heart of Asia, and ultimately down the Amur if not through China, to the western shores of the Pacific.

No allusion has yet been made to the isolation of China by sea; but up to the days of navigation by steam it was almost as difficult to reach that distant country by water as by land. It is true that the adventurous Greeks made their way through Asia Minor to the Arabian Sea, and pushed their explorations and conquests eastward along the coast as far as India, but there is no trustworthy evidence going to show that there was any intercommunication whatever, by water, between either the Greeks or the Romans and the Chinese. During the middle ages there is reason for believing that an occasional merchant, like the Polos, more adventurous than the rest, may have reached or left the Chinese coast in the frail sailing-craft of that period ; and it is certain that, after navigation became an exact science and sailing-ships of stronger build were introduced, they made their way in increasing numbers to that remote quarter of the globe, and carried with them many hardy and adventurous Jesuits ; but it was not till after steamships were invented and brought to a high state of perfection that communication with China became intimate enough to bring us any exact knowledge of the country, or to enable us to exert any influence or to produce any change whatever upon its civilization.

A moment's consideration of the foregoing facts is sufficient to show why Chinese civilization, which was developed on lines exclusively its own, and entirely free from all extraneous influences, should be unlike any other, except in so far as similar causes operating upon human beings, however remotely separated from us, but subject to the same natural wants and laws as ourselves, might produce similar results. The Chinese require shelter and food, like ourselves, and, like ourselves, live in houses, wear manufactured clothing, and eat the products of the earth ; but, in nearly everything else, they are as unlike Europeans and Americans as if they came from another planet. As might be naturally supposed, their manners and customs, their literature, and habits of thought are entirely different from ours, and these differences, together with the surrounding circumstances, must be kept in mind, in considering the chances of inducing the Chinese to abandon their own and adopt the appliances of an alien civilization.

China proper is called, by its own inhabitants, the Middle Kingdom, or the Central Flowery Land; but by the Russians and other people of Northern Asia it is called

Katai, whence comes the name of Cathay. The Persians designate it as Tsin or Chin, easily changed by foreigners into China, but the significance of this word, or the root from which it is derived, I have not been able to discover.

The country, as before stated, is subdivided into nineteen provinces, each presided over by a governor-general, and sometimes by a viceroy, appointed by the throne. These provinces, beginning in the northeast and sweeping westward around the Great Wall, are Chihli, Shansi, Shensi, Kansuh, Sechuen, and Yunnan; then, sweeping back to the eastward, and along the sea-coast, come Quei-Chow, Quangsi, Quang-tung, Fo-kien, Formosa or Taiwan, Che-kiang, Kiang-su, and Shantung. The center is occupied by Honan, Hoopé, Hoonan, Kiang-si, and Nganwhei. The entire area of these provinces is not materially different from that of the States lying east of the Missouri and Mississippi Rivers, with Arkansas and Texas added. It is included between about the same parallels of latitude, and, so far as cold is concerned, it has about the same climate; but, the two great rivers of the country running generally eastward to the ocean, have formed an extensive delta of low, alluvial lands nearly seven hundred miles long from north to south, and from three to five hundred miles in width, so that the prevailing south and southeast monsoons coming in from the tropical regions of the Pacific Ocean laden with watery vapor find no high ranges of mountains to intercept them, but carry their refreshing rains far inland during the summer months. These rains last from three to four months only, but are frequently excessive, and, when such is the case, the great plains are often swept by devastating floods. But in the fall, winter, and spring, or for two thirds of the year, the prevailing winds are from the north or northwest, and almost constant sunshine prevails. It hardly ever rains, and still more rarely snows; the atmosphere becomes remarkably dry, the thirsty northern winds drink up the water of the ponds, pulverize the grass and scanty vegetation, and occasionally carry clouds of dust from the arid steppes lying beyond the borders across the eastern provinces, and far out to sea.

I arrived at Shanghai in the month of October, and traveled constantly, in all parts of Northern China, till April, and during the whole time it did not rain at all, nor did it snow sufficiently to cover the ground. Throughout the winter the weather was clear and bright, except for three or four days only, when it was cloudy, and for five or six more when violent dust-storms were prevailing. It was, however, quite cold at all times, though, from the lack of moisture in the air, the cold was not so keenly felt as an equally low temperature would have been in the United States. Of course, it is impossible to carry on any out-door occupation during the dust-storms, but, as they rarely ever prevail with violence for more than two days, the winters are remarkably favorable to work and travel, and especially so for the latter, as the frost is destructive to all kinds of insect-life. It is hard to imagine a more bright and bracing winter climate, or one in which life in the open air is more enjoyable. The summer, however, makes up for it, as it is not only hot but wet ; the air becomes saturated with water, and the humid heat is almost unbearable to those who are not accustomed to it.

The surface of the country throughout China proper is divided into a succession of plains, hills, and mountains. The drainage is generally eastward, but the great rivers which rise in the mountains of Thibet are tortuous in the extreme till they are clear of the higher lands and approach sea-level.

The scope of this work does not warrant a description of the Amur, which touches the northern borders

HWANG-HO, OR THE YELLOW RIVER. 33

of the empire, and is in some degree a Chinese river, but it also has its source in the table-lands of Central Asia, and flows eastwardly to the Pacific Ocean.

In many respects the most remarkable but at the same time the least known river of China, is the Hwang-ho, or Yellow River. It rises in Northern Thibet, between the Shuga and Bayan-kara Mountains, in latitude 35° north and longitude 96° east, and not more than a hundred miles from the sources of the Yang-tse-kiang. It was long considered by Chinese writers as entitled to special reverence, and by some foreign scholars as being one of the four sacred rivers of the world, but all efforts to identify it with either of the latter have failed, and even the Chinese themselves have come to consider it rather as a curse and source of sorrow than as a sacred stream, from which blessings and happiness might be expected to flow. Its course from the lakelets in the narrow plains at its head, called by the Chinese the Starry Sea, is at first south, then west, and then north and northeast, for about seven hundred miles, till it reaches the Great Wall, which follows it northwardly for about four hundred miles. It then crosses the Wall, makes a great bend north and eastward around the country of the Ortous Mongols, and impinges against a spur of the Peh-ling Mountains, which turns it again almost due south, in which direction it flows for over five hundred miles between the provinces of Shensi and Shansi. In this part of its course it traverses the loëss plains and receives no tributaries worthy of the name. It is also in this part of its course that it changes its character from a clear mountain stream and takes from the loëss clay the yellow color which gives it its name. At the southwestern corner of Shansi, and about 1,850 miles from its source, it receives its greatest affluent, the Wei, and changes its course to the eastward again, in which direction it flows for about two hundred miles, to the vicinity of Kai-fung-fu, the capital of Honan. The place of its confluence with the Wei, is about five hundred and fifty miles on the shortest line from the sea, and may be regarded as the head of its delta. From Kai-fung-fu it now flows northeasterly to the southwestern corner of the Gulf of Pechili, but in this part of its course through the plains it has had many channels to the sea, though so far as is now known never more than one at a time. Since the beginning of the historic period it is certain, if we may rely upon Chinese chronicles, that it has changed its bed at least six times, but no one can now do more than guess how many times it did the same thing in the countless prehistoric ages, during which, aided by the Yang-tse farther south, it was slowly pushing back the borders of the ocean, and building up the delta plains which constitute so great a portion of the China with which we are now concerned. It is clear, however, that the wanderings of the river were coextensive with its delta, which extends from Shan-hai-Quawn, in latitude 39.30° north, to the mouth of the Yang-tse, in latitude 31° 45' north.

It is known that it has occupied in succession the beds of what are now called the Pei-ho, the Old River, and the Tatsing-ho, all entering the Gulf of Pechili north of the Shantung promontory, and that prior to 1853 it followed a former bed to the sea, in latitude 34° north, south of the promontory. The distance between those mouths, measured along the sea-coast, around the Shantung promontory, is about six hundred miles, while the distance from the northernmost limits of the delta to the mouth of the Yang-tse, measured in the same way, is nearly one thousand miles. But the deltas of the Hwang-ho and of the Yang-tse are conterminous, and not separated by highlands, and the total distance from the northern limits of one to the southern limits of the other, on the seacoast, is about eleven hundred miles.

Winding its tortuous course, as it does, for twenty-seven hundred miles, through an arid and treeless region, the Hwang-ho carries, during the dry season and for two thirds of the year, but a small volume of water, compared with that carried by the Yang-tse, or the Amazon, or even with the Mississippi. It is so shallow and narrow, and its bed has so great a declivity till after it enters the delta, that it is entirely unfit for navigation. At many places it is broken by rapids, and its current is so swift that it can not be crossed except at considerable risk. Its width, even after it enters the Great Plain, does not generally exceed fifteen hundred feet, though at one or two places along its new bed, where it has not yet excavated a well-defined channel for itself, it spreads out to a width of several thousand feet, and is filled with sand-bars. It is navigable to Yushan, near the western border of Shantung, for light-draught junks, and steamboats drawing ten feet of water might readily ascend it to Chinan-fu, the capital of that province, and even a hundred miles above, if they were authorized to run, and could get over the bar at its mouth, Generally, the river resembles the Missouri at and above Bismarck, in width, color, and volume of water, and even in the character and appearance of its fore-shores ; but, after it enters the delta, unlike the Missouri, it has no river-valley, with hill-sides near by, rising to the higher level of the rolling prairies. To the contrary, its shores are never higher than ten or twelve feet, and at places not more than five feet, even in the driest season. The plains are almost perfectly level, and stretch away in either direction from the river's margin hundreds of miles, without the slightest rise or depression that can be detected by the most practiced eye. They are absolutely as level as flowing water.

But, however insignificant and harmless this remarkable river may be in the dry season, and for the greater part of the year, its character becomes entirely changed during the rainy season. Its water-shed, which is estimated by Williams at 475,000 square miles, is almost entirely bare of trees, and hence the water which falls upon its upper portions in the short rainy season, runs rapidly into the main river, and causes the most destructive floods. When there is a concurrence of heavy rains in the delta-plains, with a descending high-water wave from the table-lands, the embankments, erected with such painful labor, and neglected with such certainty everywhere, are frequently broken and swept away, and whole districts, many miles in width, are laid waste by the devastating and irresistible inundations. Houses are melted down, crops are destroyed, and, at times, thousands of people, with all their flocks, are drowned.

The erection and repair of the embankments are now and have been, from time immemorial, matters of the greatest solicitude to the provincial and imperial governments; but, when the floods have come and gone, and the long dry season is at hand again, the improvident or corrupt officials, and the still more improvident people, seem alike to forget that the embankments can ever be required again, or that there is any necessity for looking after or repairing them. Some of them are laid out and constructed with great care, but many of them are badly located and aligned, and poorly built in every respect. They are generally placed from one to two miles back from the river, and are from twelve to fourteen feet high, twenty to twenty-five wide on top, and have slopes of two base to one perpendicular. They are not habitually protected by willows, reeds, or grasses, and whatever vegetation grows upon them is scrupulously raked off in winter for fuel. They are freely used for roads and paths, and are rarely provided with ramps or suitably constructed road-crossings. The consequence is, that they are not only injured and weakened at many places, but frequently, where the traffic crossing them is considerable, they are cut through to the level of the plain upon which they stand. They are at all times the favorite resort of burrowing animals, and during the dry season the river, wandering from one side to the other of the space included between, frequently impinges against and undercuts them. Nothing is ever done beforehand to repair or prevent such injuries, so that when the floods come again the weak spots are found, and the neglected embankments, as might be expected, are broken through and swept away, notwithstanding the most strenuous exertions at the last moment to prevent it. Large detachments of the army are hurried to the spot, and thousands of men, and even women and boys, are gathered in from the neighboring towns and villages, after a break has taken place. Frantic efforts are made and great expenses are incurred to repair the embankment, through which a cataract is pouring, and which might have been maintained intact by the exercise of a little timely foresight and the honest expenditure of a little money.

In the middle ages the embankments seem to have been placed closer to the river margins, and to have been given a stronger profile than at present. The practice now, however, is to place them farther back, as before described, but near important towns where the local circumstances seem to require it, a smaller and lower embankment is sometimes constructed close to the river-front. The most remarkable embankment examined by me was one built by the great Emperor Kien-lung, whose long and prosperous reign was contemporaneous with the life of George Washington. It is located on that part of the river near Kai-fung-fu, and extends many miles in either direction. It is from forty to fifty feet high, and from fifty to sixty feet wide on top, has the usual slopes of two base to one perpendicular, and was exceedingly well laid out and constructed. A better idea of its enormous dimensions can be had by considering its solid contents, which I estimated on the ground to be an average of a million cubic yards per mile, and to have cost, even with the abundant labor of China, fifty thousand dollars per mile. At the place where I crossed it, it was surmounted by the walls and gates of a fortified city, and, after two weeks' travel in the dead level of the plains, seemed to be a mountain commanding an almost illimitable view of country spread out below it. What is still more curious is, that it was this enormous embankment which was broken through by the extraordinary flood of 1853 at Lung-mun-kou, about thirty miles below, and from which place the river completely abandoned its old bed, and made a new one for itself, across the plain, to the Tatsing-ho, and thence along that river's bed to the Gulf of Pechili. But no intelligent and thoughtful person can examine the broken embankment and the surrounding country without coming to the conclusion, as I did, that the breach must have been due to negligence, aided by such causes as I have described as being everywhere prevalent. Williams, Martin, and Ney Elias, all distinguished scholars and travelers, together with others of lesser note, have generally cited this incident as a conclusive argument against the diking of a river's banks to resist floods. The distinguished Jesuit traveler, Abbé Huc, many years before either Martin or Ney Elias had visited the scene of the disaster, predicted that it would certainly occur, sooner or later. He alleged that the river-bed, in that part of its course, had become so filled up with silt brought down from the table-lands, as to be higher than the adjacent country ; but, having no leveling instruments, and

RIVER EMBANKMENTS.

therefore making no exact measurements, so far as I have been able to learn, I am persuaded that his statement does not rest upon data of sufficient accuracy to justify the world, and still less the engineering profession, in receiving it as correct. I shall refer to this subject again in another chapter, and give my own views more fully, as to the present condition of the river-bed and embankments, and of the causes which led to the great breach, the complete change of direction, and the erosion of a new channel to the seas.

CHAPTER IV.

The Yang-tse-kiang—Its navigation—Its various names—Its tributaries—Its floods—Canals and creeks in the delta—Area of its water-shed—The Chukiang or Pearl River—The Min—The Pei-ho and its tributaries—The Peh-tang—The New-Chwang and the Ta-wen-ho.

GREAT as is the Hwang-ho or Yellow River, it is exceeded in length, as well as in depth, width, and volume of discharge, by the Yang-tse-kiang, which also rises in the mountains of Thibet, within a hundred miles of its neighbor, and after flowing to the south and southeastward through an interminable maze of mountain-gorges and valleys, it crosses China proper from the extreme western border of Sechuen, in a generally east-northeastwardly direction to the Yellow Sea, which it enters within a hundred and twenty miles of the old mouth of the Yellow River. It, however, traverses a region in which the snows are heavier and the rains more frequent and deeper, and it has in addition a water-shed of much greater area than the Yellow River, and consequently it discharges a much greater volume of water at all seasons of the year. Its discharge has never been measured, but enough of it is known to justify the statement that it is one of the greatest rivers of the world—a broad, stately stream, navigable to the Great Rapids, thirteen hundred miles from the sea, for ocean-steamers, and for those of the greatest draught to Nanking, while river-steamers can ascend five or six hundred miles farther into the heart of

NAVIGATION OF THE YANG-TSE-KIANG. 41

Sechuen. The rapids, which are found just above Ichang, have hitherto been regarded as impassable by steamers under their own motive power, but it is now known that the current does not exceed nine miles per hour, and that the channel is sufficiently deep and clear of sunken rocks to admit of free navigation by boats having enough power to make head against the current. The rapids are habitually passed by junks, which are warped through them by means of ropes and man-power. It is understood that the China Merchants' Steamship Company are now building a boat to ply through them and along the river above, to the head of navigation. This boat will be promptly followed by others, for, when the upper river is once opened, foreign steamers will surely rush in. Under the treaties, they are entitled to enter and ply upon all parts of the river without restriction, after it has been shown that the rapids can be safely passed. Effective steam communication fully established on this magnificent water-way wherever practicable, will give a new impulse to trade with the central and western provinces, and will enable the Imperial Government to transport troops and military munitions in either direction from one side of the empire to the other, with much greater speed and safety than have heretofore been possible. The value of this river for such purposes has never been understood by the Chinese Government, and, even if it had been, the Government could not fully utilize it, so long as junks were the only disposable means of navigation. The day must, however, be near at hand when, should occasion call for it, the river will become a much more important factor in the problem of binding the empire together and protecting it against external as well as internal enemies.

It is not possible to give the exact length of this river, for its course through the mountains of Thibet has never been explored or accurately laid down, much less has it been correctly measured. It, however, approximates three thousand miles, and flows through every variety of land and climate met with in China. Each new province that it waters gives it a new name. The main trunk in Sechuen is called by the natives Kin-sha-kiang, or the River of Golden Sand, until it is joined by the Yalung, after which it is called Ta-kiang, as far as Wuchang in Hoopeh. Below this point it is designated as the Chang-kiang, or Long River, and finally, in its reach next the sea, as the Yang-tse-kiang.

Unlike the Hwang-ho, it has many large tributaries, the most important of which is the Kan-kiang in the province of Kiangsi. This affluent drains the water of the Poyang Lake, and continues the navigation of the Grand Canal and the Yang-tse River into the southern part of the empire. There are many other streams flowing from the southern mountains into the river and swelling its enormous flood. The Han-kiang in Hoopeh, draining a rich and populous valley of great extent, is perhaps the largest tributary from the north, and its junction with the main river marks a spot of great commercial and strategic importance known as Han-kow. It is open to foreigners as one of the treaty ports, and in the future development of the country, especially as to railroads and manufactures, will doubtless become one of the greatest centers of activity.

The Yang-tse differs from the Hwang-ho in many other respects than those already mentioned. Its outflow is more regular, and this is due as much to the configuration of its water-shed, and to the occurrence of lakes like the Poyang and Tung-ting, which hold back the water of the region tributary to them, as to the meteorological conditions which obtain in that part of China. The floods are very great, because the annual downfall of rain is also very great, but the river-banks are generally not so low as to be frequently overflowed, even by freshets which rise thirty feet as they sometimes do. The bar at its mouth permits the passage of large, ocean-going steamers at all times, and although the estuary contains shoals and flats at several places, they do not interpose any serious obstruction to navigation. At a distance of about a hundred miles from the sea, the shores although low, approach near enough to each other, and are so broken by detached but commanding hills, that they lend themselves readily to the defense of the interior by fortifications, a number of which have already been located and constructed.

The Grand Canal, which has lost much of its utility and importance since the Yellow River changed its bed in 1853, and to which I shall refer more fully in another chapter, enters the Yang-tse from the north, about three miles above Chin-kiang, an important city, admirably situated on the south bank of the river, one hundred and seventy miles above its mouth. The river is also connected at this city with Shanghai, Hang-chow, and many other important cities south of the Great River by a continuation of the Grand Canal, or by other canals, creeks, and rivers, leading out of it. Indeed, the whole region between Chinkiang and the sea, on either side of the Yang-tse, is a network of canals and creeks with their necessary embankments, which so cut up and divide the land as to make it almost impassable for an invading army. These canals are everywhere the same in general characteristics, and hence the description of the Grand Canal, which will be found farther on, will answer for all.

The water-shed of the Yang-tse is given by Williams at 548,000 square miles, and by the "American Cyclopædia" at 750,000. Various estimates, which perhaps, are but little better than guesses, have been made by foreigners, of the annual discharge of both the Hwang-ho and the Yang-tse, but none of them are based upon accurate measurements or systematic observations. The Chinese themselves have no conception of the science involved in such an estimate, or of the use to which the data connected therewith could be put, and hence have never wasted any time upon it.

The next great river of China is the Chu-kiang, or Pearl River, which, with its three principal branches, drains a water-shed of about 130,000 square miles, lying south of the Nan-ling or South Mountains. It enters the sea near Canton, and its western branch, rising in Quangsi, drains and affords communication to nearly all the country on the southern border of the empire. The middle or northern branch heads near the Che-ling pass, on the direct route to the Poyang Lake, and the Yang-tse River at Kiu-kiang, and at no distant day will doubtless be occupied by one of the principal railroad lines of the empire. Both of these and also the eastern branch are navigable for steamboats, and are important arteries of trade, as well as noticeable agencies in shaping the topography of the region drained by them.

There is another considerable river known as the Min, which enters the sea at Foo-Chow, about midway between Canton and the mouth of the Yang-tse, but its water-shed is of much less extent than either of those heretofore mentioned.

The Pei-ho, which enters the Gulf of Pechili at Taku, is a considerable river, and at times discharges a large volume of water, but it is principally remarkable from the fact that it lies, with all its tributaries, entirely in the Great Plain, and has at widely separated intervals constituted the bed of the Yellow River for many years at a time. It drains but little mountain or hill country, notably small areas lying northwest of Peking, west of Pau-ting-fu, and in Southeastern Shansi. It consequently has had but little influence in shaping the topography of the country, but as it is navigable, notwithstanding its great crookedness, for ocean-steamers of ten or twelve feet draught to Tientsin, fifty miles from its mouth, and is the principal means of access for both native and foreign officials to Peking, as well as for nearly all the foreign goods consumed in the country north of the Yellow River, it is of great importance to the Chinese, in connection with commerce and also with the national defense. Its southern branch, the Wei-ho, is occupied by the Grand Canal from Tientsin to Lintsing, a distance of about three hundred miles by its tortuous course. Its northern branch is similarly occupied for about one hundred and fifty miles between Tientsin and Tung-Chow, fifteen miles east of Peking. Tientsin, situated at the meeting-point of its various branches, is a city of nearly a million inhabitants, and being a treaty port, as well as the port of Peking, it has a flourishing foreign settlement, and is a city of great importance as a center of commercial and political influence. While it is not the capital of the province, it is the chief seat of the viceroy, Li Hung-Chang, and derives great additional importance from that fact.

The entrance to the Pei-ho is obstructed by a bar, which effectually closes the river against steamers except at high tide, and even then they can not enter, drawing more than twelve or thirteen feet, but it is fully within the range of modern engineering skill to remove the bar, and make a port at Taku, just within the mouth of the river, accessible at all times for vessels of even twenty feet draught. The river carries but little water into the gulf at any time, except during the rainy season, and as it lies altogether in the Great Plain, and has but little fall, it silts up rapidly, as soon as the outpour of flood-water has ceased, and then even the light-draught ocean-steamers which ply between it and Shanghai have the greatest difficulty in ascending it more than fifteen or twenty miles. It is entirely devoid of rocks, and, there being no forest-trees anywhere on its banks, it is also free from snags and sawyers, such as used to make the navigation of our Western rivers so difficult ; hence steamers suffer no danger and no inconvenience even from running ashore or getting aground, except from the delay and expense which follow.

The Peh-tang, which enters the gulf about ten miles farther north, has a deeper channel across its bar than the Pei-ho, and is of some importance from a military point of view on that account. The sea-coast between these two rivers, being only about one hundred and ten miles from Peking by the traveled roads, has been selected more than once, notwithstanding the shoal water along it, by foreign powers at war with China, as a landing-place and base for hostile operations against the capital, and this circumstance must always cause the Chinese Government to regard it as well as the Pei-ho and the Peh-tang Rivers with peculiar anxiety. They occupy important positions in connection with both the invasion and defense of the country, and hence have been carefully surveyed by foreigners, and elaborately fortified at their entrance and at various points higher up by the Chinese. In the future development of the country, the entrance to the Pei-ho must necessarily be improved, the dry-docks and other facilities for repairing ships at Taku must be increased, and, last, but not least, a railroad must be built from Taku to Tientsin, Pau-ting-fu and Peking. There is no other route in the empire where a larger passenger and freight traffic require to be accommodated, and certainly none where the contingencies of the national defense so imperatively demand the construction of a first-class railroad.

There are many other rivers shown on the maps of the Great Plain, but with the exception of the New-Chwang, in the province of Shinking and the Ta-wen-ho, which rises in the western part of the Shantung Hills, and supplies the Grand Canal south of the Yellow River with water, they nearly all dry up during the rainless season, and are indicated generally by a swale in the plain bordered by embankments to restrain the water during flood-time. I have crossed many of them, so faint in outline and so perfectly dry, that I had great difficulty in locating them at all. The great rivers of the country are the Yang-tse-kiang and the Hwang-ho, which have through countless ages been slowly cutting down the mountains and loëss terraces, and building up the great delta plain. The Chu-kiang and Min have in a lesser degree been doing the same kind of work upon the southern and eastern slopes of the mountains and borders of the sea south of the Yang-tse. Keeping these facts constantly in mind, the outlines and natural subdivisions of the land will also be easily understood from the description which follows in the next chapter.

CHAPTER V.

The surface of the country—Sinian Mountain system—The highlands and hill country—Origin of the loëss terraces—The outlying dependencies —Corea, Manchuria, Mongolia, Ili, Turkistan, and Thibet—The Great Plain or delta—Coal, iron, and other minerals—The Kaiping coal-mines and railroad—The first locomotive built in China—The coal-mines of Formosa and Shansi—Coal transported in wheelbarrows— The development of coal and iron receiving Government attention— Foreign experts required—Conservatism of the Government.

THE surface of China is naturally subdivided into mountainous and hilly country, the loëss terraces or plains, and the Great Plain or delta of the Hwang-ho and Yang-tse-kiang.

Beginning in the high mountain-region of Thibet, into the borders of which the daring and resolute Colonel Prejevalsky has recently pushed his explorations, but which is still a great geographical puzzle, the mountain system of China, buttressed upon the lofty Himalayas, branches off into four principal ranges with many spurs and outliers, the general trend of which is at first east and west, and afterward, as they pass through Central China and approach the ocean, northeast, and southwest. Roughly speaking, everywhere in China proper, as well as in Formosa and Japan, the upheaval is parallel with the direction of the Chinese coast and is designated by Pumpelly as the Sinian system. Its trend is particularly noticeable in the southeastern provinces, and again in the northern and western part of the northeastern provinces. There is a great congeries of

CHINESE MOUNTAIN SYSTEM. 49

mountains in Southern and Eastern Thibet, of which the principal drainage is to the southeast into the Meikon and the Yang-tse-kiang. The principal outliers of these mountains, to the eastward are the Peh-ling or North Mountains which separate the valleys of the Hwang-ho and Yang-tse-kiang by more than four hundred miles, on or near the 105th meridian east of Greenwich.

The Nan-ling or the South Mountains, in the southeastern provinces, seem to be a separate upheaval, and to be broken up into short ranges, which give to all the country, except the delta, south of the Yang-tse a rough if not mountainous surface. The highlands touch the coast everywhere, from Hanchow Bay to Canton, and, being bare of trees, give it a bold but uninviting appearance. They also strike the Yang-tse near Chin-kiang, and at many other points along the river to Ichang. There are a few bits of table-land in this hill-region, and two considerable river-valleys containing the Poyang and the Tung-ting Lakes. It is about four hundred miles wide by one thousand miles long, and much of it is covered with trees, and is susceptible of cultivation. On the eastern and southeastern sea-coast the hills are bare and ragged, and look like the hills of New Mexico rather than those of our Eastern States.

The region between the Yang-tse and the Yellow River is similar to that just described. Its drainage is almost all toward the Yang-tse, although a considerable river draining the greater part of Shensi, joins the Hwang-ho at the southwest corner of Shensi. North of the Peh-ling divide the loëss terraces are found; they cover a great part of the two provinces just named, and are noted for their inexhaustible fertility. This curious formation is also found at the foot of the Shan-tung Hills, and there, as well as elsewhere, has been a puzzle to geologists, some of whom, including Pumpelly, the Ameri-

4

can *savant*, ascribe its orign to lacustrine or subaqueous deposit. The investigations of Baron Richthofen, a learned German, sent out by the Shanghai Chamber of Commerce, have led him, however, to formulate the theory that it is composed of subaërial dust deposits, which have been laid down through countless ages of the past by the winds which, sweeping over the plains from the northwest, become laden with the dust of the dried-up grasses and vegetation, and of the mineral substances which are broken down and pulverized by the action of frost. This dust is so fine that it sifts through every crack and cranny, and while it settles everywhere in times of calm, it is, of course, almost impossible to detect the slow growth of the earth's surface from that source. Wherever the loëss deposits are found, they present the same curious features. They have a uniform yellowish-clay color, very like the soil of Mississippi between Vicksburg and Jackson, and their surface is nearly level. Where cut into by roads, or by the action of streams, the exposed cut stands vertical and presents a series of columnar pipelets of irregular polygonal cross-section, which also stand vertical, are readily cleavable from one another, break easily, and are filled with capillary tubes of carbonate of lime. This loëss clay pulverizes quickly in the roads, and the wind blows it away. The consequence is, that the roads are constantly being lowered, and in many places are sunken far below the level of the country. They not infrequently become the bed of a torrent caused by the outflow of rain-water, and when this is the case they are still more rapidly deepened. The banks of rivers in the loëss region also stand vertical, and are found in more than one district several hundred feet high. In such cases the inhabitants burrow into them, and dig out houses more or less commodious, in which they dwell, and excavate granaries, in which they store their crops.

THE LOËSS TERRACES.

The capillary tubes mentioned above are almost invisible, except by the aid of a microscope, and are supposed to have been formed by the slow decay of the lowermost grass-rootlets, due in turn to the slow rising of the surface, as the impalpable dust settles upon it, and to the consequent exclusion of light and heat. The tubes serve to bring the moisture of the earth below to the surface, and along with it the salts necessary for the sustenance of the growing crops. Cultivated land in the loëss region, therefore, withstands drought much better than any other land known, and retains or renews its fertility, without the application of artificial manure, in a very remarkable manner. It is thought that farms in this region have been producing crops of wheat for thousands of years, practically without rotation, or the assistance of fertilizers of any kind.

In Shan-tung, the loëss terraces are situated next to the foot of the hills, and just above the level of the Great Plain. They present all the characteristics of those in Shansi and Shensi, but are not so wide or thick. The color of the loëss substance is brighter than the soil of the Great Plain, but it is easy to see that they might have had a common origin, the difference being that the loëss was laid down by the wind and has undergone no change except that produced by the vegetation growing on the surface, while the soil of the Great Plain is alluvial, and was eroded from the loëss terraces and and tablelands and intermixed with other materials by the action of running water, partly dissolved, held in suspension, transported and finally laid down in salt-water. The first when dry is a bright-yellowish color like ordinary clay, and the second a yellowish-gray color. Either will make sun-dried or burned bricks.

There is also a range of hills in the eastern and northern parts of Shansi, Northern Chihli, and Shinking, which extends to and beyond the Great Wall, and is said to contain rich deposits of coal, iron, and other minerals. They are entirely bare of trees, and when viewed from the plain are ragged and serrated in outline, variegated in color, and full of cliffs, crags, detached bowlders, and broken materials. On the whole, they remind one of the hills of New Mexico, Colorado, and Arizona, and so far as one can now see, were never covered with trees or luxuriant vegetation. This is doubtless due in part, if not entirely, to the extreme aridity of the climate.

Outside of China Proper, beginning on the north, at the sea-coast, is Corea, formerly a tributary kingdom; then, proceeding west and northwest, come Liautung, Shinking, Kirin, and Tsitsihar, constituting Manchuria, from which came the present imperial Chinese dynasty as conquerors. Sweeping farther to the westward, we have Inner and Outer Mongolia, separated from each other by the sandy desert of Shamo or Gobi, and subdivided into many khanates. Beyond, and still farther to the west, in the very heart of Asia, lies Ili, or Chinese Tartary, a vast, cheerless, arid region, divided into Tien-Shan, Peh-lu, or Sungaria, and Tien-Shan Nan-Lu, by the Tien-Shan or Celestial Mountains. This region contains Barkul, Urum-tsi, and Kuldja, all widely separated, but on the road from China to Europe, and celebrated of late years as points in the remarkable campaign made by the late Tso Tsung-Tang for the purpose of repossessing this remote corner of the empire, and reducing it to obedience to the throne.

The southern part of Ili is known as Eastern Turkistan. It contains the cities of Kashgar, Yarkand, Khoten, and Kirrea, and is separated from Bod or Thibet by the Kwan-lun Mountains. This last dependency is subdivided into Ulterior and Anterior Thibet, and is broken up into many smaller districts by the numerous mountain-ranges which make it the most inaccessible country in the world.

These outlying regions, and especially Thibet, are thought to be rich in minerals of all kinds, and, although thinly populated by semi-civilized tribes, subsisting mainly on the products of their herds, will, when brought into communication with the rest of the world by railroads, afford homes and occupation for a population many times larger than they now support. They contain over three million square miles of territory, and while the most of them have been visited and more or less carefully described by European travelers, they yet remain to be scientifically explored, and brought under the domination of modern uses and ideas. So far as I can make out, they are, in many respects like our own Rocky Mountain regions, arid, inhospitable, and barren. Vegetation is everywhere scarce, great tracts are sandy wastes, almost impassable by man, and forsaken even by birds and beasts, but abounding in mineral resources, which will some day give occupation to millions of people. Thibet is said to be specially rich in precious stones, and some idea may be had of the possible extent and variety of its resources when it is remembered that it is eighteen hundred miles long from east to west, by nearly nine hundred miles wide.*

The northern part of Mongolia, bordering on the Amur and its tributaries, is now known to contain placer gold-mines of great richness, and there is already a rush of both Chinese and Russian miners into that region. It is not impossible that it may soon prove to be as great a source of gold as California was in the first decade after it came under the sway of the Americans. Should this prove to be the case, it will greatly influence the construction of railroads into that region, both from Europe and Northern China. The great want now of all the border-region of China is efficient transportation and

---

* See the Travels of Abbé Huc and Rockhill.

some idea can be had of the influence of this want upon the spread of civilization, when it is remembered that the Kuldja expedition, starting from the capital of Kansuh, took three years to reach its destination, and was compelled to halt at the proper seasons, and grow and garner the crops which constituted its main source of supply. At present the camel is the sole means of transport, but, as his average burden does not exceed four hundred pounds, and the country affords but a scanty supply of the coarsest forage-plants, the cost of transport by such means is beyond all proportion to its efficiency. Nearly all the tea used in Siberia and Russia is carried by camels, and, in order that the cost of such carriage may be reduced to its smallest relative limit, the tea when properly cured is compressed into solid "bricks," from which circumstance it is known as "brick-tea."

But by far the most interesting part of China is the Great Plain, which consists of the united deltas of the Yang-tse-kiang and Hwang-ho, and extends from Hang-chow in latitude 31° north, to Shan-hai-Quan, in latitude 40° north, or a distance of over six hundred and fifty English miles in a right line. Measured on its longer axis from the hills northeast of Peking to the Poyang Lake, the length is about seven hundred miles. It has nearly eleven hundred miles of sea-coast, and its greatest width is nearly five hundred miles, while it averages about three hundred miles. Its superficial area is somewhere between one hundred and fifty thousand and one hundred and eighty thousand square miles. It is everywhere as level as a floor, and almost entirely bare of trees. A few are found along the margins of the streams, and around the larger fields, or in clumps about the graves of the richer families, but there is no such thing as groves or forests. Willow, which is used for roofing-poles, and elm, which is used for the construction of carts and agricultural implements, are by far the most common. The ailantus, and the jujube, a tree somewhat like the Osage orange, but bearing a fruit which, when dried and preserved in honey, resembles the date, are also common. A few evergreens, such as the pine and the arbor-vitæ, are used to shelter the graves of the richer mandarins, and, as these are generally planted in a double row around the graveyard, they present an inviting object to the eye of the traveler, weary with gazing upon the dead and unbroken expanse of plain which constantly surrounds him.

The absence of trees from the plain is natural. Its soil is hard, and frequently so impregnated with salt, and baked by the sun, that trees would find but little encouragement, even if left free to grow undisturbed by man, but in view of the fact that every vestige of vegetation, even to the roots of the millet-stalks, is raked off the fields and plains by the people, and burned for fuel during the winter, it is evident that neither shrub nor tree can escape, unless it has special protection. Grass and reeds are cut and raked up wherever they are found, and all the waste places are invaded, and swept clean of the dried and withered vegetation. Even the leaves are gathered, and the outer bark of the few trees is in some cases scraped off and scrupulously housed for the winter's use. One of the most characteristic scenes of the plain and hill country, after the cold weather begins, is to see men, women, and boys combing the sere and yellow grass from the surface of the ground, with ingeniously constructed bamboo rakes, wherever a blade has made its appearance. I have seen adventurous boys far up the craggy sides of the sacred mountain in Shan-tung, hanging over beetling cliffs, and exploring every nook and bench and every stony fissure for dry gorse and grass, with which to cook the scanty meal in the cheerless hut of their parents miles away.

Williams, in describing the hill-country, south of the Yang-tse, says that all the raking and scraping which is practiced there also is followed by burning over the land for the purpose of fertilizing the soil; but my observation tells me that, when the raking and scraping are done, there is nothing left to burn. Of course, there are remote and uncultivated regions, either too low or too salt, or too frequently overflowed, or too poorly drained for cultivation, or too far out of the way to be entirely despoiled of their coarse reeds and grass, and these are sometimes burned over, but burning is not a common practice anywhere, and it is generally too wasteful in the Chinaman's estimation to be resorted to for the purpose of fertilizing his land. But with the raking and burning, much or little, as the latter may be, the aridity of the climate, and the condition and character of the soil, I doubt if any considerable part of North China has ever been covered by trees, and I am sure the Great Plain has not been since the beginning of the present geological epoch at least, any more than have the prairies of Illinois or the great plains west of the Missouri.

China proper is sometimes called by the Chinese the Central Flowery Kingdom, and somehow or another many foreigners have an idea, more or less distinct, that it is a land of flowers and shrubbery, if not of sylvan scenery, but this is not the case. I have visited the province of Honan, which may be regarded as the very heart of the "Central Flowery Land," and the earliest home of the Chinaman, but there is absolutely nothing in its generally flat and cheerless landscape to give the slightest foundation to such an idea. There are no farm-houses or farm-yards in all the Great Plain, and absolutely no such thing as hedge-rows or wild flowers, or flower-gardens, so far as I could discover, in over two thousand miles of travel in the interior. Flowers would, of course, grow there, if cultivated and cared for, but it is not the habit of the Chinese to waste their efforts on such matters, and my judgment is that they do so less than any other people in the world. I do not doubt that the few thousands of foreigners and missionaries, residing in and near the treaty ports, grow more flowers than do the whole Chinese race outside of them, and yet the Chinese, when properly taught, become very skillful gardeners, and excel especially as florists.

Coal and iron are found in nearly every Chinese province, except those lying in the Great Plain, and it is said by Richthofen that the extent of the workable coal-beds, and the quantity of coal contained in them, are greater than those of any other country of the world. Both anthracite and bituminous coal abound, in all qualities, from the best Lehigh to the poorest lignite, but the measures are not extensively or systematically worked, although they have been opened in the hills near Peking, and perhaps, elsewhere, from the time of Marco Polo. There is only one mine in the whole empire, that of Kai-ping, about eighty miles east-northeast from Tientsin, at the edge of the plain and the foot of the hills, furnished with European machinery, and worked under European supervision, and even that one, although it mined and sold one hundred and thirty thousand tons of excellent bituminous coal last year—perhaps half of it to the steamships visiting the Pei-ho—has not proved to be a business success. This is due mainly to over-capitalization, aided by Chinese inexperience and mismanagement. It has a most excellent plant, consisting of houses, shafts, hoisting and pumping engines, compressors, and a well-constructed but light, standard-gauge railroad seven miles long, for transporting the output of the colliery to the canal which carries it through the plain, twenty-one miles to the Peh-tang River. This railroad, the only one in China, was opened in 1881, and is exceedingly well built. It is laid with thirty-five-pound steel rails, furnished with broken stone ballast, and first-class appliances of every sort, including two locomotives built in England, and one, the "Rocket of China," the first one ever operated on the road, built at the company's works at Kaiping, out of old materials. Both the road and the engine were built and put into operation surreptitiously and without proper government warrant or authority. The coal-mining company, composed exclusively of Chinese capitalists, was authorized to open its mines, and to employ foreign experts and foreign methods, in mining and hoisting its coal, but it was never dreamed by them that any other means of transport except those of canal and river would be necessary to get the product to market. The Chinese authorities, and perhaps even the Chinese promoters of the undertaking, assumed that it would be feasible to dig and operate a canal from the company's shaft to the Peh-tang River; but when the foreign engineers took the levels of the place, and of the uncertain stream in the neighborhood, it was discovered at once that the mine-opening was nearly eighty feet above the level of the plain, that a canal was therefore impracticable, and that a tramway or railroad seven miles long would be absolutely necessary. This was made known to the Chinese authorities, who reluctantly authorized a tramway to be substituted for a part of the canal, but the company was specially enjoined to use only horses or mules in hauling the coal to the canal. The English engineers, however, went quietly to work to build a locomotive, knowing full well that nothing else would answer their purpose. Knowledge of this leaked out through the Chinese mechanics, and reached the ears of the authorities shortly afterward. Orders were at once issued to stop work on the "strange machine," and this was done; but after a while, when suspicion had been allayed, work upon it was resumed, and in due time it was finished and put successfully in operation. The railroad being in an out-of-the-way region, and remote from all the principal highways, was ignored by the authorities, and no notice has yet been taken of its existence, or of the operation of locomotives upon it by the Imperial Government. Curiously enough, no high Chinese official has ever been near it, and so long as it remains unrecognized by the imperial authorities, no great official is likely to visit or inspect it, and yet it is to be extended immediately to the Peh-tang River, under some kind of license from the provincial government, based upon the need of the northern fleet for coal and the fact that the canal from the end of the railroad to the river has proved to be entirely unequal to the business for which it was intended. It is both too narrow and too shallow, and although it could be both widened and deepened to the requisite extent, for much less money than the railroad will cost, the fact still remains that it freezes up for over three months every winter, and for that period becomes entirely impassable and useless.

The company has constructed extensive buildings for the accommodation of a school of engineering and mining, which has never been opened, and another set at either end of the railroad, for the reception and entertainment of distinguished official visitors, who have never made their appearance. It employs, besides, a large number of useless Chinese servants, and conducts its business in a wasteful and extravagant manner, subject to the countless squeezes and exactions which characterize all Chinese undertakings of a public character. The foreign officials are exceedingly capable and clever men, but their functions are strictly technical, and do not in any way involve or control the commercial affairs of the company.

A coal-mine, under English management, was opened

60   CHINA.

and furnished with foreign plant, near Kelung, in the Island of Formosa, several years ago, but it was abandoned and destroyed, to prevent its falling into the hands of the French during their recent occupancy of that island. These mines are now worked by the natives in the old way, as are others in the hills near Peking, in the provinces of Shan-tung and Shansi, and also on the Yang-tse-kiang.

The coal from the hills near Peking is an excellent anthracite, but it is understood that the measures are too thin for extensive workings with foreign plant and appliances. The coal of Southern Shansi is of the very finest variety of anthracite, and exists in thick beds of great extent. It is hauled in wheelbarrows to the Hwang-ho, and transported to Kai-fung-fu, and other points farther down the river, in considerable quantities. It is also distributed throughout the surrounding country for several hundred miles in wheelbarrows, each of which is directed by a man between the handles, and hauled by one or two donkeys, and carries from three hundred and fifty to four hundred pounds. Notwithstanding the cheapness of labor, and of food for both man and beast, coal transported in this way for any considerable distance becomes a costly luxury, entirely beyond the reach of the common people. It is used in small quantities by the rich, and by the public cooks. Coal is also sent to market by water from the mines on the banks of the Yang-tse, and will, of course, bear transportation in that way to much more considerable distances than by land, as above described.

Notwithstanding the great abundance of coal, and the cheapness with which it can be mined, its consumption is in its infancy in China, and nothing but the introduction of railroads and modern methods of mining can bring it into general use by the people.

MINERAL RESOURCES UNDEVELOPED. 61

Iron-ores are almost as widely distributed as coal, but little or nothing of their character and economic value is known. No systematic surveys or exploitations have been made of the ore-beds, and there is not a blast-furnace in the whole empire. What little iron is used by the Chinese is either imported from foreign countries, mostly in the form of nail-rods and old scrap, or is made in the remote districts in the most primitive manner. Other minerals, and especially copper, silver, and gold, exist in various parts of the empire, but they have neither been sought for nor worked in any systematic or scientific way. Special exploitations and examinations have been made by foreign experts, and some efforts based thereon have been made to establish smelting-works for the reduction of copper-ores, large quantities of which metal are used for making *cash*, the only currency of the country, but I failed to learn that any of the copper-mines or smelting-works had yet been worked at a profit. Much of the copper used is imported from Japan and other foreign countries.

The fact is that China, notwithstanding its abundant supply of ores and coal, is behind every other civilized country in mining and metallurgy. She has no experts, and no scientific knowledge, and has made absolutely no progress in respect to these matters for the last five hundred years; but there are some faint indications that a few of her leading statesmen, and especially Li Hung-Chang, the Marquis Tseng, and such as have visited foreign countries as ministers and consuls, have come to recognize the importance of these industries to the commercial and manufacturing interests, as well as to the national defense. They at least have begun to ask Western powers for geologists, mining-engineers, metallurgists, and iron-masters, and it is safe to say that large numbers of such men must sooner or later find employment in

China. It will be many years before that country can educate its own youth for such occupations, not only because they have no competent teachers or schools, but because the language itself has no scientific nomenclature whatever connected with it. Not only the scientific ideas, but the words themselves, must be introduced into the Chinese mind and language, and this, in a country where no system of popular education prevails, and no universally spoken dialect exists, is an exceedingly difficult task to accomplish.

A greater difficulty, however, than that remains to be overcome before any substantial advance can be made in mining or metallurgy, or, in fact, in anything else progressive, and that is, such a regeneration of the Imperial Government as will make it the leader of the Chinese people in the march of modern progress, instead of the jealous guardian of their conservatism in self-conceit, ignorance, and superstition, as it now is. So long as the present condition of affairs prevails, no scientific or professional man should go to China for employment, except under contract with the Government or some properly authorized and responsible official. The time may come when all this may be changed, but it has not come yet.

CHAPTER VI.

Population of China—No complete census ever taken—The country not overcrowded—Influence of famines, rebellions, pestilence, and floods —Reproduction normal and active—Population probably greater than ever before—Country capable of supporting three times as many inhabitants—Origin of the Chinese race—Physical characteristics— Compression of feet—Manchus do not practice the custom—Its origin—Failure to practice it looked upon as evidence of abject poverty and distress—Food of the Chinese people—Domestic animals.

THE population of China has never been accurately enumerated, and no such thing as a scientific and complete census, such as is now regarded as absolutely necessary by all modern governments, has ever been conceived, much less undertaken, by the Imperial Chinese Government. All statements concerning the population of the country are, therefore, but little better than mere guesses, based upon partial enumerations, for purposes of taxation. All authorities agree in saying that the best one ever made was that of 1812, at which time the eighteen provinces (Formosa was then included in Fo-kien) of China proper were estimated to contain 362,447,183 souls, or an average of about 200 to the square mile. In 1868 the Russian statistician Vassilivitch gave the population at 404,946,514 ; and in 1881 the Imperial Maritime Customs reports gave it at 380,000,000. None of these reports include any estimate of the population of Corea, Manchuria, Mongolia, Ili, or Thibet, but as they are all thinly settled, except Corea, which claims a *quasi*-independence, the actual figures, even if they could be had, would probably not materially change the grand aggregate, while figures obtained by guessing are worse than useless. Withal, some travelers' have estimated the entire population of the empire as high as 500,000,000, while others have placed it as low as 300,000,000. As to the probable correctness of these estimates, and for various interesting details connected therewith, reference should be made to Williams's "Middle Kingdom," where they are fully set forth and discussed. I have no data not found in that admirable work, or in other books of travel, but I have a decided conviction, based upon my own observation, that the population of the entire empire can not exceed 360,000,000. I have traveled extensively in Northern China, and especially in the Great Plain, which is considered by all authorities as one of the most thickly settled regions of the empire, and yet I saw no evidence whatever of overcrowding, or, indeed, of any extraordinary density of population. The hamlets, villages, and towns, into which the entire population is gathered, are thickly studded over parts of the plain, but they are neither so plentiful nor so large as to convey the idea that there is not room for more, or for greater growth of those which already exist. Besides, there are considerable reaches of unsettled or thinly settled country in which the villages are small and widely separated. In the hill country, much of which is rough and not arable, the population is still thinner, and, notwithstanding the fact that, with all deductions and allowances, China contains from one fifth to one third of all the people in the world, I do not doubt it could support three times as many as now inhabit it, if all its land were brought under proper cultivation, and it were provided with a properly located system of railroads between the various provinces and outlying dependencies, for the purpose of interchanging their different productions one with another.

Frightful famines have occurred frequently in Shansi and Shensi, and in various other parts of the Empire, and owing to the peculiar meteorological conditions which prevail, especially in Northern China, are likely to occur again, at intervals, for all time. It is estimated that over ten million people died from starvation about ten years ago in Shansi and Shensi alone, while abundance and plenty were prevailing in other parts of the country. Every effort was made, both by the foreigners and by the Imperial Government, to send food into the stricken region, but owing to the great distances to be traversed, and the entire absence of river and canal navigation, as well as of railroads, but few of the suffering multitude could be reached in time to save their lives. Religious and political disturbances and rebellions have also prevailed in various parts of the empire, especially in the southern, southeastern, and western provinces, and the wars for their suppression have carried off many millions of people. As before stated, the Taiping rebellion alone is estimated to have resulted in the death of over ten million people in the fourteen years of its duration. Pestilence and floods have also aided in the work of destruction; and, besides all these, it is undoubtedly true that in some regions population has crowded close upon the limits of the regular food-supply, and that, with the aid of infanticide, which is prevalent, especially in the south, has strongly tended to prevent any rapid increase of population. At all events, the common impression is, that the population has not materially increased since 1812. How far this impression is well founded I do not undertake to say, but I must add that my own observations would rather discredit than sustain it. It seems to me far more likely that neither the census of 1812, nor any other, was accurately taken, than that reproduction has been suspended in any degree, or that famine, pestilence, and war, all combined, could have killed faster than the tremendous aggregate force of that instinct in a population of 360,-000,000 human beings could increase the race under any circumstances which could possibly exist, even in China. It is a perfectly well settled custom that every male Chinaman must marry soon after he comes of age, and that presupposes at least one wife for every such male. Polygamy is allowed, but not generally practiced among the common people, hence the influence of that institution may be ignored. It is also well understood that every man must have at least one son, either of his own body or by adoption, to reverence him while living, and to worship him after death; therefore reproduction is a religious as well as a natural and political duty, and as a matter of fact it seems to flourish as well in China as elsewhere. In all my travels I saw children of both sexes in abundance, and they seemed to be as healthy, happy, and well cared for generally, as in any other country I ever visited. The fact is, that the Chinese not only possess the same instincts which characterize the human race in other countries, but the same virtues and the same vices in about the same degree as other people of the same grade of civilization. They appear to be naturally fond of children, and to take as good care of them as of themselves; and while it is true that girls are not so highly prized as boys, and are consequently more frequently made away with, there is no scarcity of them, so far as I could perceive, in any region visited by me.

From all these circumstances I believe that the population of China is now greater than ever before; that it is steadily, though perhaps not rapidly, increasing; and that, with the introduction of the appliances and varied industries of modern progress, it will increase more rapidly hereafter than ever before. The introduction of railroads, the opening of mines, the construction of furnaces and rolling-mills, and the establishment of manufactories, will be followed by a rise in wages, which, in turn, will bring increased comfort in clothing and habitation, as well as an increased demand for and a wider and more perfect distribution of food of all kinds now grown by the Chinese, and of many kinds produced only by foreign nations. The appliances for the support and conservation of life will become greater and better exactly in the same proportion as the progressive movement, after it is once well under way, develops itself. This is the result which has followed in every other country, and there is no reason whatever for supposing that a different one will follow in China.

I shall not undertake to give the ethnographic history of the Chinese race, further than to say that it belongs to the great Turanian or yellow stock, and it has doubtless inhabited China from the remotest ages of the past. Some writers believe that it was created or originated on the soil which it now inhabits, and in view of the complete isolation by the sandy and arid region which surrounds it on the land-side and separates it from Europe, and by the boundless sea which separates it from the rest of the world, there is nothing improbable in this suggestion. It has always seemed to me much more natural that the various branches of the human race should have been evolved in countries perfectly adapted to their wants, than that they should have had a common origin in a remote, inhospitable, and inaccessible region of Central Asia, as is so commonly believed to have been the case.

Such writers as believe that the race came into China from the northwest—and the Chinese themselves seem generally to share this belief—contend that its line of progress was down the valley of the Hwang-ho rather than that of the Yang-tse, and that they first took firm root in the rich plains of the province of Honan, from which "Central Flowery Land" they spread over and possessed all of Southeastern Asia. Be this as it may (and there is no trustworthy historical evidence upon which to affirm or deny the theory), the race has certainly displaced or absorbed all others of the land, and seems to be one of great vigor and vitality. The people of the north are in some degree fairer, larger, and stronger than those of the south, and this is not inconsistent with a common origin and substantial freedom from adulteration. Whatever differentiation has taken place, may have been and doubtless was, due to climatic influences, rather than to intermixture with autocthonous or Maylasian races.

So far as an observer untrained in ethnological studies can perceive, the Chinese are a remarkably homogeneous people. They differ but little in face or feature, whether they belong to one class or another, or to the same or different provinces. They are generally up to the average size of Europeans, and I should say considerably above that of the French. Curiously enough, there is nothing but rank and station to distinguish the Manchu mandarins from the Chinese. They all wear similar costumes in similar grades and stations of life, and look as though they might belong to exactly the same stock, although the Manchus are a conquering race, or, should I not say, a conquering tribe of the same race? Their eyes, hair, and skin are about the same color, and to all casual observers their manners and customs are the same in nearly every respect. The males all shave their heads and wear queues, but this custom is said to have been distinctly Manchurian in its origin, and to have been forced upon the Chinese at the time of the Manchu con-

COMPRESSION OF THE FEET. 69

quest, which took place between 1635 and 1644 A. D., as a sign of subjugation and submission.

There is one notable difference in the customs of the Manchus and the Chinese. The women of the latter, everywhere and in every station of life, rich and poor, mandarin and coolie alike, have their feet compressed, while those of the Manchu women, from the empress down through the imperial clan, to the wives and daughters of the common soldiers, permit their feet to grow to their natural size. The custom of compressing the feet has prevailed for several hundred years, and is said to have had its origin among the Chinese from the circumstance that a beautiful princess had club-feet, and that she concealed the fact so completely by the skill with which she disguised her deformity that she was not only greatly admired, but it became the fashion for all the ladies of the court to imitate her in everything, even in the effort to make their feet look small. Tradition has it that compression was resorted to for this purpose, and that the fashion spread to the people, and gradually became a confirmed custom. This explanation is the most commonly accepted one, but it is not entirely satisfactory to me.

There is also a tradition that the practice was at first resorted to by some cruel and crusty husband for the purpose of keeping his wife and daughters from "going a-gadding," and that it was found to work so well that his neighbors also adopted it, and that it spread throughout the country. Finally, it has been suggested that, whatever may have been the origin of the custom, it is retained because the male sex has come to admire the effect of it upon the female figure. The physical result of the practice is to bring the feet down to mere callous points, to reduce the size of the ankle correspondingly, and to obliterate the calf of the leg entirely, so that the figure tapers rapidly from the hips to the ends of the toes, and the more completely this is done the more nearly the form approaches the highest Chinese ideal of beauty.

I have heard it asked if the practice had produced any influence in decreasing the size of the normal Chinese foot, and, while this raises a curious question in heredity and natural selection, I can not say that it can be answered in the affirmative. Both Chinese men and women, in their natural condition, have hands and feet which might be properly called small, but I could not perceive that the feet of the men are unusually small, nor do I believe they are so.

As before observed, the custom of compressing the feet of the girl-children is universal among the people of North China. The common belief among foreigners who have never been in China is, that the custom is confined to the better classes, but such is not the fact. It is practiced by every walk and condition of life, from the highest and richest to the lowest and poorest. Occasionally, a poor little houseless and homeless waif may be seen with natural feet, but this is looked upon as the crowning evidence of her abject poverty and friendlessness. I once heard a most intelligent and sympathetic missionary lady, in the interior of Northern China, declare that nothing so moved her pity as to see a Chinese girl so utterly bereft of every human care, so lonely and abject in her poverty and distress, as to have no one in the world who thought enough of her to compress her feet! When I expressed my astonishment at her remark, and asked her if she did not regard the custom as about the worst and most cruel of all Chinese customs, she promptly said : "Oh, yes ! it is as bad as it can be, when practiced by a whole people, and, if I were empress, the first edict I would issue would be to abolish it ; but so long as it is the custom, I only know one thing worse, and that is not to follow it in the individual case, for that betokens a depth of sorrow, loneliness, and poverty, beyond which there is no lower depth possible for even a Chinese child."

After seeing the Chinese people under all conditions of life, and in many remote and widely separated parts of the empire, I am compelled to say that they seem to me to be remarkably strong, robust, and healthy, and to be specially free from consumption and all other forms of constitutional disease. It is quite true that diseases of the skin and scalp prevail, but they seem to be altogether due to an insufficient use of water and soap, if not to a positive aversion to those hygienic necessities. They also seem everywhere to be well fed and comfortably though cheaply clad. Their food is mostly composed of vegetables and fish, rice, of course, forming the chief dependence, especially in the southern and eastern provinces, where it is grown, and indeed everywhere else, within reach of the means of transportation. Wheat is grown and used extensively in the country adjacent to the Yellow River, where it matures and is garnered generally before the coming of the summer floods. It is ground into a coarse flour by the primitive means employed in all Oriental countries, and made into unleavened cakes, or into bread, which, owing to the scarcity of fuel, is boiled instead of baked. The loaves, if I may call them loaves, are about the size of apple-dumplings, and look more like them than anything else. They are said to be a very good substitute for the bread of the foreigners when sliced and toasted. In out-of-the-way places, where neither rice nor wheat can be had, millet is used, and that is also ground, boiled, mixed with dried fruits, principally the jujube, and sold in slices, cut from the mass as called for. Cabbage of various kinds is grown nearly everywhere, and, boiled with sea-weed, in order to increase the volume and season the cabbage with the salt which it contains, enters largely into the diet of the people. Sweet-potatoes are grown and consumed in the greatest abundance. Radishes and pulse-foods of various sorts are cultivated; persimmons as large as tomatoes are common; but, generally speaking, the country is not rich in fruits. The jujube is, perhaps, the most common fruit in North China. It is called the date by foreigners, but grows upon a tree which resembles the Osage orange more than any other in shape and size. The fruit itself when dried and preserved in honey is very palatable, and not at all unlike the date. Excellent peaches are grown on the Yang-tse, and both apples and pears are found farther north, but they are of inferior quality. Grapes are also found in the north, and are kept through the winter by burying. There are several varieties of them, two of which are large and luscious. Oranges, prunellos, cumquats, loquats, lychees, and lemons grow in the south, and are carried in small quantities by itinerant fruit-venders to the principal cities of the country. Berries and small fruits are unknown except to the foreigners, for whom they are grown in small quantities near the settlements. The extended sea-coast, and the great number of canals, rivers, and ponds, are peculiarly favorable to fish, and they are caught and used in great numbers. The Chinese are skillful, and have many ingenious methods of taking fish. Nothing that lives in water can escape them, or comes amiss when captured. They use every kind and variety of fish, and, what they can not use fresh, they dry and salt for transportation to the interior, so that the average Chinaman's most regular and constant diet is rice and fish. The best fish known to him is the sam-lai, which is identical with our shad. It is highly prized by the mandarins and grandees of Peking. Meat is but little used.

Beef is practically unknown, except near the principal foreign settlements. Mutton is much more common, especially in Northern China, where the broad or fat-tailed Mongolian sheep are raised in sufficient numbers to supply the foreigners, and the richer Chinese, who use it sparingly. It is of excellent quality, quite equal when in proper condition to the best Southdown mutton. Pork is the national flesh-food of the Chinese, and roast sucking-pig the *pièce de résistance* of every feast, but as the hog is a natural scavenger, and permitted to roam at large in the dirt and filth of every town and village, the idea of eating pork in China is particularly offensive to most travelers. Ducks and common barn-yard chickens are found everywhere, and enter largely into the food of the people. Eggs can always be had in abundance and good condition. Game-birds, especially pheasants, partridges, ducks, and snipe, abound in the country along the Yang-tse and its tributaries, and are very good. Venison, hare, pheasants, and an occasional bustard, are brought to the Peking market from Mongolia, but such food is reserved for foreigners and wealthy mandarins, and is hardly ever eaten by the common people. But little milk is produced, and that only for the foreigners. Generally speaking, food is cheap and good, and the natives appear to be well fed, while the foreigner can get practically everything he would find in the most favored regions of Europe or America.

The Chinese keep but few domestic animals. Dogs are found everywhere, and of many kinds, but the common dog of the country is a mongrel of decidedly wolfish characteristics, although he is noisy rather than fierce. He seems to receive but little care, and to be regarded rather with indifference than interest. No one pays much attention to him, and when he flies out, after the manner of dogs in all countries, at the passing stranger, and receives a slashing cut with a riding-whip for his pains, as he frequently did from my party, he yelps with mingled fury and astonishment, but, instead of arousing the sympathy of his owner by his outcry, he generally finds himself laughed at by the by-standers, as though his misfortune were a good joke.

The most common beast of burden in Central and Southeastern China and Formosa is the water-buffalo, or *Bos bubalos*, though common domestic cattle are found in small numbers, and without reference to sex are used for plowing and working in carts. Ponies of the Mongolian or Tartar type are found nearly everywhere; donkeys of excellent breed are still more common, and are used both for riding and draught purposes. Some of them are extremely agile and well broken to the saddle, but they are used only by the common people. Mules are extensively bred in the north, and are as fine as the finest of Kentucky. They are greatly prized in Peking and the other chief cities, where they are used exclusively in the carts of the upper classes. There are no flocks or herds of any kind, all domestic animals being held and cared for in small numbers. I have frequently seen a pair of sheep, or a single cow, or donkey, or a couple of geese, watched over, while feeding in the field, by a boy or a grown man, but never more than a half-dozen animals of any kind (except chickens or ducks) at one time or in one place. All the coal brought into Peking, and all the tea and merchandise taken from Peking into Mongolia and Siberia, is carried on the backs of camels, but they are not found or used elsewhere in the Great Plain.

CHAPTER VII.

The houses of the Chinese—The clothing—The great public works—The walled cities—The only crystallized and accumulated labor of the Chinese—The effect of depopulation—The common people everywhere poor—No system of popular education—No conception of or vocabulary for science—Diversity of dialects—The classical or literary language of the country—The greater wall of China—Chinese civilization—The characteristics of the race—Arrested development —Future progress.

THE houses of the common Chinese are nearly everywhere built of sun-dried brick, and covered with thatch of millet-stalks resting on rafters of willow poles. In the hill country, where rock can be had, it is substituted; and, in the extreme south, bamboos are used for building purposes. The richer people, who are very scarce, as compared with the multitude, build of fire-burned bricks, which are generally of a gray color and much larger than the bricks used in foreign countries. When the house is built of burned bricks it is covered with tiles of the same material, laid on a bed of mud mixed with cut straw. But little wood is used in the construction of houses. The doors, sashes, and scanty furniture, are made of boards, but the floors are either of clay smoothed down, or of burned paving-tiles made of the same clay and laid in about the same way as the roofing-tiles. The windows of the common houses are small, and filled with thin white paper, while those of the better class are larger, and occasionally have a single pane of glass in the center surrounded by paper. There are no fireplaces, but nearly every house is furnished with a *kang*, or a raised, solid platform, of the same materials as the wall. It extends across one end of the room, and is furnished with a small furnace and flue, for the purpose of heating it during the night when it is used as a sleeping-place for the family ; but I am compelled to say that, in nearly three thousand miles of travel in midwinter, between the Yellow River and the Great Wall, I never saw one of these kangs which had been warmed up, or in which my servants could even start a fire. Whether there is a kang or not, there is an open furnace in every house, or connected with it, and which may either have a flue or a short clay chimney, and this is used for heating water and cooking, but these furnaces and their appurtenances are exceedingly rude, and frequently smoke about as badly as would an open fire built on the floor. Fuel, as before explained, is everywhere scarce, and hence fire is used only for cooking, never for warming the house, of even the rich, and this renders it necessary for the people to keep themselves warm during winter entirely by clothing, although the best houses sometimes have an open basin of charcoal burning in the best room ; but even then they are cold and cheerless, for while the walls and roofs are close and tight, the windows and doors are poorly made, loosely fitted, and nearly always left open or on the slam. To add to the national discomfort, nothing is ever repaired, so that when decay begins it continues till the ruin is complete, and the discomfort becomes unbearable even to a Chinaman.

The clothing of the poor in China is made of cotton, and never anything else. It is nearly always dyed blue, and in winter is wadded and quilted. Occasionally, men whose occupation requires them to live out-of-doors in

CLOTHING OF THE CHINESE. 77

Northern China, wear sheep-skin overcoats and hoods. Woolen cloth, which is now being imported in small quantities, is but little worn, and never by any except rich people. Silk and furs constitute the dress of the high officials and mandarins, and also of the well-to-do merchants, *compradors* and upper servants in public, or while engaged in receiving visitors or making calls, but it is said that they are laid aside even by the richest for cotton garments as soon as the special occasion which demanded their use has gone by. To people accustomed to the warm and abundant woolen clothing of Europe and America, the mere suggestion of cotton for winter use conveys an idea of chilliness; but, so far as I could ascertain, it proves ample, when wadded and worn in a sufficient number of layers, to keep the Chinese warm and comfortable.

Cotton is grown in nearly every province of China, but it is of short fiber, and good only for the rougher and coarser fabrics. Every Chinese family in the interior does its own spinning and weaving, and nearly all its own dyeing. But, of later years, cotton sheetings, drills, and jeans, from the United States, have come into general favor, and their importation is rapidly on the increase. With proper enterprise this trade can not only be held but largely extended. The English and Germans are doing everything in their power, even to the imitation of brands and trade-marks, to take it away from the Americans, but a strict adherence to the high standards heretofore established, with a close observance of the requirements of the Chinese consumers, by the American manufacturer and merchant, can not fail to keep them in the lead, at least in this line of business.

While there seems to be but little want or suffering even in the poorer districts of China, except during the prevalence of floods or famine, it is evident to the most casual observer that there is never any great surplus of food or clothing, and that the masses live literally from hand to mouth now, as they have always lived. They are a strictly agricultural people, and have neither mines, furnaces, rolling-mills, nor manufacturing establishments. They live in poor habitations, and have no grand buildings constructed of stone and iron. Even their largest temples and government offices are badly designed, built of perishable materials, and are poorly kept. They have no enduring monuments, and no public works, except the Great Wall, the Grand Canal, and a few large river embankments. The first is a work of stupendous magnitude, and, although now out of date, must have been, when honestly defended, entirely efficacious in keeping the northern hordes out of China proper. The Grand Canal, although extending almost from one end of the empire to the other, must have always been a disappointment and an expense to the Imperial Government, if not to the Chinese people, and principally for the reason that, having no locks, and no proper means of regulating and economizing the water-supply, it must have been subject to frequent and vexatious interruptions and breaks, to the serious detriment of navigation.

There is one other form of public work which strikes the traveler with wonder. I refer, of course, to the walls of fire-burned brick which surround every great city throughout the empire. They are generally from thirty to forty feet high, from twenty to forty feet thick, surrounded by wide moats, and surmounted by crenelated parapets, broken by towers and buttresses at frequent intervals, pierced by arched and carefully fortified gateways, in which strongly framed gates, covered with iron plates and studded with iron spikes, swing heavily every night and morning, now, as they doubtless did a thousand years ago. Some of these walls are as much as forty miles around, and, like those of Nanking and Kaifung-fu, include within them many hundreds of acres of land upon which there are no buildings whatever. It might be supposed that these walls were all erected during the time corresponding to the feudal period of Europe, and certainly many of them were; but I doubt not more than one has been built in this century, and that if a new capital were selected for any one of the provinces, even at this late day, the governor-general would surely surround it with a wall exactly in the style of those built during the reign of Kublai Khan. This is no vague supposition, but is based upon an actual occurrence which took place in Formosa since the close of the last Franco-Chinese war. It was found that the old capital of that beautiful and fertile island was too far south, and had too poor a port, to permit its being reached readily, and so the governor-general was authorized to select a new one farther north. In the exercise of sound judgment, he selected a spot on the open plain near Twatutia, on the Tamsui River, about twelve miles from the sea, named it Tai-pak-fu, and at once surrounded it by a cut-stone wall of full dimensions, over two miles around, built in the style and furnished with all the ancient and antiquated glories of the hoary past. The interior is dotted about by the buildings of the governor-general's *yamen*, but nine tenths of the space inclosed is covered by a paddy-field.

Whether this wall was erected at the special direction of the Peking Government, or merely by its tacit permission, in pursuance of immemorial custom, I could not ascertain; but in view of the fact that it is within a mile of two cities, either said to contain over a hundred thousand inhabitants, it may be that the governor-general thought he would be safer, within its *enceinte*, from insurrection, or a sudden rush of the people, than he would be in either city or in an open camp, and in this he is clearly right, if he can only depend upon the fidelity of his guard.

The great works just enumerated constitute the only crystallized and accumulated labor of the Chinese people, through all the ages of their residence in China; and while they are really great, and represent the toil of many millions of men, they are all of a public character, and bear testimony rather to the slavery of the subject than to the intelligence of the Government. When one considers the unlimited authority of the Chinese Emperors, and the countless millions under their control, and which have been under their control for so many generations, the only wonder is that still greater works, of a higher and better class, have not been left as monuments to their wisdom and power. As it is, it is hardly too much to say that, if China should become depopulated and remain so for ten years, the traveler could discover but few traces of human occupation anywhere within her far-reaching limits, except the ruins of these great works. Barring its undeveloped mineral resources, and its inexhaustible supply of docile and patient labor, China is an exceedingly poor country. What little wealth it contains is in the hands of the literary and official class, and of the merchants, who are at most and altogether only as one in ten thousand. Even they are compelled to conceal it as much as possible. They generally live modestly and quietly, avoiding state and display, and putting their surplus money into clothing, embroideries, porcelains, notes, mortgages, and such things as do not unduly attract the attention of the tax-gatherer, the imperial or provincial authorities, or of the curious and evil-disposed.

The common people are everywhere poor, and have

but little surplus money and no surplus productions. Whatever may be the case in foreign countries, in these days of railroads and steam-machinery, there is no over-production in China. To the contrary, it could readily buy more, produce more, consume more, and lay up or accumulate more, if it could only sell more. It would buy more cotton cloth, more iron, more matches, and needles, and thread; more and better building materials and machinery; more guns, and steamships, and iron-clads; and in the end it would live better, build better houses, erect furnaces and rolling-mills, and lay out and construct railroads, if it could only sell more tea and silk. These articles constitute at present the greater part of what it has to sell; but the Chinese are like the rest of mankind, and may be depended upon, in the long run, to produce whatever they can sell, either at home or abroad, at a profit. They can not be said to want what they can not form any conception of. Ignorance is everywhere an effectual bar to aspiration and improvement, and the Chinese are especially ignorant in reference to everything which goes to make up what foreigners call modern progress. They have no conception of science, and no vocabulary in which to formulate its principles, or to make known its wonderful revelations. They have stood absolutely still in knowledge since the middle ages. The discoveries of Galileo, Newton, and Laplace are a sealed book to them. They have but little conception of mathematics, and none of chemistry, mineralogy, and geology. They are entirely ignorant of thermo-dynamics and of mechanics, and almost so of mining and metallurgy. They do not pretend to understand political economy as it is taught in Western countries; and, what is worse than all else, they have no system of popular education. According to the best authorities, not over one man in every hundred, nor one woman in every thousand, can read and write ; but even if this were not the case, there is no popular or common language which is everywhere understood. Every province has its own dialect, which is not only different from that of every other province, but is still more widely different from the literary language of the country, which is also the language of Peking and the imperial court. But then, again, the colloquial language of the official class and the *literati* is entirely different from the written language of the classics, in which every great idea must be clothed and every great man must express himself. So it will be seen that science and religion are alike fettered in this curious country, the civilization of which is as separate and distinct from ours as if it had originated in another planet.

The Great Wall of China was built of earth and stone over two thousand years ago ; it has been enlarged, extended, and repaired many times since, but, notwithstanding all this, it has been often broken through by the Tartars in their onward march of conquest and plunder ; but the greater wall of China is its language, which has never, within the historic period, been changed or improved, but stands now as firmly as when it first took form, an inflexible monosyllabic barrier to modern thought and modern progress. It is far more difficult for the teacher of modern science to cross effectively, even without opposition, than the wall of stone and earth ever was to the Mongolian or Manchu conqueror, defended by the whole Chinese race ; and yet the example of Japan, which, forty years ago, was the most exclusive nation in the world, with a language as antiquated and difficult to master, should encourage us to believe that even this greater wall of China can not stay the march of modern progress much longer, or even turn it from its destined course.

NEED OF MODERN IMPROVEMENTS. 83

It is folly to contend that the Chinese, as a people, want any of the things to which I have alluded, for want in this sense presupposes an intelligent understanding of the things wanted, which I have shown to be impossible to the average Chinaman, in the present condition of his language and education; but, as I shall point out more particularly hereafter, he has as great a need of railroads, furnaces, rolling-mills, mines, and factories, and will receive as much benefit from them, as any other human being, and, under the guidance of the enlightened statesmen who are coming to the front, will surely accept them as the greatest blessing ever bestowed upon him or his country. After all, it is true in China, as well as elsewhere, that "those who think must govern those who toil"; and, while the multitude can neither think deeply nor see far into the future, there are a few men of sufficient wisdom to comprehend what is good, and of sufficient height to see over the wall which has so far shut out progress, and kept their country in ignorance, stagnation, and poverty.

It has been suggested, by more than one thoughtful student of Chinese civilization, that it presents a case of decay from extreme old age; but, while it is indubitably old, though perhaps not so old as it is commonly regarded, I can not perceive that it presents any of the indications of senility. The Chinese race is certainly strong and vigorous, and shows no sign whatever of decay. It is prolific, frugal, and industrious, and these are the physical virtues which betoken youth rather than declining manhood. It seems to me that, inasmuch as China has never had the higher arts of civilization, either in architecture, engineering, navigation, mining, metallurgy, or manufacturing, or even in warfare, it rather indicates a case of suspended national development, if not of prolonged youth. The peculiar civilization of the Chinese people is merely an accident, due to isolation and other causes to which I have alluded, and may be confidently expected to give place to another and a better civilization whenever the latter can secure opportunity to demonstrate its superiority. The Chinaman's natural intelligence, although dwarfed and misdirected by a peculiar if not pernicious system of social and political government, is quite as great as that of other races. He is full of the conceit and prejudice engendered by ignorance, but is no fool, and has never been charged with being one. He is shrewd and bright at whatever he turns his mind, and whenever relieved from the incubus of old custom, and allowed to show his natural tendency and aptitudes, neither asks nor needs favor at the hands of his competitor, no matter who the latter may be. Having health and strength in addition, he may be expected, under proper leadership and education, to play his full part in the future history of the world. I have no fear that he will conquer it, for he is far behind it in skill, trained intelligence, and even in mere brute force. He may, at no distant day, as time goes, reach the point that the other nations have already attained in the march of progress, but they will meanwhile pass on, and perhaps all the faster, because he is no longer content to stand still, but has resolved to be up and doing.

CHAPTER VIII.

Voyage from Shanghai to Tientsin—China Merchants' Steam Navigation Company—American house of Russell and Company put the first steamboats on the Yang-tse—Sold them to the China Merchants' Company—Coast of Shan-tung—Chee-foo—Naval station at Port Arthur badly located—The northern fleet—Board of Admiralty—Command of the northern fleet—Need of educated officers—The Taku forts and dock-yard—"Heaven-sent barriers"—Chinese troops drilled by foreign officers in English—Chinese army badly organized, armed and administered—The Pei-ho—Villages on its banks—Grave-mounds, and burial of the dead—Fung-shuy or geomancy—Difficulty of laying out railroads without removal of graves—How that can be managed.

As before stated, it is not my purpose to give a detailed account of the manners and customs of the Chinese, nor of their language, literature, philosophy, or religion, for these have been exhaustively considered by the writers to whom reference is made in the preface. What I wish to bring into view here are rather the broader and more prominent aspects of their country and civilization, and I do not care to deal with even them further than may be necessary to give the reader a clear conception of their past and present condition, together with an insight into the character of their leading men and of their government; and this I shall endeavor to do in connection with my own travels and observations, rather than by going over ground which has been fully covered by others.

My first trip from Shanghai to Tientsin was made in the latter part of October (1885) on the China Merchants' steamship "Hae-an," a stout English-built vessel of about 1,200 tons burden, commanded by an English captain, with an English first-officer, an American second, and Scotch chief-engineer and assistants. The trip required only three days, including a stop at Chee-foo, the chief seaport of the Shan-tung promontory.

The China Merchants' Steam Navigation Company is composed exclusively of Chinamen, and was organized under an imperial edict. As it is the only Chinese joint-stock company of which I have any knowledge, except the Chinese Engineering and Mining Company, which owns and operates the Kaiping coal-mines and railroad, and to which I shall refer more fully hereafter, its history is a matter of importance.

The first steamboats used in China were built in the United States for the old American house of Russell and Company, who ran them successfully many years on the Yang-tse River, and along the Chinese coast between Canton, Shanghai, and Tientsin. In or about the year 1862 they organized the Shanghai Navigation Company, and transferred their steamers to it. In 1872 the Chinese Government authorized the formation of the China Merchants' Steam Navigation Company, which in 1877 took over all the steamships of the Shanghai Steam Navigation Company, and enlarged their fleet by the purchase of a number of new steamers. Upon the outbreak of the Franco-Chinese War, the China Merchants' Company, fearing the capture of their ships by the French, after much negotiation with various foreign houses, sold them to Messrs. Russell and Company, who raised the American flag over them, on the 1st of August, 1884, and continued them in the trade for which they had been built. Shortly after the declaration of peace between the belligerents, Russell and Company, at the earnest solicitation of the Chinese authorities, but without any previous pledge or obligation to do so, resold the ships to the China Merchants' Company, and that company rehoisted its flag over them on August 1, 1885, and now operates them on the Yang-tse, and in the various coastwise routes starting from Shanghai. The ships, of which there are twenty, are all iron, and in excellent condition, well found and managed, but, owing to the competition of various other ships, operated on the same routes by foreign companies, it is doubtful if they are making sufficient money to keep up repairs and pay dividends. It is known that a pool, or an arrangement equivalent to a pool, exists between the various companies, and that the China Merchants' Company is practically controlled, if not supported, by the Government, and yet it is not in a flourishing condition. The business of the company is managed exclusively by Chinese mandarins, designated by the viceroy, Li Hung-Chang, who, in addition to other high offices, holds that of Minister Superintendent of Trade for the Northern Sea-board. The ships are, however, officered exclusively by foreigners, most of whom are English and Americans, and it would be difficult to find, under any flag, a more capable set of men. They are mostly in the prime of life, strong, vigilant, and trustworthy, and in every way show that they belong to the dominating race of the world. The quartermasters are generally old and weather-beaten Manila men, but the stewards, firemen, and sailors are exclusively Chinese.

On this trip we ran out of the yellow water of the Yang-tse, within a hundred and seventy-five miles of its mouth, and continued our voyage in sparkling blue waves and clear, crisp air. We sighted the southeast promontory the second day, and steamed along between barren, rocky islands and the broken and picturesque coast-line of the Shan-tung province, with a range of rugged, sierra-like hills in the distance, till we passed into the Gulf of

Pechili. The hills are entirely devoid of vegetation, and show scarcely any sign of being cultivated. They have a warm and reddish hue, and look for all the world like the hills of Utah and the Humboldt Valley. After passing through the Straits of Miau-tau, entering the Gulf of Pechili, and taking our course for the Taku bar, I expected to see the clear and sparkling waves, which we had had since leaving the Yellow Sea, again discolored by the loëss-stained waters of the Hwang-ho, which enters the gulf at its southwest corner, but, much to my surprise, no trace of it was perceptible, and I was told by the captain that, so far as he knew or could learn, the volume of water discharged, and the effect produced by it, are inconsiderable, except during floods. Even then they are in no degree comparable to those of the mighty Yang-tse. In view of the fact that the rivers are of nearly the same length, rise in the same region, flow in the same general direction, and are mentioned by geographers, generally on the same page if not in the same paragraph, as among the great rivers of the world, my curiosity was still further stimulated, and I determined to find out, at some future day, something more of the mysterious Hwang-ho than I had so far been able to gather from books and shipmasters.

We stopped for a few hours at Chee-foo, about midway between the southeast promontory and the straits, to discharge passengers and freight. It is a gray, dirty, uninviting Chinese city, straggling around the shore of a pretty bay, and overlooked by a few outlying hamlets and missionary residences between it and the hill-tops in the distance. In the middle foreground, projecting out into the bay, which is nearly landlocked, is a high, rocky hill, occupied by the foreign consulates, and perhaps a dozen gray-brick and stone houses belonging to merchants or missionaries. There is also a pagoda-like signal-station on the hill. To the left of it are a club-house and several hotels, for the accommodation of summer visitors. The beach is a safe one, the sailing good, and the air comparatively bracing, hence the place is resorted to by foreign ladies and children from Hong-Kong, Shanghai, and Peking during the hot summer months, on which account it is frequently called the Newport of China. Back of the hill and foreign settlement is the junk-anchorage, custom-house, and Chinese town. The latter, crowded by junkmen and coolies, all dirty and hard-looking, and many of them clad in rags, but all good-natured and cheerful, is an interesting but not at all a savory or inviting place. It is important, however, as a distributing point for foreign goods, and the outer harbor is the resort of foreign men-of-war on the Chinese station.

Chee-fu was at one time considered by the Chinese authorities and their foreign advisers as the possible site of the great naval station for North China, but that honor seems to have gone by it to the far less eligible point of Port Arthur, on the north side of the Strait of Pechili, where the Government has located and is now busily engaged in constructing an extensive navy-yard, docks, and fortifications, laid out by German engineers, but afterward under the supervision of French engineers and contractors.

From the fact that these important and costly works lie almost at the extreme northeastern end of the empire, on an exposed and easily detached sea-coast, across a gulf at all times open to a hostile fleet, and can not be connected at all with the capital of the country, except by a line of railway running close along the coast for several hundred miles, it is obvious that they will have to be abandoned at no distant day and relocated at some spot which can be much more easily reached and defended. Several million dollars have already been expended at Port Arthur, and several more will be needed before the place can be made useful even in times of peace, or defended against any first-class maritime power for a single day in times of war. It is difficult to imagine why such an exposed position could have been preferred to Chee-fu, or even to Wei-hai-wei, about thirty miles to the eastward, and near the end of the Shan-tung promontory. Either of these positions can be much more easily connected with the interior by rail, and with the excellent coal-beds of the province; and either, if strongly fortified, would afford a much more advantageous base of operations against a foreign fleet menacing either North China or Corea.

It is said that a much better place than either of those named above is offered by the harbor of Kyan-Chan (lat. 36° north, long. 120° 15′ east), on the southern shore of Shan-tung, in a great re-entering angle of the sea-coast, and it is obvious, if the depth of water and the configuration of the land are favorable, that the situation in respect to its connection with the coal-fields and the interior of the country by rail is altogether superior to any other port north of the Yang-tse River for such purposes.

Since the Chinese have been buying the iron-clads from England and Germany, nine of which constitute the formidable " Northern fleet " now assembled at the mouth of the Pei-ho, the question of a naval station for it has been one of great moment to the Viceroy, Li Hung-Chang, and the Seventh Prince (so-called, because he is the seventh son of the late Emperor Tau Quang). This prince is also the father and tutor of the young Emperor, who has recently reached his majority and assumed personal charge of the government.

On the 13th of October, 1885, an imperial decree was issued, setting forth that—under the advice of the Superintendents of Trade for the Northern and Southern Seaboard, the Princes of the Grand Council, the Prince and Ministers of the Tsung-li-Yamen, or Board of Foreign

THE NORTHERN FLEET. 91

Affairs, aided by Li Hung-Chang, all of whom had reported upon the subject—a Board of Admiralty would be established, and that Prince Chun, the Seventh Prince, should assume the chief control of naval matters, "the fleets along the coast being placed under his control and at his disposition." The same decree appointed Prince Ch'ing and Li Hung-Chang as coadjutors in the management of naval affairs, with Shan-Ch'ing a Lieutenant-General of the Red Han-Chun Banner, and Tseng Chi-tse* Junior Vice-President of the Board of War, as assistants. It then concludes as follows: "The formation of a northern navy being at present in the initiatory stage, we commit the special control thereof to Li Hung-Chang; but all new arrangements that have to be made, and matters that have to be considered, must receive the careful attention of the above-mentioned princes and high ministers, who will devise systematic plans, and draw up regulations for submission to the Throne, and to be carried out in successive stages."

Inasmuch as all the princes and ministers named in the decree are residents of Peking, and entirely ignorant of naval administration, the meaning of all this is, that Li Hung-Chang, who resides at Tientsin, and is already overburdened with work, is also to become the actual head of the navy. The formal decree in this case, as in many others, followed rather than preceded the march of events, for the Great Viceroy had been practically in control of the naval defense of the Northern sea-board for the last eight or ten years. He was at first aided by Captain Lang, an officer of the Royal English Navy, but at the outbreak of the Franco-Chinese War that officer resigned or was recalled by his Government, and Captain Siebelin, an under-officer in the United States Navy during the late rebellion, but now a captain in the German Navy, was engaged under a three years' contract to act

---

* Commonly known by foreigners as the Marquis Tseng.

as Admiral and Instructor-General of the fleet. Since the conclusion of peace, however, his services have been dispensed with, and Captain Lang has been reinstated and in turn dispensed with. He is an accomplished and experienced officer, and if left free to act, with a proper staff of assistants and instructors, would doubtless have proven himself to be a most valuable factor in the organization, instruction, and administration of the Northern fleet. In view, however, of the aggressive policy of England in the East, and the constant danger of the disruption of peaceful relations between her and China, it is difficult to see upon what grounds of enlightened self-interest the employment of an English naval officer to build up and instruct a Chinese navy can be justified. To the casual observer, it seems to be self-evident that the Imperial Government would have done far better to select a Dane, a Hollander, or, better still, an American, for such an important position. By doing so, it could certainly have obtained as good an officer, and it would have been much less likely to lose his services by the severance of friendly relations with the country of which he was a citizen.

In this connection, I feel justified in saying that, while the Chinese Government has bought ships of the very latest design, armed with excellent guns of heavy caliber, and furnished with full complements of men, they are yet far from having an efficient navy. They have but few competent foreign instructors, and scarcely any competent native officers. Contrary to the commonly accepted opinion, the Chinese are by no means bold or adventurous seamen, and although the common sailors, like the common soldiers, are a robust and hardy race, they are far from being competent to handle an iron-clad without the supervision of well-trained officers. The recent destruction of the Chinese fleet by the French iron-clads under Admiral Courbet, at Foo-chow, is but a

THE NORTHERN FLEET. 93

sample of what may be expected, in case of war with any first-class naval power, unless the Chinese Government shall meanwhile employ competent instructors, in sufficient numbers and with sufficient authority, to educate officers as fast as they are required to man their warships. Neither one English captain nor a dozen can create a navy without this help, and for this no ample provision has yet been made, although a naval school has been organized in a small way at Tientsin.

I refer to this subject now, somewhat in detail, because the Chinese Government, in the decree above mentioned and in the steps taken to carry it into effect, have gone farther in imitation of foreigners than in any other branch of their public business, unless I except that of the maritime customs, which was organized and brought to its present high state of efficiency by Sir Robert Hart and a corps of able assistants, all of whom are foreigners, and to which I shall refer more fully in another chapter.

We arrived at our anchorage off Taku the morning after leaving Chee-foo, but, as our ship was drawing fourteen feet aft, and there was only eleven feet of water on the bar at high-tide, we had to discharge into lighters most of our cargo, which was composed of rice, "brick-tea," and copper "cash," before we could enter the Pei-ho. While this was going on, the captain and I, with his gig and a crew of four Chinese sailors, rowed through and around the "Northern fleet" of iron-clads which were lying within four miles of us, looking bright, new, and formidable.

Late in the afternoon we weighed anchor and entered the mouth of the river with the flood-tide, between the massive and heavily armed earthworks, famous in history as the Taku forts. The river which separates them is not over four hundred yards wide, and turns and twists its way through the low, marshy land, on either side, to

Tientsin, fifty miles above. The fortifications are well supplied with Armstrong and Krupp breech-loading rifles, strongly garrisoned by troops partly drilled in foreign tactics by competent German officers. They are spread out along the river for a half or three quarters of a mile, and, to render them still more difficult of assault, they are covered, front and rear, by wide wet ditches. They were taken by the allied French and English forces, August 21st, 1860, who landed at the mouth of the Peh-tang-ho, ten miles farther up the coast, and, after several slight skirmishes with a covering force, entered the works from the rear, much to the disgust of the Chinese commander, while the allied fleet was thundering away at long range in front. It was from a front attack upon these same works that the English were repulsed with such heavy loss the year before. And it was during this attack that Commodore Tatnall, of our navy, from the deck of a small steamer hired for the occasion, but taking no part in the action, seeing some English sailors struggling in the water, after their ship had been sunk by the Chinese guns, exclaimed, "Blood is thicker than water!" lowered his cutter, and, rowing into the thickest of the firing, rescued the drowning men from a watery grave.

Just beyond the fortifications we passed an excellent dock-yard, and anchored in front of the city of Taku, built entirely of mud-houses and containing a population of perhaps fifty thousand souls. There is plenty of water in the anchorage in front of the city, and for eight or ten miles farther up, and it is quite evident, from the softness of the mud on the bar and the volume of water discharged across it, that the entrance could be readily and inexpensively deepened so as to admit ships drawing twenty feet at all times, and it is also probable that that depth could be maintained without great difficulty. There is, however, a prosperous "tug and lighter" company, composed of foreigners, whose business would be ruined by such an improvement, and the Chinese themselves do not believe much in taking liberties with nature. They are rather disposed to regard the bars at the mouths of their rivers, and especially those at Taku and Wu-sung, as "Heaven-sent barriers," specially designed to keep out foreign men-of-war.

Owing to the absence of beacons and the crookedness of the river, we were compelled to lie at anchor till the moon rose. All around us we heard the hum and roar of noisy villagers, and the shouting of soldiers, and in the early evening the air seemed full of foreign bugle-calls, in which the Chinese buglers have certainly been well instructed. Another curious fact that may be mentioned here is that all military commands to the foreign-drilled Chinese troops are given in English, no matter what the nationality of the drill-master may be. Every drill-master is accompanied by an interpreter, who explains the meaning of each command till the troops thoroughly understand its significance and foreign sound, and can execute it exactly as required. This is of course a great limitation upon instruction, and, as the tactics are by no means uniform, and the discipline far from rigid, it may well be taken for granted that, notwithstanding a number of the troops serving in the maritime provinces are armed with excellent breech-loading fire-arms, they could hardly be expected to stand up before well-disciplined foreign troops, no matter how great the disparity of numbers.

In my travels through the interior I saw no troops, except a few about Peking, with improved fire-arms. They all had matchlocks of the most primitive pattern, and of every size and length. It is true that I paid no special attention to military matters, but, having had ample experience in them, and kept my eyes open wherever I went, I am perhaps justified in saying that I saw nothing formidable in a military sense anywhere in the empire, and have no hesitation in adding that it is entirely unprepared, in my judgment, either in military administration, organization, or equipment, to resist invasion from any first-class military power, with even an ordinary force. It has neither transport, commissariat, nor an adequate quantity of military munitions, and, barring its inexhaustible population from which to draw fresh soldiers, it is simply a huge boneless giant, which must fall a ready prey to the first great power that attacks it in earnest. Some of its great leaders and statesmen, like the Viceroy Li and the late Tso Tsung-Tang, years ago began to perceive this truth, and have done what they could to arouse the Throne to a realizing sense of its danger. Something has been done, in a small and unsystematic way, toward arming and drilling the troops in foreign style, and more in buying and equipping the Northern fleet, but, withal, scarcely a beginning has yet been made toward putting the country in a position to resist attack, and absolutely nothing toward conducting a successful foreign war.

The distance from Taku to Tientsin is about thirty-five miles by land, but it is full fifty by the river, which, as before stated, is about as crooked as it can be. Although it has been the bed of the Hwang-ho at least twice within the historic period, and remained so from fifty to one hundred and fifty years, it narrows down within ten miles of its mouth from four hundred yards, which is about the average width of the Hwang-ho, to scarcely more than as many feet. Were it not for its soft and stoneless sides and bottom, its navigation by steamships would be impossible. As it is, it is extremely difficult. The country on either side, as far as the eye can reach, is a perfectly level plain, unbroken by even a high embankment. It is covered next to the river with a continuous succession of vegetable patches and millet-fields. At every turn of the river a village of one-story sun-dried brick houses, all thatched with millet-stalks and straw, presents itself to the view. Here and there is one of greater importance surrounded by walls and guarded by fortifications, overlooking the river and the road; but the most curious sight to the traveler is the great number of hemispherical grave-mounds looking very much in size and color like hay-cocks, which surround every town and village immediately outside its limits, and the larger the town the more thickly are the fields next to it covered by the mounds. Some of these are as high as ten feet, and look exactly like hay-stacks from a distance, and it is the same everywhere else in the Great Plain. And yet I think there is some misconception of this subject existing in the minds of people who have obtained their knowledge of China entirely from books. The general impression seems to be that the whole face of the country, wherever you go, is dotted over by graves, and that these graves are regarded with great reverence and maintained with pious care from generation to generation, and such, perhaps, is the theory of the Chinese, but, like many theories even among more highly civilized people, it is not rigidly adhered to. In the first place, it should be borne in mind that the Chinese do not live in farm-houses on the land, even when they own it, but all classes are gathered together in villages, towns, and cities, and naturally the larger these are, the more numerous and thickly placed are the graves about them. Where the country is thinly settled, the graves are infrequent, and they are never scattered about in the open country. In the second place, there are no common grave-yards devoted exclusively to burials; rich families have their own ground, in which they set off a lot and surround it by evergreens for the family graves; but the common people bury in the fields, under a license from the owner, for a limited number of years, usually not over three. Such as can not pay for a license, encoffin their dead and lay them alongside the highway, thinly covered with earth, and sometimes only with matting. The result is, that every considerable town seems to be surrounded by graves thickly, and sometimes oddly enough, strewn about the fields for a mile or even two miles out; but great as may be the confusion, each grave is laid out with due regard to "fung-shuy," which may be regarded as a system of geomancy or superstition by which the common people are largely governed in the important transactions of life. In the third place, while the custom of ancestral worship requires that the father's grave should be carefully preserved, in order that his male descendants may worship before it, the graves of the women, unmarried people, and children, are not so well made nor so scrupulously looked after, and, as a matter of fact, not only the graves of this class, but of the heads of families, gradually fall into decay and become obliterated. Even in the case of the best-established families, it must, with the lapse of time, become difficult to say whose duty it is to keep in repair the ancestral grave, and this fact, together with the additional one that while it is provided by law that families shall neither change their occupation nor place of abode, they do so quite frequently, without let or hindrance, and thus put it out of their power to keep the old graves in order. Besides all of this, the fields around and between the graves, however small the space, are cultivated yearly; and especially throughout the Great Plain where plowing is resorted to, or where the ground is subject to overflow, the grave-mounds are gradually encroached upon, lowered in height, and ultimately disappear, or are covered up and effaced entirely. In my travels I tried to obtain trustworthy information as to the average duration of common graves, but could not make myself understood sufficiently well, even through my interpreter, to get at anything exact enough to justify me in speaking with confidence about it. My impression is, however, that it can not possibly exceed ten years, and may not exceed five.

It has been commonly supposed that the difficulty of laying out railroads without interfering with the graves and violating the sacred customs of the people would prove an insuperable obstacle to the introduction of railroads into China, and I am free to confess that if the graves can not be moved, the difficulty will at least compel the location of the railroads at considerable distances from the present towns and cities. It would be impossible to enter the most of those in the Great Plain without running over or encroaching upon many graves. In the hill-country it is different. The graves are located in such regions on the hill-tops and sides, and the lowlands and valleys, where railroad lines would naturally be located, are reserved for farms and roads. But, so far as I can learn, there is no reason for supposing that the graves can not be moved, when necessary, if the proper measures are taken to conciliate the people and to compensate them for the damage inflicted upon them. Of course the primary condition to be observed in China, as in other countries, is that no person's private property shall be taken for public or corporate use except by due process of law and with prompt payment for the amount taken. Under this rule, all lands actually set off for railroad use would have to be paid for after valuation by disinterested parties, but in the case under consideration there is more to be provided for than the mere value of the land. The graves should not only be moved, but ground for new ones should be furnished, and all expenses connected with the reinterment should be paid for by the railroad company on a just and liberal scale. If this is done, and all steps of the business are taken with due deliberation and decorum, as well as a due regard for the customs and prejudices of the people, there is little doubt that most of the difficulty on this account will rapidly disappear, especially if the Imperial sanction be given to the proceedings and some appropriate recognition be extended to the people whose places of sepulture it has been necessary to interfere with for the public good. A simple tablet of wood erected over the remains, or in some neighboring temple, by Imperial decree, would go far toward allaying the prejudices of the most superstitious and obdurate Chinaman. After all, he is not unlike other people, and if he is well and kindly treated and his natural rights are respected, he is easily managed. Besides, there is reason for believing that while reverence for the dead is a part of the Chinaman's daily life, it is not a cult of such great vitality nor of such fixed and unbending rules as to prohibit the application of common sense to such cases as may arise affecting it. Later during my travels I made inquiry as to the average cost of coffin, ground, and funeral for the average Chinaman, and learned that it varies in the Great Plain from five to eight dollars.

CHAPTER IX.

Races at Tientsin—Chinese band playing American airs—No social intercourse between Chinese and foreigners—Removal of grave-mounds to make way for the race-course—Political and commercial importance of Tientsin—The foreign settlement—Foreign gunboats—The Viceroy Li Hung-Chang—His American secretary—First call upon the Viceroy—His official residence or Yamen—Subjects discussed—Railroads and canals—Intelligence and interest displayed by the Viceroy—Ceremony of leave-taking—"Setting the watch."

ALMOST immediately after my arrival at Tientsin I was taken to the race-course, where I found nearly every gentleman and lady, and most of the children of the foreign settlement, and a thousand or more Chinamen assembled, all eager and excited over the coming contests. The entries were all Mongolian ponies, owned and ridden by foreign gentlemen residing in the settlement, each of whom was dressed in a fancy jockey suit of gayly-colored silk. The ponies were well trained, hardy little fellows, from twelve to fourteen hands high, and very spunky. They belong to the breed from which the Tartar and Chinese cavalry draw their mounts, and have not yet been improved by crossing with European horses.

The Viceroy's band, composed of about thirty musicians, clad in gay red uniforms of Chinese cut and conducted by a foreign leader, was in attendance, and, much to my surprise and gratification, it played an assortment of familiar American airs in a most spirited manner, such as "Old Blind Joe" and "Marching through Georgia." It was a gay and animated scene, in which the manners and customs of the old and the new civilization were sharply contrasted. There were many Chinese looking on, but I was at once struck by the fact that there were none taking any part whatever in the races. And it is worthy of note that neither here nor elsewhere is there any social out-door intermingling of natives and foreigners. The English custom of non-intercourse with all inferior races prevails here as everywhere else in India and China. Occasionally a mandarin invites a distinguished foreigner to dine with him, and the compliment is duly returned, but there all social intercourse ends. Most of the foreigners residing in the treaty ports are merchants or missionaries, and neither of these classes has any social standing with the official class in China. They are simply ignored, unless they have private or public business which must be attended to, and even then they are generally required to present it through the consul of the nationality to which they belong. So far is non-intercourse the rule that no Chinaman, however high his rank, is ever invited to enter a foreign club or permitted to take part in foreign games and sports, and in some cases, as in the settlement at Shanghai, they are even prohibited from entering the grounds and public gardens set apart for foreign use. Whether they are ready to do so or not if invited and permitted, is by no means certain, but the practice is as I have stated, and this is in marked contrast to the rule in Japan, where native and foreign gentlemen belong to the same clubs, and treat with each other on all business and social matters on terms of perfect equality.

I was particularly struck, while on the race-course at Tientsin, with the fact that the track, which is elliptical and about a mile round, occupies a field thickly studded with grave-mounds, many of which must have been removed in order to make room for it. At a rough estimate I should say that it incloses five thousand graves, and that there are twice as many in sight of it on the outside. Another curious fact is that many of these grave-mounds were occupied by Chinamen irreverently standing on top of them and eagerly straining their necks and eyes to see the sport going on around them.

I made inquiry as to how the ground covered by the race-course had been disencumbered of its graves, and was told with a smile that "old China hands" know how to manage such matters. And I have no doubt they did it by using common sense and money, and not very much of the latter.

Tientsin, or the Heavenly Ferry, is a point of great interest, not only on account of its being the port of Peking, eighty miles farther inland, but, as before stated, because it is the principal residence of the Viceroy Li, with and through whom nearly all foreign business must be conducted. It is situated mostly on the south bank of the Pei-ho, just below the confluence of its three principal branches, and is said to contain nearly a million inhabitants. Its site is as low, flat, and uninviting as any other in the Great Plain. It is of course subject to overflow, and is in fact almost surrounded by shallow ponds, in which the flood- or rain-water stands all the year round. Close to the river-bank below, on either side the ground is given up entirely to gardens, in which cabbage, onions, garlic, sweet-potatoes, and millet are the principal crop. Like Shanghai, it has a thrifty foreign settlement extending along the river-bank for nearly a mile, and containing a number of fine residences and warehouses. It also contains several churches, a club, two hospitals, a bank, and with its own government under the consuls of the treaty powers, an excellent police, well-paved streets, and a wharf or bund reveted with cut stone, presents almost as strong a contrast with everything in the Chinese city above as does the settlement at Shanghai with the Chinese city there. Last year two hundred and forty steamships entered and cleared at the port of Tientsin, and it is estimated that they carried into it at least two hundred thousand tons of freight. The outbound cargoes were much lighter, as the export from this part of the country consists mostly of straw braid, camels' wool, hogs' bristles, and a few other articles of no great moment. The heart of the Chinese city is surrounded by a high crenelated brick wall of the usual Chinese type, built several hundred years ago, but the suburbs lying about the junction of the Grand Canal or south branch, with the main river, and outside of the wall, are of greater extent than the old city itself. The foreign settlement, suburbs, and the old city are all inclosed, however, by a high earthern embankment of irregular trace, derisively known as Sankolinsin's Folly, built by the Tartar prince of that name, who commanded the imperial forces confronting the allied French and English in 1860. This great embankment, having a command of about fifteen feet, although laid out without any regard to flanking arrangements, would have been a very formidable bar to the advance of the allied forces had it been properly manned and defended, but, inasmuch as the Imperial commander fled from it without making a single effort to hold it, the allies took possession of it, and found it useful as a fortified base for further operations against Peking.

Since the outbreak of the mob which destroyed the French mission and orphan asylum, and massacred the Sisters of Charity at Tientsin, in 1873, the port has been occupied every winter by foreign gunboats—generally one American, one French, and one English—and is as orderly and quiet a place as there is in China. It is the seat of the naval administration provided for in the late imperial decree, and of incipient naval and military academies. It is also the headquarters of the imperial telegraph system and the telegraph school, and has two arsenals, managed by foreigners and provided with foreign machinery. While far inferior to Shanghai as a commercial city, it is, perhaps, superior to that place, and even to Peking, as a base of operations against the conservatism and ignorance which control the entire country. Although Pau-ting-fu, about a hundred miles west-southwest, is the official capital of the province of Chihli, and Peking, eighty miles northwest, in the same province, is the capital of the empire, it is quite certain that Tientsin is the center of all progressive movements which have shown themselves of late years in North China, and this arises solely from the fact that the Viceroy Li makes it his home and principal place of business. He goes to Pau-ting-fu whenever the provincial business requires it, and to Peking whenever called there by Imperial mandate, but nine tenths of his time is passed at Tientsin. In addition to being the Governor-General, or Viceroy of the Province, and administering the government of thirty-five million people, he is First Grand Secretary of the Empire, and conducts the foreign affairs of the whole nation. He is also practically the head of the Northern fleet, or Secretary of the Navy, and is absolutely Minister Superintendent of Trade for the Northern Seaboard. He is, besides, the leading military adviser of the Throne, and it was mainly through his efforts and those of the foreign officers used by him in organizing and commanding the "Ever-Victorious Army" that the Taiping rebellion was suppressed after it had overrun two thirds of the empire, and cost the lives of ten million Chinamen. Although he can not speak or read a word of English, he has been for many years in almost daily contact with foreigners, and especially with Americans and Englishmen, and is familiar with their ideas on all subjects of importance. He received General Grant, during his late tour around the world, with every honor and attention, and owing, perhaps, to a certain similarity of tastes and mental qualities, as well as to the fact that each had been the final and successful leader of his countrymen in the suppression of a great rebellion, these two distinguished men came to be intimate personal friends.

One of the Viceroy's foreign secretaries is an American, of rare modesty and attainments, who not only reads and writes literary Chinese as well as it is possible for any one except a native scholar to ever read or write it, but at the same time keeps himself abreast of the world's current thought on all questions. This gentleman, after serving through the rebellion as a private soldier in a New York cavalry regiment, went to China when still a boy, with a letter of introduction from President Lincoln to Mr. Burlingame, then our minister at Peking, and has resided in the country ever since, devoting himself conscientiously to its literature and art, and to the furtherance of whatever promises to improve its material condition. He established intimate social and official relations with the Viceroy and his family, and has rendered them much effective and disinterested service, especially in familiarizing them with the foreign way of looking at all questions. He enjoys the Viceroy's personal confidence and friendship to a high degree, and is one of the few men, whether native or foreign, who has access to him at all times.

I made my first call upon the Viceroy on the day after my arrival at Tientsin, in company with the American vice-consul, and, thanks to my credentials, and also to my services as a soldier and an engineer, with which the viceroy had been made acquainted beforehand, I was received with every mark of respect and consideration. During that and my subsequent visits to Tientsin it was my good fortune to see the Viceroy often, to enjoy his hospitality, and to establish with him an exceedingly pleasant and cordial friendship.

As the ceremonies and incidents of these visits were novel and interesting to me, I venture to describe the first one as a sample of all, in the hope that it will also prove interesting, and in some degree instructive, to others.

Custom requires that all ceremonial visits from persons of rank should be made in a sedan-chair, covered with blue or green cloth, lined with silk, and borne upon the shoulders of four coolies, clad in official costume. If occasion requires it, the chair is preceded and followed by mounted retainers, for the purpose of clearing the way and bearing proper evidence to the rank and consideration of the visitor. In this manner I proceeded from the settlement, through the narrow, crooked, and dirty streets of the Chinese city, to the Yamen or official residence of the Viceroy, on the bank of the Grand Canal, three miles away. It is situated in a compound or high wall of gray, burned bricks, pierced by a portal with high granite posts and heavy timber doors, opening into an outer court-yard in front of the residence. As my *cortége* turned into the court-yard, which was by no means cleanly swept, we were met by the vice-consul, who had arrived before us and given the necessary notice that we were near at hand, so that everything was arranged in order according to the requirements of Chinese etiquette. I sat for a few minutes in my chair, waiting in front of another pair of large, double doors, gorgeously decorated in red, yellow, and gold, with huge figures, one looking like a herculean king of clubs, and the other like a queen of the same suite. This slight delay gave me time to look about, but I saw nothing particularly striking, except a granite column or tablet to the left, about twelve feet high, three feet wide, and a foot thick, standing on the back of a granite tortoise about five feet long, three feet wide, and two feet thick, half buried, with its head stretched out upon the ground. The face of the tablet was deeply cut with Chinese characters from top to bottom, but their significance I never learned. While engaged in looking at this singular object, many of which I afterward saw near the graves of great men about Peking, the great central doors were thrown open with a bang, and my bearers were motioned to advance, which they did for about twenty paces, and then sat me down again. My footman then came forward, lifted out the yellow-silk curtain which closed the front of the chair, and indicated that I was to step out. The vice-consul joined me at once, and then—preceded by an official of the Yamen, carrying our Chinese cards, pieces of bright-red paper about seven inches long and three and a half wide, containing the Chinese characters which had been selected to represent our names—we were shown into the reception-room reserved for foreigners. The farther end of it contained a platform or dais, lighted by a window back of it, and furnished with a divan, two seats, and a sort of low table, all covered with red silk. On either side was a row of chairs and small tables, also covered with red silk ; back of them were a lot of Chinese screens hung with pictures, and the floor was covered with an English Brussels carpet. The front of the room was separated from an open corridor by a screen of glass and carved wood, and the ceiling was also of wood, all in its natural color. In one corner of the room was an American coal-stove of the base-burner pattern, made at Troy, New York, and in the other a portrait of the

LI HUNG-CHANG, VICEROY OF CHIHLI. 109

Viceroy done in oil, by a German artist, from a photograph.

I had hardly taken in these details when the Viceroy made his appearance through the door by which we had entered, bowed with grace and dignity, and then cordially shook hands with me in European style. Bowing again, he turned and led the way into a little private office opening into the reception-room, and, seating himself at the head of a large table, he showed me a chair to his left, the post of honor in China, and the vice-consul, who is also his American secretary and interpreter, a chair to the right. A pretty little porcelain tea-cup, containing freshly made tea of excellent quality, was placed in front of each of us; a box of cigars, another of cigarettes, and a box of Austrian matches were put on the table. At the same time a pipe-bearer, with a water-pipe of steel and ebony, took his stand near the Viceroy. By this time I had taken a good look at him, and was pleased with his manly and dignified appearance and his grave but benevolent and kindly countenance.

He is about six feet high, and strongly built, but by no means fat. His figure is erect, and indicates that, if he had been properly trained when young, he would have been a very strong and active man. His skin has the usual yellowish but somewhat swarthy cast which characterizes the pure Chinese race to which he belongs. His eyes are dark, piercing, and rather small, but they nevertheless show both acuteness and intelligence, and seem to sparkle with amiability and kindness. His hair is gray, shaved back from his forehead, and plaited into a queue of medium length and thickness, according to the unvarying Chinese fashion. His teeth are somewhat uneven and discolored by tobacco. He has a gray, drooping mustache, and rather thin, gray chin-whiskers, or imperial, which come to Chinamen generally late in life. His age is now sixty-six years, counting him a year old at birth, as is the custom in China. He was clad in a gray astrakhan outer garment or surtout, with long, flowing sleeves, into which he could withdraw his hands when cold, loose silken trousers, felt shoes, and a black turban-shaped hat with flaring sides and flat top, surmounted by the button of his rank, with a peacock's feather sticking straight out behind.

We had hardly taken seats before he asked me how old I was. This question is always asked by the Chinese of foreigners, and is fully justified by the rules of their etiquette. When I had answered it satisfactorily, he said, with some surprise: "You must have been quite young in the wars. What position did you hold when you were in the War Department at Washington?"

Perceiving that he wanted an account of my public services, I replied that I had been chief of the cavalry bureau, charged with the supervision of the organization and equipment of all the cavalry troops, had commanded a cavalry division, and, still later, a cavalry army. I added that after the restoration of peace I had returned to my legitimate duties as an officer of regular engineers, and taken charge of the improvement of the Mississippi, the Illinois, and the Rock Rivers, and finally had resigned from the army for the purpose of building and operating railroads, in which business I had been engaged, in various parts of the United States, for the last fifteen years. This recital drew from him an expression of surprise at the extent and variety of my services, whereupon I explained to him that, previous to reaching the rank of brigadier-general, I had also served two years on the staff of General Grant as an engineer officer, and as the inspector-general of the army under his command, and that the aim of our system of military education at West Point is to teach all sciences useful in the military profession, including drill, tactics, engineering, and the art of war, so thoroughly that the graduate is competent to serve efficiently wherever he may be placed.

This reference to General Grant drew from the Viceroy an expression of profound sorrow at his untimely death under such sad and distressing circumstances, and that after retiring from his high public employments he should have been drawn into business relations with men who had proved themselves so unworthy of his confidence and had betrayed him in such a shameful way. He expressed the greatest sympathy for Mrs. Grant, coupled with anxious solicitude for her comfort, and the sufficiency of her fortune to provide for the wants of herself and family. When I told him of General Grant's struggle during the last year of his life, while suffering under a painful and incurable disease, to write his memoirs for the purpose of providing, by its sale, another fortune for his family, and called attention to the fact that it was, on the whole, the most heroic year of his life, and had been crowned by success as complete as any he had ever gained, the Viceroy expressed his gratification in the highest terms, and said it was a noble ending to a noble career.

He then asked me if I knew General Upton, whom he had met during the visit of the latter to China and the other nations of Asia and Europe for the purpose of inspecting and reporting upon their armies, and who had proposed to establish a military academy for the Chinese Government. I explained that I had known him intimately from boyhood, that he had commanded a divison of cavalry under me during the closing days of the rebellion with marked ability, had died only a few years ago under distressing circumstances, and had left behind him a great reputation as a military man.

After expressing sorrow at the sad ending of a career which promised so much usefulness to his country, the

Viceroy then reverted to my own services and varied employments, and said, "With all you have done, you must be very rich." I replied, "No, not rich, and yet not altogether poor," adding that "I had rather striven to do things and accomplish what I had undertaken than to make money out of them, and yet I had made some money." He asked at once, "How much?" It seems that this is quite the question to ask a foreigner, but that it is hardly ever asked of a Chinaman. Not feeling quite like putting a fixed value upon the usual assortment of American assets, I replied, "I have enough to keep the wolf away from the door, and yet not so much but that a man of my age, with wife and children to care for, might properly want more." And this seemed to satisfy him. At all events, he dropped the subject, and asked if I had brought my family with me to China, and how long I intended to stay. This gave me an opportunity, which I availed myself of at once, to explain in a general way the objects which I had in view in visiting China, and that, while I had hoped they would not keep me away from home more than six months, I should stay longer if necessary. I then adverted to the fact that he was not only the first statesman and soldier of China, but also its recognized leader in intelligence and progress, and asked him to explain the policy of the Chinese Government in regard to railroads and other industrial undertakings. He replied, without hesitation, and apparently with perfect frankness: "China must build railroads, open mines, and put up furnaces and rolling-mills, but the great question is where to find the money with which to pay for them." I rejoined that I had no doubt the money could be got on reasonable terms if the Chinese Government would ask for it; that its credit was good, that money, and especially silver, were abundant in both Europe and America, and that the times were favorable for getting it. I added, I had even heard it stated by a distinguished American statesman that he would be glad to see the silver, which was accumulating in such large quantities in our Treasury, used for building railroads in China.

This remark excited his interest at once, and he asked eagerly if I could not induce our Government to lend a part of its surplus silver to China for this purpose. I of course told him that such a thing were hardly possible, but added that, being only a private citizen, with no authority whatever to discuss a matter of such serious importance, I could only express my private opinion about it, and that was that it could not be done directly, although it was doubtless possible that our bankers, who had larger deposits than ever before, might make a loan which would indirectly accomplish the same object. His Excellency then asked : "What is your Government going to do with the large quantity of silver accumulating in its Treasury ? I understand it amounts to hundreds of millions, and that they have to build new houses of iron and steel to hold it." How he got his information I never learned, but I was struck with its general accuracy, as well as with the question he asked about it. I replied that of course the Government would use so much of it as necessary to pay its current expenses and maturing debts, but had not decided, so far as I knew, upon a definite policy for disposing of its surplus. He smiled, and came back quickly with the remark, "Well, it might get rid of some of it by paying its diplomatic and consular agents in China larger salaries than they now get," and in this I concurred most heartily.

A pause now occurred in the conference, during which a servant brought in and opened a bottle of champagne and poured out a glass for each. He then struck a match, with which he lit a twisted paper lighter, and carefully placing the mouth-piece of the water-pipe be-

tween the lips of the Viceroy, who had his hands spread
out on the table before him, and was looking intently at
me, without seeing the pipe-stem. As soon as he felt it,
however, between his lips, he closed them, took a long
deep pull at it, blew out the smoke, and then took another, still deeper if possible, and exhaled it through his
nostrils. The pipe was then withdrawn, cleared of smoke,
recharged, and returned to his mouth in the same deliberate and careful manner, and he smoked again in the
same way. The operation was repeated several times,
and then the conversation was resumed by the Viceroy's
asking if I knew Colonel Denby, the newly arrived American Minister, or had served with him in the rebellion.
Upon my replying in the affirmative, he expressed himself much pleased with the colonel's distinguished bearing
and intelligence, and said he would like to see him appointed as Minister to Corea also, not only as an honor
to the colonel, but because it would be a convenience to
all parties concerned, and there seems to be but little
doubt that such an arrangement, if it were allowed by
our Government, would not only be an economy, but it
would be productive of excellent results. I explained to
his Excellency that Congress controls all such matters,
and that neither the President nor the Secretary of State
would feel at liberty to do what he had suggested without the authority of a law specially authorizing it. I
assured him, however, that I would take an early opportunity to make his views known, and this I did by cable.

The conversation now took a wider and less formal
range, champagne, of which the Chinese are very
fond, was drunk, and although this is generally the
signal for closing an interview, it was not intended
as such in the case now under consideration. To the
contrary, the Viceroy then returned to the subject of
railroads and asked many questions as to their use, their

probable cost in China, the best system for the Chinese to adopt, and also what would be the relative cost of transportation by railroad and canal. In reference to the last-mentioned subject he said : "General Grant told me when he was in China that transportation by canal was cheaper than by railroad. How is this?" I gave him my views fully on that subject, and illustrated them by reference to the facts and statistics, which are familiar to all students of the subject and need not be repeated here; but when I told him that even if there were any doubt as to the relative merits of railroads and canals, when speed as well as the actual cost of transportation for freight and passengers were considered, and expressed the opinion that he could surely entertain no doubt as to which was best when he remembered the additional and important fact that in a climate like that of Northern China the canal must necessarily freeze up and remain closed for three or four months of the year, while the railroad would remain open all the year round, he frankly admitted that the considerations I had cited were conclusive, and reiterated his declaration that China must have railroads.

He then made some practical suggestions as to the way in which I could most profitably spend my time while in China, pointed out several expeditions which he thought I ought to make in order to get a practical idea of the country, and of the difficulties which would be encountered in building railroads in it, and, after expressing the wish that I should see him often, he indicated that the interview was closed. It was now about sunset, and the room had become so dark that lights would have soon been necessary. We accordingly rose to take our leave. The Viceroy was then standing, and, seeing us ready to start, he turned and passed out into the corridor. I took my place by his side and walked with him toward the main entrance of the Yamen, and during our progress the stillness was broken by a sudden but muffled roll of drums and a blare of brazen trumpets from the court-yard, which was very weird and impressive. It continued till we had reached the inner court-yard, where we had left our chairs. The Viceroy stopped at the edge of this court, and, turning toward me, grasped my hand most cordially in foreign style, saying: "You are my friend and I am your friend," and then bade me good-by in a most polite and courtly manner. He did not turn away at once, but stood bowing to me, with his own hands clasped and raised to his chin, until I had re-entered my chair, which I of course did not do till I had turned and recognized his civility as best I could.

At a subsequent interview, just as I was entering the Yamen, I again heard the roll of the kettle-drum near at hand, but this time, instead of a "flourish," it was the signal for the close of the official day, and "setting the watch" about the premises for the night. On stepping outside the waiting-room, I saw the drummer standing at the right of the door, beating a large sonorous drum like those used in Western orchestras; his hands were flying with the greatest rapidity, but every now and then, with measured regularity, he would strike a heavier blow. Farther out in the dim twilight there were two trumpeters clad in white robes, and each playing a long, straight brass trumpet, of the kind depictured in Old Testament scenes. Each raised his instrument in unison with the other, till it was nearly perpendicular, and, while lowering it slowly to the level, blew a long, quavering blast, now soft and low, now loud and strong, but always in harmony with the drum, and always with a strange weird sweetness of tone, which impressed me profoundly. Pausing a moment, they raised their trumpets as before, repeating the strange, semi-barbaric and yet pleasing music over and over again for perhaps five minutes, after which they let it die away as though they were disappearing in the distance. The drummer, with softening beat, closed the ceremony by giving three measured taps, which, after a short pause, were followed by three strokes of a musical bell. And then the watchmen marched away to their various posts for the night. This ceremony, I was told, is conducted daily at every provincial Yamen, and at the headquarters of every army. If a modern musical composer could give it, with proper scenic accessories and instrumental accompaniment as I heard it, I am sure it would prove to be a striking and interesting entertainment to a Western audience.

CHAPTER X.

Li Hung-Chang—His public career—Influence of Generals Ward and Gordon—English misconception of their character—The career of Burgevine—The influence of the war threatened with Russia—Gordon revisited China—The introduction of telegraphs—Messages sent in English, or cipher—Memorial of Liu Ming-Chu'an on the introduction of railways—Referred to Li Hung-Chang and Lin K'un-Yi—The memorial of Li Hung-Chang and Lin K'un-Yi—Tso Tsung-Tang's dying memorial on the same subject—No official action yet taken thereupon—The essence of progress and the death-knell of conservatism.

LI HUNG-CHANG, now by far the most conspicuous figure on the Chinese theatre of action, is a pure Chinaman, with no trace of Tartar blood in his veins. He comes of a family, six or seven generations of which have attained high literary rank but only moderate fortune, was born in the province of Ngan-whei, and early gave promise of decided literary ability, which in China is the only test of fitness for office—having successfully passed the three public examinations, and obtained in the last one at Peking the highest degree known in the hierarchy of Chinese scholarship. He is a fellow of the Hanlin College—the most learned body of men in the empire. By the time he had reached middle age he had passed through the various grades and public employments open to men of his attainments. Shortly after the Taiping rebellion reached his native province, he was appointed to the staff of the general acting against the rebels, and was engaged in the various operations in the Kiang prov-

LI HUNG-CHANG, VICEROY OF CHIHLI. 119

inces, from 1853 till the close of the rebellion, during the latter part of which he was in chief command of the imperial forces. In February, 1863, he was made Superintendent of Trade for the southern ports. In 1866 he was appointed special commissioner for the suppression of the Nienfei rebellion, and in 1870 he was directed to settle the difficulty with the French and Russians arising from the Tientsin massacre. He has since that time been special commissioner for the settlement of the Yunnan question, and for readjusting the various treaties and arrangements with foreign powers; and, in all matters intrusted to him, has acquitted himself with such marked ability, that the Empress Regent bestowed upon him, January 9, 1875, the office of Senior First Grand Secretary, which is equivalent to saying that he is the first civilian of the empire.

Chinese custom and law require a public official to retire from all public employments for three years upon the death of his mother. Having been appointed Governor-General of Chihli in 1870, on the death of his mother (in 1882) he retired from office, but was ordered to return to his post as Viceroy after the expiration of only one hundred days of mourning. Shortly afterward, at his earnest request, he was allowed to vacate his posts as Grand Secretary and Viceroy, but was again compelled to resume office in August, 1883.*

In this connection it is worthy of note that no Chinaman can hold office in his native province, nor can any near relative hold office under him. It is also worthy of note that in China, as in America, the civil functions of government are supposed to be superior to

---

* Biographical table of the high officials composing the central and provincial governments of China, published as an Appendix to the translation of the "Peking Gazette" for 1884.

the military functions. The scholar, therefore, looks down upon the soldier, but is frequently called upon to perform the highest military duty. The governor-general of a province is *ex-officio* the commander-in-chief of its military forces, and, whenever necessity requires it, is compelled to lead them in the field. In accordance with this rule, Li, who had come to be one of the leading scholars of the country, also became in due course of time its most conspicuous if not actually its ablest soldier. In the terrible struggle which ensued for the suppression of the rebellion, he had Tso Tsungtang, Tseng Quo-fan, and Tseng Quo-chu'an for coadjutors; but, without disparaging these able men, it is safe to say that he received by far the most valuable assistance given to him from the "Ever-Victorious Army," which was organized by the American Ward, and consisted of native Chinamen, instructed and led by foreign officers. Ward, it will be remembered, was killed at the head of his force after an extraordinary career, in which he showed skill, courage, and organizing capacity of a high order. He was succeeded by Burgevine, another American of great bravery, but of bad habits and an ungovernable temper, which soon brought him into disgrace. The force then fell temporarily under the command of an Englishman, who proved to be incompetent, and was in turn succeeded by Gordon, an officer of the Royal British Engineers, who had the qualities of a true soldier, and speedily restored the discipline and prestige of the force. He adopted the methods of Ward, even in the matter of leading his men into action with a walking-cane or wand in his hand as the sole sign of his authority. By great activity and rigid discipline, combined with a thorough knowledge of the theatre of war, gained by actual surveys which he had previously made for the British authorities, he soon brought the rebellion to desperate straits. Of course he had the co-operation of the imperial commanders in all combined undertakings. He was especially subject to the orders of Governor-General Li, and made no campaign except with his consent and under his control. This fact has been too frequently ignored or glossed over by English writers, to the disparagement of Ward, who was undeniably an able man, and without whose untimely death it is more than likely that the English commander, great as were his abilities, would never have become known to history as Chinese Gordon, and also of Li, whose intelligence and sound judgment enabled him to perceive, even at that early day, the vast superiority of foreign organization, discipline, and arms, and, in spite of the prejudice of his ablest coadjutor, induced him, in desperate undertakings, to put his main reliance upon the "Ever-Victorious Army." In other words, it was Li who upheld Gordon and gave him the chance to use, with such terrible effect, the organization which had been fashioned to his hand in all essential particulars by Ward, the intrepid Yankee sailor. Another circumstance in connection with Gordon, frequently overlooked, is, that he was not intrusted with the exclusive control of the force, but had a Chinese *adlatus*, who, nominally at least, had as much to say as himself. How far this was an actual limitation upon the independence of Gordon does not appear in the histories of that period, all of which were written by Englishmen; but there is reason for believing that he was not wholly trusted either by Li or his lieutenants.

The final surrender of the Taiping chieftains was made to Gordon on his assurance that their lives should be spared, but this was an innovation upon Chinese methods of concluding such matters, and it was repudiated; the prisoners were slain, and a hot feud arose between Gordon and Li in reference to it. Gordon charged Li with bad faith, and is said to have sought for him three days with a revolver, openly avowing that he would kill him on sight. Fortunately for China, and probably for himself, his anger was evanescent, and soon friendly if not intimate relations were re-established between him and Li. High honors, including a yellow jacket and a gratuity of ten thousand taels, were bestowed upon him by the Imperial Government, but he rejected the latter with the plain though perhaps unnecessary intimation that he was no mercenary soldier of fortune. Still feeling aggrieved at the execution of the Taiping chieftains, and perceiving that the rebellion was over, he resigned his commission and the force was disbanded. This was perhaps a wise measure, for it had come to regard itself as the only respectable military organization in the empire. Its officers had from the first been more or less inclined to be insolent, and Burgevine at least had threatened more than once, when he got through with the rebels, to turn the force against the imperial armies, and, after overthrowing them, to drive out the reigning dynasty at Peking, and make himself master of China.

The subsequent career of Burgevine was romantic but unfortunate. After being relieved from the command, he went to Peking and protested against the treatment he had received at Li's hands, and so much interested Mr. Burlingame, the American minister, and Sir Thomas Wade, the British minister, in his case, that, through their intercession, the Peking authorities sent him back to Li, with a vague sort of request that he might be restored to command. Li, who doubtless knew him better than his diplomatic friends, or had some secret understanding with the Government, declined to reinstate him, and after a short time he made his way through the lines and joined the Taiping rebels. They in turn failed to treat him with that consideration which he regarded as his due, or he saw that they could not possibly succeed even with his help, and consequently he left them, making his way back through the imperial lines, probably by consent, to the sea-coast, whence he sailed for Japan. Remaining in that country for several months, he again became discontented, and returned to China, it is said, in violation of a tacit agreement with the imperial authorities, under which he had been permitted to depart from China without molestation. At all events, he was speedily apprehended and sent into the interior under escort. Efforts were made by foreigners, and especially the American consul at Shanghai, to secure his release ; but, whether by design or accident has never been clearly established, he was drowned by the upsetting of a boat while crossing a river.

Li's experience with Ward, Burgevine, and Gordon, and also with the foreign ministers, consuls, and naval officers, during the closing days of the rebellion, was of such character as to put him somewhat on his guard against foreign influence, which was by no means at all times entirely disinterested ; but, nevertheless, it inspired him with a high opinion of foreign skill and ability in military and naval matters. It familiarized him with foreign methods, and must in some degree have shaken his confidence in those of his own countrymen. As a reward for the craft and discretion displayed in his management of affairs in Che-kiang, he was, as before stated, appointed Governor-General of the metropolitan province of Chihli in 1870, with the enlarged powers of a Viceroy, and the high offices of tutor to the young Emperor, Grand Secretary, and virtual Minister for Foreign Affairs. In this position he was thrown more and more into relations with foreigners, by whom he soon came to be regarded as an exceedingly able diplomatist. As special commissioner, he negotiated new treaties with most of the treaty powers, and, notwithstanding the fact that he was confronted by men of great skill and experience, it is now apparent that he was by no means overmatched by them.

When the difficulties arose with Russia in 1881, in regard to the northern boundary, and war appeared to be imminent, he sent for Gordon, who had been many years in England, and it is said offered him command of the imperial forces. Gordon revisited China, and remained in conference with Li for several months, but finally returned to Europe when it was evident that the war-cloud had passed away. There is the best of reason for believing that Gordon, at the time of this visit, had not only entirely forgiven the viceroy for putting the Taiping chieftains to death, but wished to secure for him the highest possible position which a Chinaman could hold, and was willing to undertake an adventure in his behalf quite as desperate as any Burgevine had ever contemplated for himself. I mention this circumstance for the purpose of showing that Gordon was not a safe adviser in all things, as well as that the viceroy's prudence and loyalty were proof against temptation, no matter from what quarter it came, nor how great an honor it held out to him.

It was during this period that the Viceroy memorialized the Throne, and obtained permission to erect telegraph lines to the principal provincial capitals and commercial cities of the northern and southern seaboards. The work was done under the personal direction of Mr. Carl H. O. Poulsen, assisted by Mr. Culmsee, formerly officers of the Danish Cable Company's service. They have now in operation about five thousand miles of line, connecting Seoul, the capital of Corea, Mukden, the capital of Manchuria and the home of the reigning dynasty, Port Arthur, Shan-hai-kwan, Peking, Tientsin, Taku, Chinan-foo, Che-fu, Chin-kiang, Shanghai, Nanking, Wuchang, Hankow, Hang-chow, Ning-po, Foochow,

Amoy, Canton, and Kin, and are fast extending it to all the provincial capitals in the interior, and also through Mongolia to the Russian border. Notwithstanding this is as great an innovation as anything which could be suggested, and was opposed at first by the conservatives, it is now desired by every governor, prefect, and magistrate, as well as by every intelligent merchant throughout the empire, and is in no way molested by the common people. All the operators are Chinese, who have been taught English and telegraphy in America, or in a school established for that purpose at Tientsin, under the immediate charge of Messrs. Poulsen and Culmsee. The Chinese written language being a language of idiographs, with a separate character for each word, instead of syllables made up of distinct sounds represented by letters, it is impossible to send by the Morse system a message written in such characters, but the difficulty is overcome by representing each character by a combination of three Arabic numerals, and then sending the corresponding figure-message, which the operator at the receiving office immediately transposes into the proper characters, by reference to a key, a copy of which is in the hands of every operator. The system is very ingenious, and, although it has certain defects, works with as much satisfaction as could be expected. Of course, it is equivalent to putting every Chinese message into a foreign language, which, in view of the fact that there are something like eight thousand characters in common use, and nearly forty-five thousand in all, each of which must have its equivalent combination of three figures, it is easy to see requires a large key, and much time for the preparation of each message. It is much easier to send an English message, because the telegraph system is specially adapted to that, and every operator is required to know enough English to read the messages fluently, and to write a good plain hand.

126   CHINA.

It was also during the excitement growing out of the probability of a war with Russia, that the Viceroy Li prepared and submitted to the Throne a very remarkable memorial, setting forth at length the reasons favoring the immediate construction of railroads. This was preceded, however, by a memorial from Liu Ming-Chu'an, at that time a general in the Chinese army, but now Governor-General of the Island of Formosa, and, besides being one of the Viceroy Li's most devoted friends and adherents, is an able and progressive man, still in the prime of life.

Although I find other allusions to railroads in the "Peking Gazette," these memorials are the first formal presentation of the subject to the Throne, and inasmuch as they have been published in the official gazette, for the information of Chinese subjects, I deem it best to set them forth at large herein. They are not only important state papers, but may have great historical value hereafter. Moreover, they show how Chinese statesmen communicate with the Throne, and also the state of knowledge existing among them in regard to this most important subject :

Memorial of Liu Ming-Chu'an, a general in the Chinese army, in retirement, recommending the immediate introduction of railways as a means of augmenting the power of the country.*

"Your Majesties' slave, Liu Ming-Ch'uan, etc., etc., upon his knees addresses the throne. Looking upward, he implores the glances of Your Sacred Majesties upon a memorial, reverently prepared, showing that as the situation of the empire is daily becoming more critical, and

---

* It is understood that this memorial was prepared at the instance of the Viceroy Li.

as difficulties from without are pressing harder upon us day by day, immediate consideration should be given to the question of introducing railways as a means whereby to augment the power of the empire.

"Your slave's merits sink into insignificance when compared with the abundant favors which have been bestowed upon him since his withdrawal from the army, in consequence of illness. Your slave, in the retirement of his garden home, has always studied the relations between China and foreign countries, with the result that he has often been awaked and brought to his feet in the hours of night to find his eyes streaming with tears from anxiety. He feels mortified at the thought that all his dog- or horse-like * exertions are inadequate to repay one ten-thousandth part of the favors which he has received.

"Recently he had the honor to be summoned by Your Majesties, and in contempt of his sickness came to the capital. On his arrival he was further honored by being summoned into the imperial presence, when he received full and complete instructions, his gratitude and respect for which your slave can not find words to express.

"Your slave conceives it to be the duty of an officer toward his sovereign to speak when he learns anything that should be known to his master, and, acting on this principle, he feels it his duty, with all diligence, respectfully to submit to Your Imperial Majesties, the Empress Dowager and the Emperor, that the introduction of changes are matters which are attended with the gravest embarrassments, and the adoption of measures which may result in benefit or in injury to the country are considerations of the gravest importance.

---

* A mode of expression designed to humble one's self when speaking of favors received. (The dog can watch its master's house, and the horse can draw or carry burdens for him.)

"The troubles which have beset China since she removed the bolts and opened her doors to engage in trade with foreign countries are by far more numerous and embarrassing than anything she has had to meet from her enemies since the earliest ages. These foreigners, in their dealings with us, are ever ready, on the smallest pretext, to create a dispute whereby they may deceive and oppress us, and, when there is a quarrel between any one of them and ourselves, the others press around and eagerly watch for an opportunity.

"Russia's southern frontier (in Asia) is very extensive; so much so, that it is contiguous to and interlocked with our northern, eastern, and western frontiers; we feel her grip on our throat, and her fist upon our back, and our contact with her is a source of perpetual uneasiness to our hearts and minds. But our long season of weakness and inaction disables us from making a show of strength, and our only alternative, therefore, is to patiently bear insult and obloquy. When a quarrel occurs we have to yield to her demands and make a compromise, regardless of money, in order to avert the dangers of war.

"It must be remembered, however, that a long-enduring peace between two countries is a thing that can not be relied upon as a certainty, and that the wealth of a nation is not unbounded. If we make no departure from our present conservatism, what strength can we hope to acquire?

"There are those who speak thoughtlessly of going to war. In this connection your slave would beg to observe that the essential point before going to war is to ascertain the condition of the enemy's forces. Russia has built railways which run from Europe to the neighborhood of Hao Han, and she purposes to build one from Hai-Shen-Wei to Hui Ch'un, and the reason why she did not proceed to send troops recently, when the quarrel with us commenced, is not that she feared to encounter our soldiers, but that her railways were not quite completed. Your slave foresees that, before ten years are passed, some immeasurable disaster may be looked for from that quarter.

"Now, Japan is an extremely small country—like a pill. Her rulers, however, have adopted Western mechanical arts; and relying on her possession of railways, she attempts now and again to be arrogant—like a mantis when it assumes an air of defiance—and to despise China, and gives us no small amount of trouble on the smallest pretext.

"Your slave is much grieved and distressed when he thinks that if the present time is allowed to go past without measures being taken to strengthen our country, how vain it will be to repent when it is too late.

"Although it is true that the proper way to proceed to strengthen our country is by drilling troops and manufacturing arms, etc., regularly in their turn, yet it must be confessed that the immediate construction of railways will be the main-spring of our country's strength.

"It would be difficult to enumerate all the advantages that will be derived from the possession of railways; such, for instance, as facilitating the transportation of the grain-tax, affording prompt and effective communication in the distribution of relief, the extension of commerce, the furtherance of mining operations, the suppression of likin* stations, and the improved system of traveling. But the principal advantage that will be derived from them is the more effective method of transporting troops, and this consideration renders it important that their introduction should not be delayed.

---

* Stations in the interior for the collection of taxes on goods in transit.

"The area of China's territory is very great. Her northern frontier stretches out to a length of 10,000 li,* and is conterminous with the confines of Russia; moreover, there are foreigners of many nationalities resident at the treaty ports, who are engaged in trade with our people. To draw a line on our frontier and guard it against invasion is a matter which, in spite of our desire, we are unable to do. 'Although we ride about on a fleet horse, and do not spare the whip, we are unable to come up in time.'† If railways are built all parts of the country, north, south, east, and west, will be within easy communication, and in case of war we can form our plans according to our observations of the enemy's movements. It will be easy to come to a given point in a few days, although the distance be 10,000 li, and a million troops can be brought together at one call; and such irregularities as confusion and hurry when troops are ordered to move and obstructions and delays in the transport of materials and supplies, and similar vexatious embarrassments will be removed. The strength of an army consists in its troops being united, and a state of division means weakness.

"China numbers eighteen provinces [now nineteen]; her troops are not few, nor are her supplies insufficient; but the troops and supplies of each province are under the control of its high provincial officers. The affairs of each province being thus confined to its own limits, the result is the division of interests that should be united in one mutual and common concern. In case of war, each province has barely time to concert its own plans, and when called upon to furnish troops or supplies has not the means wherewith to meet the demand. They are un-

---

* A li is equal to about one third of an English mile.

† Metaphor for "Our movements are too slow to guard the vast extent of our country."

able, moreover, to come forward with the necessary relief in times of adversity, although an edict be issued from the throne visiting the responsible officers with severe punishment. With the construction of railways the power of the country will be concentrated, its arteries will be unobstructed, the number of soldiers may be diminished, supplies curtailed, and several regiments converted into one effective corps. In the protection of our frontiers and seaboard, the necessary materials, such as artillery, etc., can be transported with surpassing rapidity [literally between the dawn and twilight]. Troops garrisoned at different stations can be converted into an effective active battalion, and the strength of the eighteen provinces will be brought into one center. One soldier may be made as efficient as ten. Hereafter the army and commissariat will be under the control of the central Government, which will become the seat of importance, while the provincial administration will remain auxiliary and secondary, and the efficiency of the army will not be exposed to be impaired and obstructed by the failures of provincial officers.

"In the present state of our affairs the expenditure required for the defenses of our frontiers makes a sensible diminution in the revenue of the country, the prosperity of the people is fettered by the lekin excise, the wealth of the country is being monopolized by foreign merchants, and the riches of the land are daily diminishing. There are signs portending some great calamity. But if railways are constructed, the profits to be derived from their working will suffice for the maintenance of troops. Some of the lekin stations may be abolished after due consideration, and the worries caused by complaints of foreign merchants regarding transit passes, etc., will be avoided. It would be difficult to devise any other plan more eminently calculated to benefit the prosperity of the country and to further the happiness of the people.

"The reasons why Russia is overbearing in her relations with us, and why Japan underrates us, are to be found in the fact that China has only one corner of her vast possessions protected, is afraid to face difficulties, and is incapable of rousing her energies, because possessed of an inordinately pacific disposition. But the day when an imperial edict is issued sanctioning the construction of railways it will be manifesting our desire to strengthen ourselves, and the life and energy of our country will instantly be roused. This intelligence will startle those countries; and while, in the first place, we shall find it easier to agree to the terms of a treaty with Russia, on the other hand the insidious designs of Japan will insensibly disappear.

"Some time in the current year, the Viceroy, Li Hung-Chang, memorialized the throne praying for the sanction of a telegraph line to be laid along the coast. Telegraphs are one of the essential requirements in the operations of an army, and if constructed as auxiliaries to and in conjunction with railways, there will be a large saving in expense, as well as increased facility of supervision. If any difficulty be encountered in raising the requisite funds for the construction of railways, and doubts arise as to our inability to proceed with the work, your slave thinks that the plan of inviting contributions from the mercantile classes is not unworthy of consideration; but if this plan be infeasible in consequence of the wide dispersion of these classes, the contraction of a foreign loan is the only plan worthy to be considered, if there exists a desire to avail ourselves of the present time for the construction of railways.

"If the contraction of a foreign loan in aid of the Government be held to be an impossibility, a loan for this purpose may be considered an exception. It is a means whereby a source of profit may be opened up, and the money expended will be represented in the materials and plant. These are considerations which will induce the foreign banker to gladly accommodate us with the loan.

"The Government will have no difficulty in repaying the debt. As the interest asked will be small and the time for repayment ample, it may be liquidated with the profit of the undertaking. The mechanics of the West are expert in manufacturing railways, and are, moreover, eager for an opportunity of displaying their skill in our Celestial country. Your slave believes the present occasion is especially opportune, and one that should not be missed.

"Two lines of railways are urgently needed in China: One to go from Chin-kiang [on the Yang-tse-kiang] through the provinces of Shantung and Chihli, having its terminus at Peking; the other to go from Hankow through Honan to Peking. There should be, besides this, two northern routes, one from Peking running eastward to Shengking, the other running westward to Kansu. But as it will be difficult to undertake all these lines at once, in consequence of the enormous outlay that will be required, your slave would suggest and prays that sanction be given for the construction, first, of the line from Chin-kiang to Peking, to be in connection with the line of telegraph which it is proposed to lay this year. As the provinces of Shantung and Chihli cover a large tract of territory through which this railroad will have to pass, and as stories are likely to be current about its interference with the family graves and homes of the people, much opposition to it must be expected from those who are ignorant that the government roads are broad, and that the space required for the permanent way will be little more than ten feet, and that the railway will in no way interfere with their homes and graveyards; but if obstacles do present themselves in the way of the line, it will be easy to avoid them by a slight *détour*.

"Your slave, while engaged in extirpating the rebels in former years, traveled all through the empire, and has frequently traversed the provinces in question. He is therefore perfectly familiar with the condition of the country, and the circumstances of the inhabitants; he would not dare to be careless or reckless in forming his opinions so positively.

"Should this business, which so closely concerns the efficiency of the army, and is so intimately connected with the weal or woe of the empire, be honored with the sanction of Your Majesties, your slave would pray that an edict be issued instructing the Board of Foreign Affairs to take the matter into immediate consideration, and to memorialize in reply. If, however, indecision and procrastination prevail, and the business be regarded as a thing that can be put off to a future day, it is much to be feared that, after the treaty with Russia is signed, the construction of railways will be indefinitely postponed, like the case of the 'man who, wanting to build a house, concerts his plans with passers in the street,'* and also that the lesson taught in ancient history by 'sleeping on straw and tasting the bitter gall' † will become a vain waste of words, and that the day will never come when an effort to strengthen our country will be made.

"Your slave has written out the reasons which have prompted him to make this request for the introduction of railways as a means of augmenting the power of the

---

* That is, does not make up his mind and go to work seriously.

† An allegory drawn from ancient Chinese history, in which the ruler of a certain state, being overcome by his enemies, slept on straw and tasted the bitter gall to inure himself to hardship, and to foster resentment and a determination for strength to be revenged, which he was eventually enabled to accomplish by vanquishing his victors.

MEMORIAL OF LIU MING-CHU'AN. 135

country in a memorial, reverently prepared, which he now submits to the throne. Prostrate, he prays Your Majesties, the Empress-Dowager and the Emperor, to cast your sacred glances thereon, and to announce your pleasure regarding the feasibility or otherwise of the recommendations set forth therein."

This memorial was referred by the Imperial Government to Li Hung-Chang and Lin K'un-Yi, northern and southern superintendents of trade, and they supported and supplemented it as follows :

"Your Majesties' servants, Li Hung-Chang, northern superintendent of trade, and Lin K'un-Yi, southern superintendent of trade, upon their knees address the Throne: Looking upward they implore the sacred glances of Your Majesties upon a memorial reverently prepared, showing that, in obedience to an imperial rescript, a satisfactory consultation has been held upon the subject of railways, and that as their construction is a question of the foremost importance in augmenting the power of the country and promoting its prosperity, measures should be immediately devised whereby to raise the necessary funds for their construction, and steps taken in the first place to appoint a competent person to make a careful study of the subject.

"Your servants would humbly state that they had the honor to receive from the Grand Council, who had privately communicated to them, the Imperial Edict of December 3d, as follows :

"'Whereas, Liu Ming-Chu'an has memorialized us regarding the formation of railways, and has recommended that steps be taken for the construction first of a line from Chin-kiang to Peking, to be in connection with the line of telegraph which Li Hung-Chang has asked for permission to establish this year, the purport of the memorial being to recommend the adoption of measures whereby to augment the power of the country :

"'Let Li Hung-Chang and Lin K'un-Yi carefully consider the proposals set forth therein, and let them memorialize the result of their deliberations.

"'Let a copy of Liu Ming-Chu'an's memorial be made and forwarded to them.

"'Respect this!'

"Looking upward, your servants behold with unspeakable respect and submission their sacred master's anxiety concerning the present troubles, and his untiring endeavors to devise plans for rousing the energies of the country, and incessant efforts to obtain information on every side.

"Prostrate, your servants beg to make the following observations:

"In the earliest ages, when mankind were first created, the nine divisions of China were subdivided into some ten thousand different states, each of which had its own habits and customs. Although within a few hundred *li* of each other, they were divided and had no intercourse with each other. When the sages came into existence, men learned to scoop out logs of wood and convert them into canoes; wood was hewed into paddles, and with the aid of these paddles and canoes they crossed over to places which were before inaccessible; oxen were yoked to carts and horses were mounted; heavy burdens were dragged to great distances, and thus all parts of the world became benefited. It is over four thousand years from that time to the present, and all parts of the country, north, south, east, and west, have the same doctrine and the same literature; a condition of things that may rightly be styled flourishing.

"The nations of the West have always studied the arts with minute care, and they all manufacture steamboats and railways. Although the earth is about ninety thou-

MEMORIAL OF LI HUNG-CHANG. 137

sand *li* in circumference, they are able to surmount all obstacles, and travel through almost every part of it. They have superseded the boats and chariots bequeathed to us by the old sages, by putting forth new ideas and producing inventions which appear to be Heaven-sent for the benefit of mankind.

"In these latter years China has derived no small amount of benefit by imitating Western nations, and building steamboats. The human intellect becomes enlightened after it has been obscure. Rough materials are transformed into utensils for use. Communities get united after being divided. These are the natural results of the laws of Nature, and it is neither wisdom nor force that can restrain them.

"Railways first had their origin in England, in the working of coal-mines. In the first year of the reign of Tao-Kwang, the tracks, which were to keep the wheels of the cars in control, were first laid down, and from that time the invention gradually improved. They were used in transporting coal and iron to the markets for sale, and the profits realized were very great. Their use was subsequently extended to every branch of industry and trade, and England came to be the champion of Europe; France, America, Russia, Germany, and other great nations then followed suit, and built railways, and it was only after they possessed them that they were enabled to encroach upon and usurp the land of their neighbors and open up and reclaim wild territory. As the populations of these countries increased, and trade flourished, they had to extend their railways in order to meet the improved circumstances of the times. From that time the two continents of Europe and America became accessible from all points of the compass, as each had constructed some hundred thousand *li* of railroads. Troops ordered to a given point reach their destination in a day,

138   CHINA.

and news and tidings travel with the rapidity of the wind.

"The daily increase in prosperity and strength that has marked the progress of these nations throughout the last forty or fifty years may be ascribed to the fact that they possess steamers that plow through the sea, and railways that make traveling by land exceedingly convenient.

"Now, to speak of Japan, she is a small, insignificant country, yet she possesses railways that run across the whole of her country. Her idea is that, by adopting Western mechanical improvements, she will have it in her power to despise China.

"Russia has railways that run from Europe to within a short distance of Hao Han, Kiakhta, and neighboring places, and she is about to build a line from Hai Shen Wei to Hui Chun. The frontiers of China and Russia are co-terminous with each other for some ten thousand li. If we build some railways now while it is time, the present force of our army will be amply sufficient to protect our frontier; but without railways all our endeavors to protect that frontier will be futile, even though we increase our troops and supplies.

"China's isolation in being without railways, when all other nations possess them, may be aptly illustrated by supposing those who lived in the middle ages to have discarded the use of the boats and chariots of their time. They could not help being behind other men in all their movements.

"Your servants estimate that the advantages to be derived by the possession of railways may be classed under about nine principal divisions :

"1. The country north of the Yang-tse and Hwai Rivers is rather destitute of water-courses, unlike the southern provinces which abound with rivers and streams, by which all manner of goods are conveyed in different

MEMORIAL OF LI HUNG-CHANG. 139

directions. It is owing to this that out of the twenty to thirty million taels of revenue derived yearly from foreign goods and lekin, the southern provinces provide about nine tenths, while the northern provinces figure for one tenth only ; whereas, if railways are gradually built, communication will be established throughout the country like the threads in a loom, commodities can be transported and interchanged between the different provinces according to their respective wants. The idle population of the northern provinces will become industrious ; no part of arable land will be allowed to remain unprofitable, nor the energies of man lie dormant, and the condition of the country will gradually become one of affluence. The customary duties and lekin can be levied at the important points of the line, so that the revenue derived from these sources will be equally divided between the northern and southern provinces. This is the first advantage that will accrue to the finances of the country.

"2. It is a well-known fact that union in an army means strength, and that weakness is the result of disunion. China's frontier on land and her seaboard are each over ten thousand *li* in extent. It is not to be supposed that defenses are to be built at every place along this line, for not only will our troops and supplies be insufficient, but this would be a plan without any sense. Railways are wanted to make military operations successful. With their aid, distances like those of Yunnan, Kwei-Chow, Kansu, and Kuldja, can be accomplished in about ten days. The troops garrisoned in the eighteen provinces may be converted into an effective active battalion ; hereafter the number of soldiers may be diminished, supplies curtailed, and several regiments converted into one effective corps. The army can be summoned at one signal, its discipline and power will be concentrated, and one soldier made as efficient as ten. This is the second advantage that will result from the possession of railways, in making military operations more successful.

"3. Peking, which may be termed the root of our country, is situated in a lonely position in the north of China, at a great distance from its center, and is very difficult to control, nor can help be afforded in time of trouble. During the war which happened in the tenth year of Hsien Fung's reign, several statesmen of that day advised that the capital be transferred to some more suitable locality, but in view of the gravity of the step it was deemed undesirable to act precipitately on that advice. Moreover, every time a quarrel occurs between foreign nations and ourselves, they threaten to shatter our capital. If railways are constructed, a distance of ten thousand *li* may be considered as at one's very threshold, for it can be accomplished in no time, and a hundred million soldiers can be moved to a given place within a few days. All parts of the country will be in a condition of protection and security, the Government will be peaceable and unmoved as a rock, and in case of danger assistance will be readily forthcoming. Officials and merchants of every province will be continually traveling to long distances by the railway. Merchandise and government grain will be transported with surprising rapidity. All will be anxious to travel by this route, and to avail themselves of the railway-depot for the storage of their goods. In time of peace it can not fail to prosper trade and to increase the activity of the multitudes. There will be no further necessity to talk of transferring the capital; moreover, the covetous designs of foreign nations will be cut short forever, and the foundation of our country will become immovable for a hundred centuries. In this way our capital city will be protected, which is the third advantage to be gained by the possession of railways.

"4. A few years since, during the disastrous famine

that raged in the provinces of Shansi and Honan, the price of grain in Shansi rose to the exorbitant rate of over forty taels* per picul. Had there been railways to convey it, the price could not have exceeded some seven taels per picul, including the freight from Tientsin. When the country is in possession of railways, if any calamity by drought or inundation should happen in any of the provinces, relief, in the shape of grain or money, can be transported as rapidly as light or sound takes to travel, and the lives of many human beings will be spared. Moreover, goods will flow easily to all parts of the country, and the evils of exorbitant prices and engrossing commodities in a market will be avoided. This is the fourth advantage that railways will bring by benefiting and preserving the lives of the people.

"5. Since the transportation of the government grain-tax was transferred from the junks to be conveyed over the sea by steamers, several officials have criticised the step, and have ever been anxious that the old custom of conveying it *via* the Grand Canal should be re-established, in order to forestall the unseen dangers of the sea. When railways are constructed, the transportation of the grain will flow unobstructed like [the blood in] the arteries of the human system, and if on some day the sea-road be rendered dangerous by war, there need be no anxiety that any obstacle will prevent the whole amount (one million piculs) of grain from being transported to its destination. Besides this, munitions of war, such as gunpowder, guns, and weapons, and Government taxes [in kind], will all be conveyed without the slightest impediment. This is the benefit that will result to measures of transportation, and is the fifth advantage to be gained by the possession of railways.

---

* A tael is worth about one dollar and thirty-three cents in Mexican silver.

"6. The speed of railways is ten times that of the fleetest horse. Henceforth dispatches can be sent with increased rapidity, Government orders and missions for purposes of investigation will travel with greater speed than is now possible by the post-horses. Exclusive of this, letters and parcels will be conveyed rapidly; soldiers sent in pursuit of robbers and malefactors will reach them in a day. Some of the Government post-stations on the main road might be abolished, and the savings appropriated to the maintenance of the railway. This is the sixth advantage that will result to the postal department of the Government.

"7. The coal and iron mines of the empire are all at a distance from the water-courses. If railways are used in transporting the products of these mines, the cost-price will be small, and their sale abundant, and in proportion as the sales increase the mines will prosper and be opened up in large numbers. The expenditure required for constructing the railway will be greatly economized by using the coal and iron of the mines, and the profits that will be derived from their working will be an inexhaustible source of supply for the army. Thus, mining operations will be developed and benefited, and this is the seventh advantage that railways will bring.

"8. It is difficult to carry goods to places that are remote from the rivers and canals, as it is difficult to bring native produce thence. With railways merchandise will be conveyed to and from places that are inaccessible to steamers, and traffic will be considerably increased. Thus, steamers and railways will aid each other mutually in transporting goods. This is the eighth advantage that will inure to the carrying-trade of the China Merchants' Steam Navigation Company.

"9. When railways are introduced, all classes of travelers, whether officials, commoners, merchants, or soldiers, traveling on private or public business, can go to great distances with surpassing speed (literally one thousand *li*) in a twinkling. The expenses of the journey will be considerably reduced in view of the rapidity with which one travels, there need be no fear of robbers on the road, and the dangers of wind and wave will be avoided. This is the ninth advantage that railways will create by improving the system of traveling in the empire.

"As your servants have shown in the beginning of this memorial, the various nations of the West have suddenly risen in importance because they have all been careful to develop and employ this new invention. It must be remembered, moreover, that the revenue of the state and military tactics are considerations of the foremost importance in planning measures for strengthening the country and promoting its prosperity.

"Your Majesties' confirmation of the purport of Liu Ming-Chu'an's memorial, viz., the recommendation of measures that will augment the power of the country, is in reality what is meant when he says that he foresees the advent of some calamity, and the daily increase of our embarrassments, and while expressing his resentment at the injustice of foreign nations toward us, desires that the energies of the country be immediately roused by the promulgation first of our intention to introduce railways, and thus cause the insidious designs of Russia and Japan to disappear.

"The railroads that are urgently needed in China are, two lines in the south, one to go from Chin-kiang, through the provinces of Shantung and Chihli, reaching Peking, the other from Hankow, through Honan, to Peking; and two northern lines, one running from Peking eastward to Feng-t'ien, the other running westward to Kansu. These four routes, if constructed, may be termed the root and stem of the railway enterprise. If branch lines are required to go to places of importance distant a few hundred *li* from the main way, your servants believe that they can easily be formed. The distances being short, and the necessary expenditure small, contributions can be invited from the merchants, who will be glad to respond to them. Thus the smaller lines will shoot off from the main way like the branches of a tree, so as to form a regular network, and there need be no anxiety that the railway enterprise will not flourish.

"As, however, the construction of these four lines will necessitate an enormous outlay, it will be exceedingly difficult to undertake them all at once. The suggestion of Liu Ming-Chu'an, that the line from Chin-kiang to Peking be first built in connection with the line of telegraph which your servant, Li Hung-Chang, proposed to lay this year is one which, if adopted, will bring two advantages, viz., facility in overseeing the line, and uninterrupted means of sending telegrams. If the construction first of this line be said to be only a partial benefit to the country, considering its condition and requirements, it must be remembered that all the nations of the West were similarly situated fifty years ago, and that it is only owing to their determined efforts to construct them and push to the front, for fear of being behind, that they are able to have the influence which they possess to-day. Liu Ming-Chu'an's idea is first to give an example, whereby a start may be made. If the enterprise is pushed on gradually, there need be no fear that it will not some day be in a flourishing condition.

"If it be argued by some that after railways are constructed it is to be feared that the road will be used by enemies to invade our country, or, again, that as foreigners have long been wishing to build railways in China, if she once makes a commencement it may give these foreigners reason to become exceedingly importunate;* it must be said that such objections can only be made by those who are ignorant that every nation uses its railways in transporting troops to defend the country against its enemies. They have never been known to serve the purposes of an enemy. This will be made plain by remembering that the railway is within our territory. Every pass on the frontier being guarded, it is not likely that the enemy will find their way through some neglected passage. If, by some extraordinary hazard, a danger like this should happen, one portion of the road can be destroyed, and the whole made useless, or if the train be kept out of the enemy's hands, the road will be of no value without it. Other nations have had no reason to be anxious on this point, since railways were built some scores of years ago. It is a condition that may be likened to the convenience of the man at home, and the disadvantage of the stranger abroad.

"By international law and the treaties, foreign nations are prohibited to build railroads in the territory of another power without the authority of that power. If we apprehend that they will rely on their superior strength and violate the treaties, and we do not proceed to construct railways ourselves, will our mere apprehensions prevent them from presuming on their strength if they desire to do so?

"Foreigners are, moreover, constantly advising us how to benefit China. If we proceed of our own motion to adopt measures that will benefit the country by constructing this important line, it will be enough to cut short all further officious advice from them.

"Again, if objections be made to the railway on the score of its interference with the welfare of carters and

---

* This fear is never lost sight of by those opposed to the introduction of railroads.—J. H. W.

other classes of laborers, who, it is apprehended, will have no way of getting their food and clothing, and that disturbances must inevitably result in consequence of these poor people having lost their means of sustenance ;* to these objections it must be answered that in England, in the early days of the railway, there were similar fears that many poor people would be robbed of their means of support; but before long the number of carts and traffic generally in the important towns on the line of the railway became double what it was formerly. Then the railway will be on the main road, and can not interfere with the villages and little towns in the by-places, which will continue as before to use carts and men to transport goods and passengers. An increase in the railway-traffic will necessarily produce a corresponding increase in the number of carts and carriers.

"If the railway enterprise reaches a condition of prosperity, it will give work to numbers of men, viz., employés to run the train, laborers to make the roads, guardsmen to watch the line, carriers to load and unload merchandise, and menials to attend on the passengers. The monthly allowances to these men will amply suffice them to support their parents and their families, and if any of them have a little surplus means they might open an inn, and, with an increase in their business, take partners, and, without much effort, have a trade with capital and profit. It may, therefore, be reckoned that every ten or twenty *li* of railroad will support and afford means of living for not less than some hundred thousand men.

"Another way in which numbers of men will be employed is in the coal, iron, and other mines, which will

---

* This argument is constantly used against the introduction of railroads.—J. H. W.

be opened in large numbers when railways are constructed. The numbers of poor miners who live by the sweat of their brow will be incalculably increased, which is positive proof of the benefit that will result to all classes of miners.

"Finally, some may argue that the railway will interfere with the fields, homes, and graves of the people, and that much opposition to it must be expected in consequence.* These arguments can only be made in ignorance of the fact that the government roads are broad, and that the permanent way will not require much more than ten feet, and therefore can not interfere with the fields, homes, and graves of the people. In places where the government road is too narrow, a strip of land can be bought and paid for liberally; and if graves do present themselves in the way of the line, they can easily be avoided by a slight *détour*. Liu Ming-Chu'an traveled all over the empire while engaged in exterminating the rebels in former years, and is thoroughly familiar with the condition of the country and the circumstances of the inhabitants.

"The introduction of railways, however, being a question of paramount importance, it behooves us to examine the subject very carefully in the first stages of its management to forestall future evils and have a good model by which to go in the long run. Your servants have been careful to gather much information on this subject, and find that the railways constructed by foreigners are of various kinds; some are strong and last a good while; others, again, are less durable and last only a short time. Their prices also differ very widely; one *li* of road may cost a few thousand taels, or it may cost ten thousand

---

* This is generally supposed to be the greatest difficulty to be overcome, but I do not regard it as at all insuperable. See page 97, *et seq.*—J. H. W.

taels. As the road from Chin-kiang to Peking is an important highway, the line which it is proposed to build should be a substantial one, so as to last for a long time. Although it is difficult to estimate in advance what sum will be required, it is certain that it will not be small.

"The money at the disposal of the Government is very limited at the present time. If the funds required for constructing the railway be called for from the provinces, the provincial officers will not know how to raise the money; or if contribution be invited from merchants, it will be difficult to collect them in consequence of the wide dispersion of these classes. The proposition of Liu Ming-Chu'an, that a foreign loan be negotiated, is the only feasible plan. China has on former occasions frequently contracted foreign loans, but some officials, fearing that each province would make this a precedent for borrowing money, and become so far involved as to be at the mercy of foreign creditors, the Board of Revenue memorialized, and the contraction of foreign loans was interdicted. It must be said, however, that a loan for starting a large, profitable undertaking and a loan in aid of the army are two different things. When railways are started, the interest on the loan can be easily repaid by the profits of their working, and the Government will have gained a lasting source of profit.

"But there are three things in the contractions of foreign loans that demand great care:

"1. As it is to be apprehended that the foreign lenders will take the direction of the railway into their own hands and exclude us from being masters in the business, a clause must be inserted, distinctly stating that they may not interfere in the matter. The interest of the money being guaranteed, and the debt being punctually paid up at the specified dates, all matters relating to employing workmen, purchasing materials, and constructing the line, must be left to our management, the foreign creditor being debarred from questioning our actions. If this condition be inadmissible, no foreign loan should be made.

"2. The next fear is that foreigners will strive unlawfully to get the undertaking into their own hands. To prevent this, the regulations of the China Merchants' Steam Navigation Company, which exclude foreigners from becoming shareholders, will have to be followed. When the railway company is formed, its management will be in the hands of Chinese merchants, subject, however, to the supervision of some government official. Regulations should be made, after consultation, providing for the repayment of the loan by the said company by installments in different years, till the whole amount, interest and capital, be cleared off. If there should happen to be failures in paying up, the government superintendent will urge payment; the company will only be allowed to mortgage the railway, but not to transfer it into the hands of the foreign creditors. The repayment of the loan being thus clearly provided for by limitation, all malpractices will be cut short. A foreign loan should not be contracted unless the foregoing indispensable condition be complied with.

"3. The third danger is, that the finances of the country will have to suffer in consequence of the railway loan. Hitherto when foreign loans have been negotiated, the revenue derived from the maritime customs has always been appropriated to repay them. Recently the customs establishments have been called upon to meet so many demands for money that they are greatly embarrassed.*

---

* They are *now* in a healthy condition, but there is a great and growing indisposition on the part of the Imperial Government to pledge the customs revenues for the security of foreign loans.—J. H. W.

It should be clearly stipulated that the loan will have no connection with the customs revenue. The Government will decide in what way the profits to be derived from the railway enterprise will be successively appropriated toward repaying the debt, which will be cleared off at latest within ten or twenty years. No foreign loan should be made without this indispensable condition for the protection of the finances of the state.

"The foregoing three provisos are important considerations in negotiating a foreign loan.

"Your servants have learned that foreigners have hitherto been very careful, in making loans, to consider what the chances are of recovering their money. If the conditions set forth above are rigorously adhered to, it is likely they will not be willing to lend; but if they are, then the construction of railways may be proceeded with at once. Instead, however, of proceeding to build them hastily, regardless of evils which a loan on any condition might entail, the business should be deferred to be maturely considered, that there be no reason to repent of errors. Your servants have also learned that none of the railways of other nations have been built without a loan. Their mode of procedure is the following: An engineer of reputation makes a survey of the road, and a prospectus is prepared, clearly showing the estimates of the undertaking and the probabilities of its success, which is a means of amply securing the confidence of the people.

"The road from north to south which it is proposed to build in China will, after it has run some time, bring considerable profit. When the public company is formed, an engineer of intelligence and reputation should be engaged to make a careful estimate of the undertaking. His estimate will be carefully considered by the Tsung-li Ya-mên and your servants, who will prepare a satisfactory and reliable prospectus, on which some wealthy foreign merchants might be induced to accommodate us with the loan.

"As regards the selecting of materials for constructing the railway, estimating how many *li* of the road are to be built, hiring laborers economically and at the same time to obtain substantial work, all these are matters that should be carefully investigated, so that the essential parts of the business be not overlooked.

"A high official should be specially deputed to superintend the management of this business, which includes inviting shareholders and raising the loan, measuring the land, hiring laborers, etc., etc., and is somewhat intricate. Without this step the business can not be expected to work satisfactorily. Your servants beg to state that Liu Ming-Chu'an is a man in the full vigor of life, and possesses a bold and resolute nature; he has gone through great hardships in the service of his country, and is very desirous to undertake the management of this business, since he has seen lately that foreign nations are ill-treating us on all sides, and believes that the country's present state of helplessness should be changed for an attitude of strength. The business, however, being an innovation, its management will be difficult, and it will require time before we experience its benefits. If any imminent danger were threatening the empire, and the court were to order Liu Ming-Chu'an to take a command, the consideration of this affair would naturally have to be postponed, but he is now without any occupation, having solicited leave to nurse his health. Should this proposition be honored with the sanction of their sacred master, and Liu Ming-Chu'an be appointed to superintend the management of the railway company, your servants would pray that he be ordered, in the first place, to make a careful study of the important points in this business, and without precipitancy to consult and deliberate thereon. Japan and Russia will be startled to hear that, in the midst of all her difficulties, China has still strength left to take this step. It will be manifesting something on which they did not reckon—a truly admirable way of first giving the sound and following it up with the reality. As Liu Ming-Chu'an is now at leisure, he might proceed to invite shareholders and form a company to consider the question of a foreign loan ; although it is hard to say whether or not a large sum can be raised, his reputation as a man of loyal merit is more likely to enlist the united assistance of men of all classes, both foreign and native, than any other official.

"There are over ten thousand men stationed in the garrisons of Chihli and Kiangsu, who served under Liu Ming-Chu'an in former years. In his study of the railway question, it might appear plain to him that an economical way of proceeding will be to employ the aid of these men in constructing the road, and if the contributions of native merchants be abundant, the surplus can be applied to some other purpose. In each case it will be the duty of your servants to consult with him and manage the business according to the shape it may assume. The question of introducing railways having been thus brought before the Throne by Liu Ming-Chu'an, its management from first to last should be intrusted to him. If, for any reason, the business be put off ten years, at the end of that time he should still be charged with it ; there is no other person on whom he could place the responsibility. Should other and more important calls of duty arise after his appointment, he can leave the railway business, and, in obedience to the orders of the Throne proceed to his new post of duty.

"When railways are built in China, she must also open up her coal and iron mines to prevent her treasure from flowing into foreign lands. The coal and iron mines in the neighborhood of Che-chou-fu and Lou-wan-fu, in Shansi, are very rich. It is matter of regret that no merchants, with large capital, are to be found to work them. If the capital for constructing railways can be raised, one tenth of the sum obtained might be employed in working the mines after Western methods and with foreign machinery, and the coal and iron obtained might be used for the railway. Thus the mines will be developed and benefited by the railway, and will in turn, help to extend the railway enterprise, and the two undertakings will bring about a highly desirable result.

"Your servants forward, with all dispatch, their memorial in reply, reverently prepared, setting forth the considerations relative to railways as a means of augmenting the power of the country, and to the necessity of first making a careful study of the question. Prostrate they submit their reply to the Throne, and pray Your Majesties, the Empress-Dowager and the Emperor, to cast your sacred glances thereon, and to issue your instructions in the premises."

There is no reason for supposing that either the Viceroy Li, or the Governor-General Liu, has in any way changed his opinions upon the important matters discussed in the foregoing memorials, but, to the contrary, they have both recently reiterated them in personal conversation with me, and both say, clearly and unequivocally, that they intend to have railroads as soon as they can obtain the imperial sanction for them. There is now a generous rivalry between them as to who shall first get permission. Liu is more remote from Peking, and naturally feels that he is less likely to be interfered with in anything he considers necessary for the defense or development of the Island of Formosa, where he is now serving as governor-general; while Li is almost under the shadow of the Throne, and is a statesman of far greater consideration than his friend. He is patient, adroit, and thoroughly in earnest, and while he is not by nature, so far as a foreigner can judge, disposed to make himself obnoxious to those in authority over him, or to seriously weaken himself by running counter either to their prejudices or to the well-established customs of the country, he thoroughly understands the arts of a courtier, as well as those of a statesman, and if he lives will surely silence the opposition and secure the imperial approval of his policy. Gradually throwing aside the principles of rigid conservatism which is the essence of Chinese philosophy and state-craft, he has put himself squarely at the head of the progressive movement. He has never for a moment tried to delude himself or others into the belief that the Western nations are barbarians, and their arts valueless. He has been too long and too intimately associated with foreigners to look down upon them with contempt, or even to treat them with discourtesy. He impresses me as a calm, far-sighted, and enlightened statesman, who, without having a technical understanding of Western arts and sciences, knows their vast superiority to any that the Chinese have, and does not fear to say so whenever occasion requires it. And yet it must not be forgotten that neither he nor any other subject of the Emperor will dare run counter to his wishes, or take any aggressive action in so grave a matter, without the express authority of the Throne.

The Viceroy Li has already had one great accession to his party, if I may use the word in writing of a country where no such thing as party is known, or can be known for many years. I refer, of course, to the conversion of the late Tso Tsung-tang, who had always been opposed to foreigners and foreign methods in everything. He was a great scholar, and also a great soldier. Throughout a long and useful career he was a bold, resolute, and outspoken adviser of the Throne, and was always a hero and favorite with the conservatives. He had military talents of a high order, and is thought by many to have been the greatest Chinese general of modern times (as Li is indubitably the greatest statesman), but he never undertook to disguise his fierce contempt for the "Western barbarians." He used Krupp guns and improved small-arms in his Turkistan campaigns, but would never admit that he needed any one to show him how to use them. He was a firm believer in the Chinese system, and, although in some degree a recluse, he did not fail to keep himself informed of what progress was promising to do for his country. He died, full of years and honors, just before I reached China, leaving Li with no living rival to dispute his supremacy either in war or statesmanship, and paying the highest possible tribute, in his dying memorial to the throne, to the superior wisdom of the great Chinese liberal leader.

This document, which was evidently prepared with the last remnant of the writer's strength, and is a most touching and patriotic appeal to the Throne, was translated for the "North China Herald" of October 7, 1885, It runs as follows :

"May it please Your Majesties ! Your Majesties' gracious favor unrequited. Your servant sick, unto death, utters these valedictory words, and implores that the sacred glance may deign to rest thereon.

"Your servant, finding his bodily ailments increasing daily, besought an extension of furlough, for the purpose of restoring his health. This was granted him on the 25th of the seventh moon, and he prepared forthwith a memorial of thanks, at the same time handing over to Yang C'hang-Chun his imperial commissioner's seal, and the business connected with the various military departments under his control. Then he would have started upon his homeward journey, but, within a couple of days or so, severe pains in the loins came on, making it troublesome for him either to sit or stand. His hands and feet were numbed; hot phlegm rose in his throat; he knew that the end was come!

"Your servant, a poor scholar of books, first attracted the attention of His Gracious Majesty the Emperor Hsien-Feng, and has held important posts under three successive reigns. He has assisted at the deliberations of the Privy Council; he has been commander-in-chief of the army. And, were his corpse to be rolled into a horse's skin, he could not complain that he had not received his due. But now, when peace or war in Anam means the weakness or strength of China, and when your servant, traveling southward, has to this date not once engaged in conflict with the foe, and made manifest the might of our arms, he feels a grief in life that will prevent his closing his eyes in death.

"Overwhelmed with imperial kindness, it is but a year since your servant took leave of Your Majesties. And now he can never again set eyes upon the divine countenance, but must wait until, as a dog or a horse, he may discharge his debt in the life to come. Now he is but a bird that sings a sadder strain as death draws near.

"At present, when peace has just been made in the regions of the west (Anam), Japan is seeking to thrust herself upon us, and the various nations of the earth watch round us like glaring beasts. Unless we make a great and united effort to close the stable ere the steed be gone; unless we keep our *mugwort* * on hand ready for use, in the event of further trouble, we shall become weaker and weaker, and less able to make an effort, until at length we shall not even be able to attain the point at which we are to-day.

---
* For purposes of cauterization.

"Therefore, let Your Majesties, out of the deliberations of the high offices on the matter of the coast-defense, come rapidly to a decision. Let railways and mines and the construction of ships and guns be undertaken at once, as a means of insuring our national prosperity and strength. At the same time, as understanding is at the root of all undertakings, let Your Majesty the Emperor attend with more and more diligence to the study of our sacred books. Be not remiss even in the smallest matter. Daily associate with men of principle, and listen to their counsels. Take what is not absolutely necessary to be spent at the moment, and apply it to the wants of national defense. Be sparing in every-day life, that there may be a fund for circumstances unforeseen. Let the Emperor and his ministers strive with one accord in what is right, to procure what is right, and your servant will seem in the day of his death to be born again into life.

"With gasping breath and flowing tears your servant humbly speaks these words, which are copied down to be submitted to careful consideration under Your Majesty's mirror-like glance."

I have not been able to learn that any official action has been predicated exclusively upon this remarkable memorial, but there is abundant evidence that it has made a profound impression upon the literary and official class throughout the empire, as well as upon the foreigners residing within its borders. The simple fact that it was not suppressed by the Empress-Dowager would alone go to prove that she is not inimical to the introduction of railroads, were there no other evidence in existence; but it is now well known that she approves them, and has expressed herself in favor of their early construction. In China, as in every other country, the Throne has its courtiers and attendants, who are loud in the declaration that it can do no wrong, and is the unfailing source of wisdom and virtue. But until it speaks in an authoritative manner, which it has not yet done, the utterances of such men as Li and Tso, however great their wisdom or exalted their patriotism, can do no more than familiarize the official class with the great ideas which underlie modern progress. The adherence of so great and conservative a statesman as Tso Tsung-tang to these ideas, although he limits their application to the national defense, is a great event, and may well be considered the sure precursor of a wide-spread though still tardy acceptance of the policy which they foreshadow. In every line of the dying memorial the surrender of life-long prejudices is written. Sadly and pathetically the "poor scholar of books" confesses that Chinese learning and Chinese arts, whether of peace or war, are alike unable to save China from conquest and dismemberment, and implores his imperial master to "let railways, and mines, and the construction of ships and guns be undertaken." This is the very essence of progress and the death-knell of conservatism, and indorsing, as it does, the memorial of the Viceroy Li, it has done more to increase his influence and popularity than any event which has happened for years. If it leads to the construction of the initial railroad, it will prove indeed the inauguration of the golden age of China, and will speedily render her invincible to the rest of the world. Withal, it will be the Viceroy's chiefest glory that he has become her greatest benefactor as well as her greatest soldier and statesman.

It must be added, however, that notwithstanding the sound arguments contained in the foregoing remarkable memorials, the ignorant and conservative censors are far from yielding. They still oppose all progress, and especially the introduction of railroads, by all the means in their power, and, having the right of memorializing the Throne at all times, they resort to it whenever occasion offers. So far they have been able to frustrate all the plans of Li Hung-Chang in respect to this most important matter.

CHAPTER XI.

Visit to Peking—The unspeakably filthy city of the world—Its origin and characteristics—No suburbs or villas—Streets not paved—The foreign legations and society—Non-intercourse between court and diplomatic corps—The young Emperor—The Empress-Dowager—Her unlimited power—The censors—The Emperor worships at the tomb of his ancestors—The influences which control him—He can hardly become a conservative—The difficulties of his situation—Unprepared for a foreign war.

OF course, no foreigner visits Northern China without going to Peking, and ultimately to the Great Wall, and I am no exception to the rule. The distance from Tientsin to Peking is eighty miles; the wall lies about forty-five miles farther north, and the journey may be made in either of three ways. The most common and perhaps the most comfortable way, for Europeans, is by houseboat, a sort of scow, about thirty feet long and six feet wide, with a small house built in the middle for the protection of the occupant. The boat is propelled by sails, poles, or by the old-fashioned method known in America as the cordelle, and generally goes no farther than Tung-chow, a city fifteen miles from Peking, on the west bank of the Tientsin River (the northern branch of the Pei-ho), where the Grand Canal leaves it. Another way is by cart, and the Peking cart is an institution peculiar to North China. It is an exceedingly rude, springless vehicle, which fairly illustrates at the same time the condition of the mechanic arts and of transportation in China. It looks like a large Saratoga trunk on a pair of baggage-skids, balanced on a pair of wheels, and drawn by two mules driven tandem. And, finally, one may go on the back of a pony, breaking the journey into two stages, and riding the same pony all the way through, or by a relay of ponies, which enables one to make the trip in a single day.

I chose the third method, as the one requiring the least preparation, but sent my baggage and servant through by cart. The country is absolutely level, devoid of trees, and uninteresting, but it is under the closest cultivation. The road is distinct enough for about ten miles, throughout which it occupies the river-embankment, but for the most of the distance it wanders about in a very indefinite and uncertain way. It shows no evidence whatever of having ever been laid out or worked, and it certainly has never been paved or macadamized. As there are no fences, hedges, or ditches about the farms, and no farm-houses, there is nothing to designate even the general direction except the telegraph-poles, and as they occupy the river-embankment, which is very crooked, one would have to travel much farther than necessary if he followed them. As a consequence, a foreigner who goes horseback requires a guide, and should be sure before starting that his *mafoo*, or horse-boy, knows the way and the stopping-places. I have made the trip several times, and was never over twenty-four hours on the road.

Peking is the unspeakably filthy place of the world. It is dirtier than Constantinople, and, although it is the capital, it is even nastier than any other Chinese city, and nothing worse can be said of it. No correct census has ever been taken, but it is claimed that it contains a population of a million souls. It is surrounded by a stately gray brick wall, forty-five feet high, surmounted by a crenelated parapet with flanking towers at proper intervals.

It is penetrated by arched gateways, and encircled by a moat which constitutes the beginning and the end of the Grand Canal.

Its origin is lost to history, but it is evident that it was selected as a central point from which to defend the northern frontier. It is practically a fortified camp, and has never been anything else. Here, in the olden days, were gathered the forces which were expected to defend the Great Plain from the ravages of the Tartars, and hence it was against this point that they directed their first attacks. Having captured it under the Great Khan in 1264 A. D., and probably many times before, they made it their own capital, not only because it gave them a safe base for further operations, but also because it covers the road which leads back into the fastnesses of Mongolia. It was visited by Marco Polo during the reign of Kublai, and called by him Kambaluc, or Khan-baligh, that is to say, the City of the Khan. It had already had many other names, and gone through many vicissitudes. After remaining the capital throughout the reign of Kublai's descendants, it was wrested from their weak and enfeebled hands by Hung Wu, the great Chinese soldier, who drove out the conquerors, and founded the strictly Chinese dynasty of the Mings. He, however, restored the capital to the much more eligible city of Nanking, where it remained till his son, Yung-loh, established it again at Peking. The descendants of the latter held it till 1644, when it was captured by the Manchus, and has ever since been retained by them as the seat of their dynasty and the capital of the whole empire. It is divided into three parts, the Chinese City, the Tartar City, and the "Carnation Prohibited City," commonly called the "Forbidden City," because it is inhabited by the Emperor and his court, and Europeans are excluded therefrom. The parts are divided from each other by separate

PEKING THE UNSPEAKABLY FILTHY CITY. 163

inclosures or cross-walls, and while they are well laid out in broad, straight streets, crossing each other at right angles, they are equally dirty and uninviting. There are no sewers and no police regulations. Dirt and dilapidation reign supreme, and, what is worse, the people seem to live almost in a state of nature, and to have no sense of shame or decency. It is claimed that Peking was much larger and finer than now, during the reigns of Yung-loh and Kien-Lung, but this may well be doubted. There is abundant evidence that some of the roads entering it, notably those from Kalgan and Tung-chow, were once paved with large slabs of granite, and kept in passable condition, but they have long since fallen into dilapidation and disuse. Like everything else in China, they seem to have been stricken by decrepitude. The houses, yamens, and compounds are generally built of fire-burned brick, but here, as elsewhere, disorder reigns supreme, and no one ever thinks of repairing or cleaning anything. Roads, city walls, temples, houses, and streets alike, betoken an inefficient administration. Dust and dirt give a dingy appearance even to the highly glazed yellow and green tiles, which cover the pavilions of the Forbidden City. The palaces, if such a word can be appropriately used, are of gray brick, but only one story high, and there is every reason for supposing they are as open, draughty, and uncomfortable as if they were the residence of ordinary, well-to-do Chinamen, instead of the Emperor, the Empress-Dowager, and their immediate family and dependents.

Peking is peculiar in having no surrounding villas nor pretty suburbs. It stands solitary and alone within its massive walls, on a wide expanse of cultivated plain, like an island in the sea, frequently buried in clouds of dust, like banks of fog; withal it is an interesting place, and as the capital of a far-reaching empire it is visited by many curious people. Its streets are filled by hurrying crowds of officials, soldiers, and common Chinese, and present to the European many strange if not inviting sights and sounds. Here camels are first seen in large caravans, transporting Mongolian products to market, and returning laden with tea, cloth, and other manufactured articles, suited to the wants of the Tartars living beyond the Great Wall. They also carry all the coal used in Peking from the Western Hills, a few miles away. Mongolians, Thibetans, and Coreans abound, and all seem to be civil and well-behaved. It is plain to see, whatever outsiders may say, that these people, one and all, are proud of their capital, and regard themselves as fortunate in being the subjects of the Chinese Emperor.

Mud and dust in their turn render communication exceedingly disagreeable if not difficult. The streets are unpaved, and there are no sidewalks. Of course there are no street-railways, nor gas-mains, nor water-pipes, but they are all sadly needed, and there can be but little doubt that the first of them would pay a handsome return on the capital invested from the start.

Peking being an inland city, and not a treaty port, has no foreign settlement in or near it ; neither foreign merchants nor bankers are permitted to reside nor even to visit there without a passport, which must be arranged for through the consul at Tientsin. Foreign ministers and *attachés* live in legations, generally belonging to their own governments. They are all situated on one street close to each other, and each is surrounded by its own high brick wall or compound. The street connecting them is broad but unpaved, and dirty like the rest. The legations have no control over it, but a movement has been set on foot to secure its cession to them for police and sanitary purposes. There is no hotel open to foreigners, but the merchant who is allowed to live near the

THE FOREIGN SOCIETY OF PEKING. 165

legations for the purpose of supplying them with foreign goods, also entertains such strangers as can not for any reason secure the shelter of their own legation or of some member of the maritime customs department, which also has its headquarters here, and the principal officers of which are foreigners, with the able and accomplished Sir Robert Hart at their head.

The foreign society at Peking, composed as it is entirely of diplomatic and customs officers, and of the foreign professors in the Tung-wen College and their families, is most attractive and charming.* It leads a gay and happy life ; tiffin, riding, and dancing parties follow each other in rapid succession during the winter season, and in the summer most of the families retire to the hills, where they live in Buddhist temples hired for the purpose.

The diplomatic corps have no relations with the Emperor, the Empress-Dowager, or the court, and never see any one connected with them, except the prince and ministers of the Tsung-li Yamen, or Board of Foreign Affairs. This board is a modern one, and has no administrative or independent powers. Its sole duty is to receive and entertain the foreign ministers and such distinguished strangers as may be presented by them, and to forward to the Throne, or to the appropriate boards, such communications as may be lodged with it. In view of the fact that none of the members of the board (except the Marquis Tseng, who has recently returned from Europe) understand English or any other foreign language, and none of the foreign ministers understand Chinese, all conversation must be carried on through the intervention of official interpreters, and to prevent mistakes all official communications must be in writing, translated into the court

---

* There are quite a large number of missionaries residing at Peking, but here as well as elsewhere there is but little social intercourse between them and the diplomatic corps or other foreign officials.

dialect, or literary language of the country. As this language is an almost insuperable obstacle to the general dissemination of Western knowledge, and as there is no social intercourse whatever between foreigners and the conservative Chinese officials, or their families, it will readily be seen that there can not be a very active interchange of ideas between them.

Now that the young Emperor, Kwang Hsu, has assumed personal direction of affairs, one of the first duties required of him under the treaties will be to receive the foreign ministers accredited to his Government; and this may mark an epoch in the history of China, inasmuch as it may lead to the breaking down of that exclusiveness which has hitherto so effectually shut out modern ideas. His predecessor, Tung Chi, gave audience to the foreign ministers only once, and the regulation of the details, and especially the omission of the *kotow*, which the foreigners insisted upon, gave rise to protracted and deliberate negotiation, much of which, of course, will have to be gone through with again. The present Emperor was born August 15, 1871, and, counting him a year old at birth, according to Chinese custom, is not yet seventeen. His personal name is Tsaitien, but he is officially designated as Kwang Hsu, which is really the title of his reign. He is the ninth of the Manchu or *Tsing* dynasty; and T'sing, which means *pure*, was chosen by the founder of the dynasty to indicate the purity and justice with which he and his descendants proposed to administer the affairs of the empire which they had captured. The surname of this family is Gioro, or Golden, after Aisin Gioro, a brave and aggressive but petty Manchurian chief, who was its progenitor, and whose great descendant, Hientsu, actually led its followers to the conquest of Peking, about the beginning of the seventeenth century. Kwang Hsu is not the son, but the first cousin, of the late Emperor, Tung Chi, who died without issue shortly after he had ascended the throne. A council of princes, led by the mother of the deceased Emperor, who was Empress-Dowager during his nonage, and her sister, who was also a wife of the Emperor Hienfung, and consequently the aunt of Kwang Hsu, adopted him as heir to the throne. He is the son of Prince Chun, seventh brother of the Emperor Hienfung, and hence commonly designated as the Seventh Prince. Exactly why or how the son of the latter was selected, instead of some other of the same generation, is not clearly understood by outsiders; but when it is remembered that the Chinese Emperor has always exercised the right of designating which of his sons should succeed him, in spite of primogeniture, and that if a man, as head of a family, has no son of his own body, he may adopt one, it will be seen how the Empresses-Dowager, in the exercise of a similar right, may have been able to control the family council in behalf of their own favorite. At all events, the selection was made and acquiesced in, and the little boy (who may have been the oldest of his generation) was duly installed on January 12, 1875, as heir to the throne. It is true that a cabal within the imperial clan undertook to control the Empresses-Dowager and the young Emperor, and through them the administration of the Government, but this was promptly frustrated by the Empresses, aided by Prince Kung, the eldest surviving brother of the Emperor Hienfung, and also by Prince Chun, the young Emperor's father. The two sisters, as co-regents, carried on the government with unusual vigor and success till the 4th of April, 1881, at which time the first one, commonly called the "Empress of the Eastern Palace," died, leaving the sole power in the hands of her sister, Tz'-u Hsi, "Empress of the Western Palace," and the present Empress-Dowager. The latter is a woman of strong character, and it is asserted by the best-informed foreigners in Peking has proved herself to be the ablest ruler of China since the days of Kienlung, whose reign was one of the longest of modern times. She is fifty-three years of age, and is said to give the closest personal attention to public business. She has never seen or been seen by a foreign official, and, so far as known, takes no notice or account of their doings, and yet she is supposed to be a liberal, or to incline toward liberalism and progress in her ideas. She has seen the entire country restored to peace and comparative prosperity under her rule, and her dominion at the surrender of it to her ward on the 5th of February, 1887, was undisputed to the very outermost limits of the empire. As the mother or guardian of the young Emperor, she has looked carefully after his welfare according to her lights, but, so far as known, no ray of Western learning has been extended to him. He has no Western teachers, nor is it likely that any of his Chinese tutors have ever studied Western science or languages. His instruction is therefore exclusively in the Chinese language and literature, and probably extends no further than to the teachings of the great sages and philosophers. Of course, in a country where everything is regulated by custom and a code, all the details of his daily occupation are strictly laid out and conducted; but, after all, it is only Chinese, and can lead, without foreign aid or influence, to nothing but Chinese results in the end.

The Empress-Dowager is said to be well educated according to the Chinese system; but, inasmuch as even the princes and great dignitaries of the empire have not been permitted to see her familiarly, or communicate freely with her, she has been left largely to the guidance of the great boards of Government in the transaction of public business. During her regency she has been for all practical purposes an absolute monarch, but, according to

INFLUENCES WHICH CONTROL THE EMPEROR. 169

the theory of the Chinese Constitution—if I may use the word where the thing itself has not yet passed beyond the rudimentary stage—she was compelled to govern according to precedent and the principles of the code. The censors may remonstrate and the grand secretaries and the boards may "advise and consent," but, after all, there is no earthly power which could control her against her will when she had once made up her mind. The process of making up her mind was therefore of the greatest importance, especially in connection with new matters, or such as do not come within the range of precedent or of the code.

Like all human beings, the occupant of the Chinese throne is more or less under the influence of the people who immediately surround his person and minister to his wants, and these are of course servants of one grade or another. They can unconsciously give his mind a bias or twist, no matter how self-poised or independent he may be; and when it is remembered that they are also strictly Chinese, and that many of them belong to an unfortunate class peculiar to Oriental countries, it will be seen that he is much more likely to be influenced by ignorance and prejudice than by enlightened and progressive ideas. Under such influences, he would naturally be inclined to let well enough alone, and to set his face against change; and so, if change comes, it must be under the pressure of some force great enough to break down the opposition of the ignorant and unfortunate, and command attention, whether the case in hand comes within the ordinary rules or not. Under the pressure of war or some great emergency, or in the face of some great public necessity, the voice of the statesman, even though he be but "a poor scholar of books," may penetrate to the innermost recesses of the palace; but, even when invited, he may not speak except when lying prostrate in "the divine presence." The common method of advising the Throne is by memorial, which must be most carefully expressed in the classic literary style; and I have been told that no verbal explanations may be offered, except in response to a direct question from His Majesty. The "Peking Gazette" is full of cases where the memorialist has been reprimanded, or handed over to the Board of Punishments for the determination of a proper penalty for the use of a careless or inelegant word or phrase.

Theoretically the censors, whose functions I will explain more fully hereafter, may memorialize the Throne, either affirmatively or negatively, upon any subject, and the memorial must go upon the record, and even the official historiographer may comment as he chooses upon the acts of the Emperor; but both must be careful to adhere closely to the truth, and to guard their language and motives against the charge of impertinence, misrepresentation, and malice. Practically the post of censor is a dangerous as well as a powerful one. Only last year a new decree was issued enlarging upon the duties of censors, encouraging them to make suggestions freely and loyally, and to be guided by "considerations of time and circumstance in what they say"; but to "avoid everything like bias or private prejudice." It also admonished them that "to offer improper suggestions to the Throne from motives of private animosity, and to vilify and abuse the object of attack at will," is not only irreverent to the Emperor, but injurious both to morals and good government. After quoting several decrees issued in past reigns severely condemning "the practice of indulging in slanderous accusations based upon private spite," the decree gives emphasis to the policy laid down in it by ordering that a censor who had the year before called one of the grand secretaries "a traitor to his country," and a historiographer of the Han Lin College, who had attacked the

Grand Secretary Li Hung-Chang "on various counts, and in involved and ornate language had hinted that he ought to be put to death, to be both of them committed to the board for the determination of a severe penalty, as an example to others who would carry vilification of ministers in high place to such extreme limits."

Although the Empress-Dowager has been for so many years the absolute head of the Government, and must always, because of the potential influence she has exerted in the selection of Kwang Hsu as heir to the throne, wield a great if not controlling influence over him, if she is so disposed, the laws and customs of the country require that she shall retire from all public participation in the business of the Government after turning it over to the personal charge of the heir, which, as before stated, she did on the 5th of February of the current year. As mother of the adolescent Emperor, she had a most important duty to perform for him, and that was to select his wife or wives, conduct the wedding ceremonies, and to see that he worships at the tomb of his ancestors both before and after marriage.

This religious duty was duly performed in the early spring of last year, at which time the young Emperor, accompanied by the Empress-Dowager; his father, the Seventh Prince; the Viceroy, Li Hung-Chang; and many of the grand dignitaries and members of the imperial clan, made his pilgrimage in state to the Eastern Tombs, and went successfully and, it is to be presumed, reverently through the solemn ceremony which had been arranged for the occasion. A new road something over a hundred miles long, with proper pavilions and stopping-places, had been built beforehand, and every effort known to the Chinese was resorted to for the purpose of making the procession imposing. The Emperor and the Empress-Dowager were carried in sedan-chairs, and were escorted by soldiers and retainers all clad in their best ; but withal the pageant was described as disappointing. The trappings and outfit were neither new nor fresh-looking, and as the column moved before daylight, and every precaution was taken to keep the streets and roads near its line of march clear of spectators, and especially of foreigners, none of the latter, except one who occupied a place of concealment in a Chinese house, obtained a sight of the procession. The spring rains had not yet begun, and the road, although quite new, and of course unused by profane feet, was very dusty. It was sprinkled by an advanced guard of soldiers, each of whom was equipped with a small wicker scoop or basket, painted pink, and which he used for dipping water from the ditches alongside.

It was of course impossible for any foreigner to witness the ceremony at the tombs, though it probably consisted of nothing more than the burning of incense, together with gold and silver paper representing money. The young Emperor doubtless prostrated himself, and knocked his head against the floor or ground in front of the tomb of the late Emperor, as any other young Chinaman would have done before the tomb of his father ; and this may have been repeated before the various tombs of the dynasty, back to that of its founder if buried there. So far as I have seen or can learn, the ceremony, whether performed by Emperor or coolie, is a perfunctory one, and generally entered into in obedience to a time-honored custom rather than to the dictates of a deep religious feeling.

The young Emperor is described by one who claims to have got a good look at him as a rather frail, sallow, and undersized youth, showing no external signs of extraordinary vitality or ability. The Chinese say it is understood among them that he is petulant and unsteady in his temper, and shows but little persistency in his studies. The chances are that he has neither the mental nor physical constitution of a reformer. His father is, however, a man of resolution and vigor, and will necessarily be an important factor in the control of affairs, although he, too, as well as the Empress-Dowager, will have to retire from the court when the young Emperor assumes personal charge of the Government. This is necessary, because the law and custom of the country are such that no subject can approach the Emperor without prostrating himself, while the higher law of the land requires that children, whether actual or adopted, shall bow down before their parents. It was said, however, that the Empress-Dowager might issue a decree before retiring, giving herself and the Seventh Prince a dispensation against the strict letter of the law, and authorizing them, in view of his youth and inexperience, to have audience with the Emperor on public and family affairs without going through the *kotow* in his presence. While this may seem quite simple to foreigners, it is really a very serious and complex matter to the Chinese. It must be borne in mind that the direct male line of the present dynasty has never before failed, and it has been on the throne nearly three hundred years. Precedents are therefore very old and scarce, and it is possible that there are none at all. So far as foreigners know, the laws may be silent in reference to such a case. At all events, even the most learned Chinese did not speak with any confidence as to what would be done in the emergency which they have just passed through. So far as I have been able to learn, no such dispensation has been issued, and it is now suggested that an able counselor may be obtained, and a part of the difficulty removed, by the restoration of Prince Kung, the senior uncle of the Emperor, to favor. He is an experienced and progressive statesman, and his influence can hardly prove to be anything but beneficial to the empire.

But one thing seems to be entirely clear, and that is, that the Empress-Dowager will remain a very important factor in Government affairs during the rest of her life. Having conducted the young Emperor safely to the Eastern Tombs and back, and, it is said, selected her favorite niece, the daughter of her brother the Duke Chow, for his first wife, it is evident that she does not intend to leave the young couple entirely to their own resources. As his mother by adoption, it is her right and duty to select such other wives from time to time as she may think the Emperor ought to have, and it is certain she has had many of the eligible young women of the country sent to Peking for her inspection. These are, of course, only the daughters of the grandees and of the members of the imperial clan. So, no matter what restrictions there may be upon free intercourse between her and the Throne hereafter, it will readily be seen that the person who selects its occupant, and the wife who alone can sit beside him or approach his person without prostrating herself, must always remain a very considerable personage.

It is possible, of course, that the young Emperor and his wife or wives may develop such independent character as to throw off all family domination, and thus get rid of both father and aunt at the same time, but this is hardly to be expected. Human nature must, after all, be the same in the Chinese imperial family as elsewhere, and hence, notwithstanding the restriction of laws and customs, it may fairly be assumed that both the Empress-Dowager and the Seventh Prince will continue, for many years, to play an important if not a principal part in the conduct of the Chinese Government. The Empress-Dowager has been practically head of the Government for over twenty years, and the Seventh Prince, as father and tutor of the young Emperor, has held a position scarcely less important. As titular head of naval affairs, he made his first visit to Tientsin and to the fleet in the Gulf of Pechihli last spring. During this visit, he not only saw foreign-built ships and guns for the first time, but personally granted audience to foreign consuls and dignitaries themselves, all of whom he received with courtesy, and impressed as being a man of liberal sentiments and fine natural abilities.

Finally, it is understood among Chinese and foreigners that both the Empress-Dowager and the Seventh Prince are in favor of progress, and especially of railroads, mines, furnaces, and rolling-mills, as well as of telegraphs, foreign-built ships, and guns, and of foreign instruction in their use.

This being the case, the young Emperor can hardly become a conservative, and turn back the hands of time, however great may be the opposition of the older men. China must move forward, and, whatever may be the natural bent of the young Emperor and his surroundings, he and they must move with her; but how it will all turn out, with special reference to him, the world can tell much better after he has occupied the throne for several years, and reached actual as well as legal manhood. With the tremendous power and influence wielded by him, by virtue of the system of which he is the center, he can greatly retard as well as facilitate the development of his country's power and resources. He will have unusual opportunities for signalizing his reign. He finds the empire united and at peace from the center to the remotest boundary, as well as with all outside nations; but it is also closely watched and crowded on all sides by Russia, England, and France, and likely at any time to become engaged in war with either of them. Germany is also alert and aggressive. She is sending out her syndicates and engineers to build railroads and her merchants to secure trade, and will not be slow to find a *casus belli* if she wants one. Each of the great powers named is keenly alive to the fact that the trade and the internal improvements of a country comprising one tenth of the habitable globe, and containing from one fifth to one third of all the people in the world, is a tremendous prize, and that no sacrifice or exertion is too great to make for it. They are all represented by able and experienced diplomatists, who not only watch one another, but watch and report everything going on within the empire. Not a ship or a gun is bought, but all compete for it. Not a military or naval review is held, but their *attachés* are present to witness it; and not a stranger arrives at the capital, or even at a treaty port, but they endeavor to discover his business, and, if need be, to frustrate it.

In the midst of all this contention, watchfulness, and distrust, the young Emperor and his advisers will have a difficult task to maintain their country's rights and to keep the peace; they will require not only great diplomatic skill and knowledge, but a great show of organization and power, which as yet they can not make. They have a few excellent ironclads and cruisers, and a few good instructors; but the results of the late war show that neither their ships nor their crews can stand against those of the French. They have a considerable armed force and many improved field-pieces and breech-loading fire-arms, but no organization adequate to the requirements of a war with even the least of the European powers. They have unlimited numbers from which to draw recruits; but the more of such undisciplined men they put into the field without commissariat, supplies, or transportation, against a well-commanded Anglo-Indian or Russian army, the greater will be the number slain and the more overwhelming the disaster. They have some fortifications, but they are rudely constructed, and in many cases badly placed; moreover, even if this were not the case, they, like all fortifications, are powerless to inflict damage upon an enemy unless they are assailed; and I know of none that can not be easily turned. Besides, there are many points on the Chinese coast totally undefended, where landings can be made by bold and resolute commanders. To make all this worse, it should be remembered that they have no railroads, and no north and south lines of inland water communication adequate for military uses; hence, they are absolutely powerless to concentrate, move, or supply an army capable of making head against a properly organized and equipped European invasion, even if they could find or create such an army in their own dominions and out of their own materials.

War is always possible; it generally comes when least expected, and may come in that way, as heretofore, upon China. Should it come soon, or even within the next decade, it can have but one result, and that will be the defeat and humiliation of the Chinese army. It will be impossible for it to defend even the capital, and it is more than probable that the Emperor and his court will have to flee into Manchuria, as did their predecessors before the allied French and English armies. This presupposes an invasion from the sea-coast; but it is now or soon will be possible for the Russians, whose railroad has already penetrated to within a few hundred miles of the Chinese boundary, and whose settlements in the Amur Valley are growing with surprising rapidity, to make a descent upon Peking from the north, as did Kublai Khan and the founder of the present dynasty. In that case, the Emperor and court will have to flee toward the Yang-tse or the interior of the empire; and, while this may enable them to continue the war longer, the result will in the end be the same. Defeat must follow, and there will be nothing left for them but to accept such terms as the conquerors may consent to grant. It is hardly to be doubted that an army of fifty thousand Europeans, with the usual proportion of artillery and infantry and a preponderance of cavalry, well organized, supplied, and commanded, can go anywhere in China, and, if so disposed, it can overrun and dismember the empire. Should such an invasion take place and meet with success, is it safe for the Emperor or his advisers to assume, or even to hope, that the terms extended to them will ever again be as favorable as those granted by the English and French allies? It has been said that the French, upon the occasion alluded to, proposed a partition of the country along the line of the Yang-tse-kiang, and that both French and English have more than once since, in contemplating "their opportunities," been "astounded at their moderation." If either should find it necessary to go to war with China again in earnest, it will doubtless go alone, and thus be free to act according to its own judgment.

NOTE.—The Seventh Prince died about December 1st, 1887, and his place as a state adviser was at once filled by his brother, the Fifth Prince. How long the latter will retain his place, or how much influence he will exercise, is a mere matter of conjecture. Only one thing seems to be entirely certain, and that is that the Empress-Dowager is still the most important personage connected with the Imperial Government.—J. H. W.

CHAPTER XII.

The Emperor an absolute monarch—The Government patriarchal in form —Liberty unknown—Slavery exists—No hereditary nobility except the imperial clan and heads of the families of Confucius and Koxinga —The literati are the office-holders—The Imperial Government— The Grand Secretariat—The General Council—The " Peking Gazette " —The Six Great Boards—The Tsung-li Yamen—The Censorate or all-examining court—The minor courts and boards—The functions of the great boards—Power greatly divided and distributed—The provincial governments—All officers selected by public examination —Defects of the system—Li Hung-Chang's position somewhat like that of the British Premier—Foreign ministers not yet received by the Emperor or Empress-Dowager—Much of the foreign business done by provincial governors—The central Government isolated and inaccessible—Difficulty of communicating or transacting business with it.

ALTHOUGH the Emperor of China is an absolute monarch, who may do almost as he pleases in any specific case, the machinery by which he carries on the government is complex and ponderous to an unusual degree. It is patriarchal in form and arbitrary in character, and yet there is a vein of high moral ethics underlying and pervading its operations. With an able and well-instructed monarch to run it, he might not only be entirely independent of restrictions, but he could hardly fail to make it a source of great blessing to his subjects. It has no constitutional limitations, but comprehends all subjects, and is the source of all power, mercy, and justice.

No government in modern times is altogether like it. It has no cabinet of responsible ministers, as in Europe and America, each presiding over an executive department, with well-defined powers and duties, and in a greater or less degree independent of the chief of state ; but, instead, its current operations are conducted by a series of great boards and courts, composed of many members, none of whom have power individually to originate measures, or to take action upon them. There is nothing elective, and no element of popularity to be found anywhere in its machinery. It is in no degree the servant of the people, but belongs exclusively to the Emperor, and exists solely for his convenience. He is head and front of all its boards and departments, the actuating and controlling force of all its branches. The whole body of the people is under him, and, like a great family in the patriarchal days, bound implicitly to obey his will. The members of this family have no rights or property of their own ; in fact, "they have nothing but what has been derived from and may at any time be reclaimed by him."* It follows, as a matter of course, that he holds the fee simple of all the land, and may, if so minded, dispose of it without let or hindrance. Commonly, however, he does not interfere with titles so long as taxes are promptly paid. The great number of his subjects, and the wide extent of their aggregate possessions, are their surest protection.

Liberty is unknown among them, and it is said that there is not even a word in the Chinese language which accurately expresses its significance. Slavery exists, and is fully protected by the laws, and to all external appearances the slaves are just like their masters in race and color, if not in condition. There is no Bill of Rights by

---

* "The Middle Kingdom," p. 411, *et seq.*

which the freeman is protected, nor any other form of acknowledgment on the part of the Emperor that the plain people have any rights which he is bound to respect. He is their sovereign lord, the son of Heaven, and reigns over them by divine right pure and simple. There are no hereditary nobility nor feudal lords, except the heads of the family of Confucius and Koxinga, and the members of the imperial clan; consequently, there has never been any meeting in China, like that of the English barons at Runnymede, to teach an overbearing monarch that there is an earthly power greater than his own. Neither is there any hereditary official class. The *literati* are the office-holders, and theoretically there is no possible road into that class, except that of learning, as tested by the public examinations. Every man's son, no matter how humble his origin, may present himself for examination, and, as the latter is so conducted that the examiners do not know the names or station of the persons they are examining, it is hardly possible that favoritism should work injustice. The system is strictly democratic and popular. Most of the defects there are in it are due to the fact that it has to deal with human nature, through human agencies and imperfect knowledge, and takes no cognizance whatever of science. There is no system of popular education, and therefore no general diffusion of knowledge. Contrary to the common belief, it is now pretty well established that not more than one man in a hundred, nor one woman in a thousand, can read and write, and hence there is no such thing as popular opinion to guide or uphold the Government. In all matters, therefore, which come within the functions of the Government, the country relies absolutely upon the Throne, and, when that fails, everything fails. It is strong in small matters, but weak in great ones. It is strong in dealing with business that is settled by custom, but weak when business arises for

182   CHINA.

which there is no precedent, and in regard to which the code is silent.

The first great branch of the Government is known as the Grand Secretariat. It consists of four principal chancellors, two assistants, and ten sub-assistants, half of whom in each grade are Manchus and half Chinese. Its duties are to receive and transmit edicts and decrees, present memorials, lay before the Emperor the business of the day, receive his instructions thereon, and forward them to the appropriate office to be copied and promulgated. The officers of the Grand Secretariat also belong to other boards and bureaus, and individually have many other duties to perform. They are the keepers of the twenty-five seals of state, each of which has its own peculiar form, and is used for a special purpose.

The General Council, or Council of State, which was organized about 1730, although nominally second, has become, perhaps, the most influential body in the Government.* It is composed of an indefinite number of princes of the blood, grand secretaries, chancellors, presidents and vice-presidents of the six boards, selected by the Emperor at his pleasure. "Its duties are to write imperial edicts and decisions, and determine such things as are of importance to the army and nation, in order to aid the sovereign in regulating the machinery of affairs." It meets daily between five and six in the morning, and at such other times as may be necessary, either in the immediate or assumed presence of the Emperor, and takes cognizance of whatever business is brought before it. It keeps the lists of officers entitled to promotion, and of persons to fill vacancies; supervises and correlates the action of the various branches of government, not only in the capital but throughout the country, and generally keeps the Em-

---

* "Middle Kingdom," vol. i, p. 418.

peror informed of such matters as should have his personal attention.

The line of demarkation between the Grand Secretariat and the General Council does not seem to be well defined, and as each is composed of both Chinese and Manchus in nearly equal numbers, there is a certain amount of dislike and rivalry between them, which doubtless causes some trouble to the Emperor, but is supposed to have a compensating advantage in enabling him the more easily to discover and thwart intrigues and conspiracies.

The common method of procedure for each of these bodies is to present its views and recommendations, in regard to such memorials as come before it, to the Emperor, upon a piece of paper attached, indicating the action to be taken, or upon more than one if alternative recommendations are made, and the Emperor signifies his approval or disapproval with the vermilion pencil which is furnished to him for that purpose, or he may write a separate opinion or decree of his own, if he is so minded.

The "Peking Gazette," which has been published daily, it is said, for eight hundred years, is the official organ of the Government, and it is made up of memorials, edicts, decrees, and rescripts, which have been presented to and acted upon by the Grand Secretariat or the General Council and the Emperor. It is sent to all parts of the country, and constitutes almost the only source of information open to the provincial authorities and the people as to what is going on in the capital and throughout the empire. Certain persons may also copy and print these documents, and abridge the same, but no one is permitted to make editorial notes, comments, or explanations. The "Gazette" is translated by the official interpreters for the various legations, and also by one of them for the "North China Herald," which publishes it entire or in part for its readers, according to its interest, and collects it year by year into separate volumes for sale to the world at large. It affords the best and only attainable means of ascertaining how the daily operations of the Chinese Government are carried on, and, although much of it is exceedingly dry reading, it also contains many interesting and instructive papers.

While the Government evidently selects the matter to be published, and can of course suppress whatever it chooses, it does not seem to screen rascality or malfeasance in office, nor to conceal in any degree the short-comings of the official class. To the contrary, it is quite as free in exposing crime, disaster, famine, and misfortune, as the daily press of our own country. Whatever comes before the Government seems to be openly and fairly laid before the people; and no moralist could deal with bribery and corruption in a more straightforward manner, or give utterance to admonitions and precepts of a higher or more exemplary character. All public business requiring further investigation and report, is distributed by the Grand Secretariat or the Grand Council, as the case may be, to whichever of the Six Great Boards can most appropriately take cognizance of the business in question. These boards are as follows:

1. Hu-Pu, or Board of Revenue.
2. Li-Pu, or Board of Civil Office.
3. Li-Pu, or Board of Rites.
4. Ping-Pu, or Board of War.
5. Hing-Pu, or Board of Punishments.
6. Kung-Pu, or Board of Works.

Each of these boards has two presidents, four vice-presidents, and from six to eight directors; several have superintendents, and all have secretaries, under-secretaries, comptrollers, clerks, writers, and servants, in sufficient numbers to carry on the business according to custom. The upper officers are equally divided between Manchus and Chinese, the theory being that, while they are alike subjects of the Throne, each will watch the other closely, and thus secure the very best results to the state. The boards are also divided into appropriate bureaus for the transaction of the various kinds of business with which they have to deal. They perform their public duties mostly within the Forbidden city, entirely beyond the sight and influence of foreigners, and both officers and members are almost absolutely unknown to the diplomatic corps residing at Peking. There are no social or official relations between them and the foreign ministers; and, this combined with the barrier interposed by the language of the country, conceals the daily working of the Government to a degree that an outsider can hardly understand.

There is also another board, known as the Tsung-li Yamen, or Board of Foreign Affairs, organized shortly after the capture of Peking by the allied English and French armies, apparently for the sole purpose of receiving foreign diplomatic agents, and listening to what they may have to say. It is composed of a Manchu prince, and four or six ministers, who are at the same time members of other boards. This board seems to have no authority whatever, except to listen to what the foreign ministers have to say, and to report to the Throne, or to the councils and other boards. It can not take conclusive action on any subject, but stands, as it were, a sort of advanced guard on the borders of the Forbidden city, to report to the Government within what may be going on among the foreigners. The prince and ministers are exceedingly civil and courteous to the foreign ministers, and at every interview entertain them with a formal feast of sweetmeats, tea, and hot *samschu*. When I was at Peking last winter, several of the foreign ministers were considering the advisability of inviting the members of the Yamen to dine with them at their legations in foreign style, and it was understood that the ministers at least would accept, though the prince had not yet committed himself.

In addition to the foregoing, there are several other important branches of the Government, such as the Li Fan Yuen, commonly called the Colonial Office ; the Tu-chah Yuen, or Censorate ; the Tung-ching Tse, or Court of Transmission ; the Ta-li Tse, or Court of Judicature and Revision ; and the Han-lin Yuen, or Imperial Academy. Besides these, there are a number of minor courts and departments, among which are the Tai-chang Tse, or Sacrificial Court ; the Hunglu Tse, or Ceremonial Court ; the Tai-puh Tse, or Horse Department ; the Kwanglu Tse, or Banqueting-House ; the Kwoh-Tse Kien, or National College ; and the Kin-Tien Kien, or Imperial Astronomical College, which prepares the almanac and selects the lucky days of the year for all the important acts of life.

Although the functions of the Six Great Boards and Censorate are indicated in some degree by their names, it will give a better idea of the workings of the Chinese system of government, and especially of its complexity, if I define them more fully.

The Board of Revenue has cognizance of the census and the admeasurement of the lands, levying and collecting taxes and duties, paying salaries and allowances, and the regulation of transportation by land and water. It superintends the mint in each province, makes conscriptions for the army, prepares lists of Manchu girls eligible for the imperial harem, and determines the latitude and longitude of places. It is also a court of appeals in cases concerning property. It is subdivided into fourteen or more subordinate departments, which correspond with and control the agents for collecting the revenue in various parts of the empire ; and, as this is paid in money, grain, silk, porcelain, and other manufactured products, a great number of subordinates is required. One of the bureaus of this board has charge of the "Three Treasuries," one for metals, one for silk and dye-stuffs, and one for stationery.

From the fact that this board controls the receipts and disbursements, it has great influence over all branches of the public business, and especially in regard to such new matters as may necessitate additional expenditures on the part of the Government. Like all persons and corporations which have to do with money, it is naturally conservative, and, with the possible exception of the Censorate, has more influence than any other board. It must be said, however, that it has never taken an exact census, nor made an accurate survey of the lands or other elements affecting the revenues and expenditures of the Government. The theories upon which it proceeds are antiquated and crude in many respects ; and yet, if the machinery for carrying them into effect were properly organized and honestly administered, the results attained would be in every respect better than they are now or have ever been. One of the great difficulties in the way of real progress in China is the poverty of the Government, and this is due in a great measure to the disorder of its fiscal system. Under a capable administration, an accurate and exhaustive census would be taken without delay. The country would be correctly surveyed, and the lands properly measured and classified. With this done, it would be practicable to assess the taxes fairly and to collect them honestly. It is no discredit to the Chinese as a nation to say that they do not appear to understand the science of political economy, as applied to levying, collecting, and disbursing the public revenues, or that in this branch of their business they have great need of foreign advice and assistance. If they could be induced by any means to employ either Mr. Goschen, Mr. David A. Wells, or General Francis A. Walker, or all of them, as a board to advise them in reference to the revision of their financial system and the reorganization of the machinery for collecting and disbursing their revenues, they would take a step which could not fail to benefit them greatly, no matter what it cost them in the way of salaries paid and honors conferred.

The Board of Civil Office is subdivided into four bureaus, and has charge of all the officers in the civil service of the empire. The first bureau attends to the selection, promotion, and precedence of officers. The second investigates and records their merit and demerit, and prescribes their furloughs. The third regulates retirement from office on account of filial duties and mourning. The fourth regulates the distribution of titles, patents, and posthumous honors. Civilians are presented to the Emperor, and all civil and literary officers are assigned and distributed by this board.

The Board of Rites has charge of all kinds of ritual observances and ceremonial forms, and of the rules and proclamations in regard thereto. It prescribes the regulations for determining precedence and literary distinction, maintaining religious honor and fidelity, giving banquets, and fixing the etiquette to be observed at court, and in the performance of official duties. It also prescribes the cut, style, color, fabric, ornaments, and insignia of official dress and accoutrements, fixes the number of followers, and defines the number of bows upon ceremonial occasions, and the degree of attention which high officials and nobles must pay to one another. It also directs the forms of written official communications, and has charge of the literary examinations, the number, privileges, and distinction of the graduates, and the establishment of government schools and academies. It superintends the rites to be observed in worshiping the gods, as well as the spirits of departed monarchs, sages, and philosophers; and saves the sun and moon when they are eclipsed. It looks after tribute and tribute-bearers, and also after all embassies sent abroad. It supplies food for banquets and sacrifices, studies the principles of music, selects and composes musical pieces, and fixes the form and number of instruments to play them.

The Board of War has charge of all the military and naval affairs of the empire, and also of the transmission of mails, both official and private; but the postal system is very inefficient, except that part of it conducted by the Inspector-General of the Imperial Maritime Customs for the benefit of foreigners, and of his own business.

This board has four bureaus, which have charge of promotions, issuing general orders, inspecting the troops, and distributing rewards and punishments; supplying and distributing cavalry-horses; and, finally, selecting candidates, preparing rosters and estimates, and supplying equipments and ammunition. It does not, however, control the household troops, nor the bannermen, which are commanded by captains-general appointed by the Throne, one to every banner of each race. It must also be remembered that the land-forces are largely under the command of the governors-general of the provinces in which they are serving. Until the establishment of the Naval Board, as previously described, under the Seventh Prince, the Viceroy Li, and the Marquis Tseng, for the organization of the northern fleet, the naval forces were controlled in the same way, so that as at present organized the Board of War has but little control over the military and naval forces of the empire, and it will be seen at a glance that its organization is entirely unequal to the efficient and economical management of the public defense. Its greatest lack is that of a responsible head, and a competent and well-organized scientific and military staff. It has neither engineer nor ordnance officers, and its artillerists are untrained; it has no quartermaster-general, no regular system of transport, no commissariat, and no surgeon-general or medical department. A young surgeon, who had had experience in the American army, went to Peking only a few months ago, and submitted a proposition to establish a medical department for the Chinese army, but he could not even obtain a hearing. He was given to understand, however, that the Board of War not only felt no interest in the subject, but held that it was cheaper to obtain new recruits, with which to replace their sick and wounded, than to organize a department for curing them.

The Board of Punishments has the control and direction of punishments throughout the empire, and partakes of the nature of both a criminal and a civil court. In connection with the Censorate and the Court of Judicature and Revision, it constitutes the "Three Law Chambers," which decide upon capital cases brought before them. These three, uniting with members from six other courts, constitute a Court of Errors, which revises the decision of provincial judges before transmitting them to the Emperor, without whose approval, expressed or implied, no man's life can be taken. An officer of this board superintends the publication of the code, with all its alterations and additions; another has charge of jails and jailers; another of fines levied in commutation of punishments; and still another registers the receipts and expenditures of the board.

THE BOARD OF WORKS. 191

The Board of Works takes charge and direction of all the public works throughout the empire, together with the expenditures for the same. It takes cognizance of all city walls, palaces, and public structures, including fortifications; it furnishes tents for the Emperor's journeys, ship-timber, pottery, and glassware, and sits as a prize court; it attends to the manufacture of military munitions and implements; has charge of arsenals, stores, and camp equipage; regulates weights and measures, sorts pearls according to value, and furnishes death-warrants; it repairs and digs canals, and has charge of water-ways and their embankments; it builds bridges and vessels of war, mends roads, collects tolls, preserves ice, makes book-cases, and takes care of the silk sent in as taxes; it has charge of the imperial tombs, pavilions, palaces, and temples, and of the erection of monuments and tablets to such great men as are buried at the public expense.

Two of its great ministers have charge of manufacturing gunpowder, and two of its vice-presidents look after the mint. It has a multitude of duties and employés, and might, if properly organized and administered, be of immense advantage to the country. I am compelled to say, however, that none of its duties seem to be well or economically performed, except, possibly, the work done at the public arsenals, of which there is one at nearly every provincial capital and important seaport. They are all constructed on foreign plans, furnished with foreign machinery, and run by foreign superintendents and experts. The greater part of the work done at them, however, is turned out by native workmen, who have been instructed by foreign mechanics.

The forts, canals, embankments, roads, and, indeed, all public structures throughout the empire, so far as I have seen, are badly designed and constructed, and in bad repair. They show clearly and unmistakably, not only a bad system of organization, but the absence of all proper supervision and responsibility.

The Colonial Office has charge of all the wandering and settled tribes in Mongolia, Ili, and Turkistan, and generally exercises control over all their affairs, civil, military, and religious. It collects taxes and tribute, makes rewards, pays salaries, and maintains discipline. Its jurisdiction extends over vast regions, and of late years has been directed specially to reducing the influence of the Begs, Khans, and Lamas, and the settlement of the people in permanent homes, as owners and cultivators of the soil.

The Censorate, or All-Examining Court, is, perhaps, the most powerful branch of the Government. It consists of two censors and four deputy-censors. Besides, all governors and lieutenant-governors, as well as the superintendents of rivers and inland navigation, are *ex-officio* deputy-censors, and generally, wherever two or three Chinese officials are collected together, one of them is sure to be connected with the Censorate, and to keep it informed of all their doings. A class of censors is placed over each of the Six Boards, to supervise its acts, and to receive and distribute all memorials and public documents. The censors have access to all public offices and courts, and to all documents pertaining to the archives and records. They are charged with the investigation of all branches of the public service, and the privilege of reproving all public officers, from the Emperor down to the lowest, is given to them by law, and Chinese history abounds in cases where the privilege with reference to the Emperor has been openly and freely exercised. The Emperor is, however, absolute, and may suspend or disgrace a censor at will, and hence it may well be imagined that only the honest and resolute members of the body ever criticise the imperial acts, or even those of the great dignitaries of the empire.

The system is far-reaching in its organization and powers, and holding as it does a position next to the throne, it is always first to make itself felt, and it certainly exerts a controlling influence in many cases. It is from its very nature exceedingly conservative, and, having the privilege of memorializing the Throne upon all subjects, and especially upon such as do not come within the range of precedents or the code, it has been potential at times, and especially of late, in staying the march of progress.

From the foregoing sketch it will be seen that the Government of China, although it has an absolute monarch at its head, is, from the very magnitude of the empire, and the multiplicity of interests with which it has to deal, a Government of boards and courts, which so divide responsibility and distribute power as in many cases to defeat the ends for which they were created. It is a great, complex, cumbersome machine, which could not exist a day in any foreign country. Espionage and surveillance prevail everywhere. Concealment and dishonesty, accompanied by conservatism and timidity, are the rule in all branches of the public service, and the truth of this is abundantly attested by the "Peking Gazette." There is neither change nor progress, except in the treaty ports and maritime provinces, where there is a limited class which comes in contact with foreigners and foreign ideas, and also except in the minds of such great statesmen as Li Hung-Chang, the two Tsengs, and Liu-Ming Chu'an.

The nineteen provincial governments are like the Imperial Government in their general features. The sons and relatives of the Emperor are excluded from holding civil office in the provinces, and no Chinaman can hold any civil office in his native province, nor can he marry or own land in the jurisdiction, nor can his brother, son, or near relative hold office under him or in the same province with him. The governors and governors-general are appointed by the Throne subject to these limitations, and nominally for only three or four years, but in many cases this period is overrun. But, when this is done, it is generally due to some great consideration of state, although remoteness from Peking, or the apathy of the Imperial Government, or the difficulty of communicating with the distant ports of the empire, has in more than one case caused the period of a governor-general to be extended indefinitely. In such cases the actual powers exercised by him are almost as unlimited within the province and over the inhabitants of it as are those of the Emperor within the empire. In such cases it has become the custom of foreigners to designate the governor-general as a Viceroy, although nominally and legally he has no higher title than any other governor.

The duties of the governor-general consist in the control of all civil and military affairs in the region under his jurisdiction, but, like the Emperor, he is supposed to govern according to the code and the precedents, or in accordance with specific instruction from the Throne.

The functions of provincial government are comprised under a number of different heads, the principal of which are territorial, financial, and judicial, but the details of organization and administration vary considerably in the different provinces. The governor-general is assisted by a treasurer, a criminal judge, a literary chancellor, and by commissioners and superintendents, prefects, and district magistrates; also, by a commander-in-chief, generals, and such other high civil and military officers as the peculiarities of his situation require—the relative rank and precedence of which are rigidly and clearly defined—subject to the general rule that civilians always take precedence over military officers of the same or corresponding grade.

The authority of the governor-general extends, in extreme or urgent cases, to life and death ; to the temporary filling of all official vacancies ; to the absolute control of the troops ; and to the issuance of such laws and the adoption of such measures as he thinks necessary from time to time to secure the peace and safety of his province. His higher officers constitute a council or cabinet, with whom he may confer whenever he thinks best, and he is always subject to regulation removal and discipline by the Throne. Any censor may report upon or denounce his administration, and altogether his place is a difficult one to fill acceptably. Each official is assisted by a multitude of subordinates, and the result is that the common people are frequently oppressed and fleeced in a shameful manner.

Theoretically, all officers are selected by public examination for the ascertainment of their literary acquirements, and this department is conducted by the literary chancellor, who is appointed directly by the Emperor, and takes rank next to the governor. He is assisted by head-teachers residing in the chief towns, and exercising a greater or less control over the colleges and academies, as well as over the studies of the students attending them. He personally makes an annual circuit through the province, and holds examinations in the chief towns, of each department, at which any student may present himself. Those who are successful may present themselves at the provincial examination, and, if again successful, they may attend the grand triennial examination at Peking. Many of the students by the time they reach Peking are middle-aged men, and, as rejection does not disqualify them from trying again, old men are not unfrequently found in the students' stall, struggling for the highest degree. These examinations are conducted, as before stated, in writing, which must be done in seclusion from the outside world, and upon subjects given out after the students have entered the stalls, and all connection with books and friends has been cut off. The examination papers are sealed and numbered, so that no one can tell who the writer is till after it has been pronounced satisfactory. Every precaution is taken to prevent fraud, and to secure absolute honesty in carrying out the system, and yet it is quite certain that means have been successfully resorted to time and again, by which unworthy men have secured degrees to which they were not entitled, and which they never could have got by honest methods.

It is a curious circumstance that the highest degree granted to a Chinese subject, when literally translated, means simply "fit for office," and not doctor of laws, as with us.

The system, it will be observed, takes but little account of character, and deals only with Chinese classics. It takes no cognizance whatever of Western learning and sciences, and hence, however honestly it is administered, can not possibly produce satisfactory results, as viewed from a Western standpoint. It is well understood that, notwithstanding this seemingly admirable method of selecting officials, the civil service of China is as bad as any in the world, and worse than that of the poorest European nation. It is not, however, entirely devoid of honest, able, and efficient administrators of every grade ; and, indeed, this is to be expected, since no plan yet devised can any more certainly select and make all officials bad than it can select or make them all good. I am inclined to believe that for the present, and, indeed, for many years yet to come, the system will prove itself to be as good as any which could be substituted for it. If Western sciences and learning be gradually introduced into the empire, and be made prerequisites along with the Chinese classics, the latter in smaller and smaller quantities, for the degrees granted at the public examinations, and if to this be added the qualifications of honor, honesty, and good moral character, before even the highest graduates can be assigned to public office, the civil service of China will be steadily improved. It will, of course, be still further elevated, if a system shall be devised for more certainly punishing malfeasance and corruption in office, and for "turning the rascals out" when once they are discovered.

It came to be the custom under the late regency, and especially after the close of the Taiping rebellion, to refer nearly all new, difficult, or embarrassing questions presented by foreigners, or growing out of their presence in China, to Li Hung-Chang, who, as the First Grand Secretary of the Empire, holds a place somewhat like that of the Premier of the British Cabinet, or of Prince Bismarck, the Chancellor and chief adviser of the German Emperor. He does not, however, reside at Peking, nor visit it often, but, as Governor-General or Viceroy, he makes his principal place of business at the treaty port of Tientsin, eighty miles away. Here he receives and calls upon all diplomatic agents who enter the country, even before they present themselves to the Government at Peking, but he does not generally see their credentials, which are addressed to the Emperor, and can not, of course, be presented to any subordinate, however high his rank or exalted his position.

It is an interesting fact that no foreign minister has yet been received by the present Emperor or Empress-Dowager, and that the credentials of the entire diplomatic corps at Peking are consequently supposed to be lying safely locked up in the strong boxes of the respective legations. This is certainly the case with our own minister, who not only retains his own credentials but those of his recent predecessors as well.

Much of the foreign business of the Government has heretofore been done by the provincial governors, or by special commissioners, and in the purchase of arms, heavy guns, and machinery, this must continue for some time to be the practice. The telegraphs have been built under the supervision of an imperial commissioner by foreigners specially employed for the purpose. Naval vessels have been bought, manned, and armed heretofore by the governors of the maritime provinces, but all such business will doubtless soon pass under the control of the Admiralty Board heretofore mentioned, although it must necessarily continue to be managed by the Viceroy Li and the foreign assistant employed by him, in all its practical details.

From the foregoing sketch it is apparent that the Chinese Government is so isolated, vague, and inaccessible, as to render it almost impossible for foreigners to reach, influence, or move it, while it is peculiarly subject to the control of conservatism and prejudice operating upon it through the Censorate, or through the large number of old and timid men, who constitute the majority of the Great Boards and Councils, and who are naturally sorry to see any innovation introduced, for fear it may put their own order in jeopardy.

In mere matters of trade a foreigner has no difficulty, for he conducts all his buying and selling through Chinese agents or *compradors*, and rarely if ever has occasion to see the people with whom he is dealing ; but, when it comes to negotiations of any sort with the Government, they must be conducted in person, and generally through high officials who have but little independent power, who hedge themselves about with ceremony, and who can not be seen at all, unless the person desiring the interview also has high diplomatic or military rank, or has such letters of introduction as will secure the kind assistance of his minister or consul. Unless he can obtain these, he had better stay at home, no matter how important or pressing his business may be.

CHAPTER XIII.

The eyes of the world now turned toward China as a field for investment in public undertakings—Its financial system—No statistics except those of the maritime customs—The revenues collected by "farmers"—The growth of the system—The sources of the imperial Chinese revenue—The land-tax—The salt monopoly—The likin, or internal transit tax—Miscellaneous taxes—Maritime customs duties—Summary—Comparison of Chinese and British Indian revenues—Estimates made by various persons—No correct account can be given of the expenditures of the Chinese Government—Approximate estimate—The funded debt—Fear of the Chinese Government to negotiate foreign loans—Its obligations good and negotiable for $100,000,000—The Chinese slow to lend to their Government—No statistics of private wealth—Thought to be capable of raising $100,000,000, if properly secured—Necessity of measures to promote confidence.

IN view of the fact that the eyes of the world are turned toward China as a field for railway-building and for the opening of mines, the erection of furnaces and rolling-mills, and the establishment of manufactures which shall utilize its boundless supply of labor, it is important that some account should be given of the financial system, revenues, and expenditures of the Imperial Chinese Government.

It must be understood at the outset that no statistics except those of the maritime customs, as the word is understood among foreigners, exist, or at least can be got at by outsiders. It must also be understood that all revenues, whether for imperial, provincial, or municipal purposes, are levied, collected, and disbursed under the orders or sanction of the Imperial Government.

In what follows, no effort will be made to account for any but the imperial revenues, for the simple reason that, while the provincial authorities collect all the revenues except the maritime customs, and, after paying the provincial expenses of every sort, they send the balance to the imperial treasury, or rather they send what they absolutely must to the treasury, and retain the "balance" for provincial uses.

All official salaries in China are small—in most cases totally inadequate to the requirements and expenses of the official, and it has therefore become a part of the national system that all officers, high as well as low, who handle money, are expected secretly, if not openly, to retain a part of it for their own use.* The collectors of the revenue are, in fact, "farmers," who must furnish the sum demanded of them by the Board of Revenue at Peking, but are permitted by custom (and this has been or is the practice in nearly all Asiatic countries, as it was formerly in Europe) to retain all they can collect over and above the amount they are called upon to account for. In China it is said that this system grew out of the practice of holding the collectors responsible for the return of a minimum sum, and compelling them to make good any deficit in the collections out of their own pockets. The "Peking Gazette" affords abundant evidence that there

---

* A remarkable case illustrating this truth has just come to my notice. In pursuance of the recommendation of the superintendent of the Yellow River works, the Board of Revenue set aside 500,000 taels for those works last winter, but, when the officer went for it, he received only 490,000, the fiscal clerk who paid over the money withholding 10,000 taels for his trouble. This raised a great disturbance, because the "squeeze" was deemed excessive; the matter came to the attention of the board, and, after much discussion, the clerk was "fined" and compelled to pay 10,000 taels, the amount he had withheld.—J. H. W.

is a continual struggle between the imperial and provincial authorities about money and its application, and that the Censorate has frequent cause of complaint against those who have to collect and disburse it.

The books on China, and especially "The Middle Kingdom," give full accounts of the system and its origin, but their figures are not altogether trustworthy.

The most authentic statement of the Chinese revenue, of which I have any knowledge, is contained in a series of articles which originally appeared in the "China Mail," and were reprinted in pamphlet form at Hong-Kong in 1885. What follows is summarized mainly therefrom.

The sources of the imperial revenue may be given as follows: 1. The land-tax. 2. The salt monopoly. 3. The transit duties collected on inland commerce, and known as the *likin*. 4. Miscellaneous, including the revenues arising from "contributions," "assessments," and "subscriptions," and from the sale of official rank and titles. 5. The maritime customs.

LAND-TAX.

In China, as in all other Oriental countries, the land-tax is one of the principal sources of revenue. It is collected by the district magistrates, and in the offices of all such magistrates there is a registry wherein the name of every landholder, every transfer of land, and the amount of tax levied on each tract of land, is required to be recorded. As a matter of fact, this is not always done, and it is said that great confusion prevails in some districts, both as to the amounts of the levy and the persons from whom it should be collected. Be this as it may, the revenue from this source has fallen off greatly of late years; and, although it is said that a part of this falling off is due to the devastations of the Taiping and Mohammedan rebellions, part to floods, and part to famine, it is quite certain that the land-tax is not now over one third of what it was in the days of Kienlung.

The practical labor of collection is performed by underlings, known as *tepaos*, and years-men, but it is worthy of note that there is no class of middle-men, like the zemindars of India. The yield of this tax for all the provinces, as given in the Red-Book, should amount to 32,845,474 taels in silver (a tael is about a dollar and thirty-three cents) ; to 4,356,382 piculs of rice, or to about 40,000,000 taels in all ; but this assessment was fixed at about the beginning of the century, and is considerably in excess of the amount actually collected. From reports of reassessments made in the provinces which have suffered from rebellion, famine, floods, and other causes, it is assumed—and the assumption appears to be altogether reasonable—that the amount collected in silver of late years does not average over 20,000,000 taels yearly.

That part of the land-tax paid in kind is comprised (1) of grain (mostly rice), sent annually to Peking, and (2) rice, beans, straw, etc., levied for the maintenance of the provincial army. The first was originally levied only on eight provinces, namely, those south of the Yellow River and along the Lower Yang-tse, but four of the eight have, since the Taiping rebellion, been permitted to commute their grain-tribute into a money payment. In 1813 the whole of this tribute was estimated at 3,000,000 piculs ; a few years later it is said to have amounted to 4,000,000. It is now estimated at about 1,900,000 piculs, including that which is commuted into money. The total value of this may therefore be put down at 2,800,000 taels. The present yield of the second part of this tax is now thought to be about 3,000,000 piculs, valued at 4,500,000 taels, and the entire yield of the taxes in kind is therefore about 7,500,000 taels. Much more than this is said to be taken from the people, and it seems to be

204   CHINA.

quite certain that, with a proper registration of the land as required by the theory of the Government, and a rigid system of accountability and collection, a very much greater revenue could be secured from this source.

The area of the nineteen provinces of the empire (including Formosa) is about 1,300,000 square miles, and of the nine provinces in or near the Great Plain, the greater part of which is a highly fertile region, is about 500,000 square miles. Throwing out one half of the whole, and counting the rest, or 650,000 square miles, equal to 416,-000,000 acres, as under cultivation; and, allowing that it should pay a tax of only a quarter of a tael per acre per year, it will be seen that the Imperial Government could raise an annual income from this source alone of 104,-000,000 taels, as against the present collections, amounting to only 27,500,000 taels.

THE SALT MONOPOLY.

The profit and tax derived from the monopoly of the trade in salt have always constituted an important part of the imperial revenue. For the purpose of distributing the salt and collecting the taxes, the country is divided into seven main circuits, the boundaries of which are carefully defined, and the salt produced in one is not, under ordinary circumstances, permitted to be transported to or sold in another. The administration is nearly the same in each circuit. The salt is made from sea-water around the coast and from brine inland, and there is no restriction upon the amount produced; but the Government requires that it shall all be sold at fixed rates to the Government agents, who establish depots near the salt-works.

The sale and distribution of the salt is managed by salt-merchants licensed by the salt commissioner in charge of the circuit. The quantity of salt required in each cir-

THE SALT MONOPOLY. 205

cuit is roughly estimated each year, and enough licenses are issued to cover that amount, and each license is supposed to be used every year. Each license entitles the holder to buy 500 *yin*, or 3,760 piculs, at a time, and, as it is perpetual, and may be handed down from father to son, it is worth, in a good district, from 10,000 to 12,000 taels. Having paid for his salt at the fixed rate, the merchant may carry it to any part of the circuit; but, having chosen his market, he must deposit his salt in a sort of bonded warehouse, which is established for that purpose in every considerable town, and enter his name in the book of the warehouse. The salt is sold in the order it is entered, and at the price fixed by the Government for all, so that the only advantage one merchant can get over another is in choosing a good market.

The Government makes a profit on the original sale, and taxes the salt at a fixed rate per picul; and this tax, which is collected at the time of the sale, is also known as *likin*. When trade is brisk, and each license can be used once a year, the profits are from twenty to twenty-five per cent to the merchant. The retail dealer is not taxed, and, after the salt reaches his hands, its sale is unrestricted. The profits on sales and the tax assessed thereon are stated at 9,680,000 taels per year; but here, as in the land-tax, there is room for a very large increase of revenue by a more careful system of administration and accountability. It is believed by close observers that the Government might thereby, and without increasing the cost of salt to the consumer, secure a revenue of 20,000,000 taels, or at least double the amount that now finds its way into the imperial treasury.

THE LIKIN.

This is a tax upon internal commerce in transit, and is frequently regarded by foreigners as illegal; but, as it is imposed by imperial decree, the highest form of law known in China, it is hardly illegal, however disagreeable it may be to foreign merchants. By the Anglo-Chinese Treaty of Nanking, it was agreed that no further inland duties should be levied upon foreign goods, whether in British or native hands, than were then authorized. This clear stipulation was, however, modified by the Treaty of Tientsin, and, since that was ratified, there has been a dispute about it, but the Chinese have continued to levy and collect the tax.

The likin, as now levied, is a modern form of taxation, having first come to the knowledge of foreigners about 1853, and became universal during the latter days of the Taiping rebellion, when the Imperial Government was forced to resort to every known means of raising money. It is levied on all classes of goods in transit, internal custom-houses, commonly designated by foreigners as "squeeze"-stations, for its collection being established on all trade routes. It is a specific and not an *ad-valorem* duty, assessed upon each bale, box, piece, or picul. The word is compounded of *kin* or *kinen*, "contribution," and *li*, nominally the thousandth part of the value.

The details of the collection and the designation of the stations along the trade routes are regulated by the provincial authorities according to the amount of trade and the frequency with which it will stand taxing. The amount collected at each station is inconsiderable, but, if the goods have to go any great distance, the tax becomes an intolerable one, and exerts a most powerful influence upon the repression of trade. There is, of course, no check upon the accounts, and it is generally believed that only a small part of the collections find their way into the public treasury. Fortunately, there is quite an array of testimony as to the amount of money from this source reaching the treasury. Without giving it in detail, it is

MISCELLANEOUS TAXES.   207

sufficient for my purpose to say that the Board of Revenue states that the collections from the whole nineteen provinces amount to "17,000,000 or 18,000,000 taels."

Likin is levied and accounted for under the three heads of salt, opium, and miscellaneous goods, and the figures quoted above include the revenue from all these sources; but in the estimate of the revenue derived from the salt monopoly the part collected from the likin-tax is included, and it is estimated that of the whole amount nearly one third is profit on sales, while over two thirds, or nearly 7,000,000 taels, are derived from likin.

The likin on foreign opium, amounting to about 1,000,000 taels, is included in the statement above, but this is accounted for in the maritime customs returns. Hence to get at the real amount yielded by the likin, these two sums, aggregating a total of say 8,000,000 taels, must be deducted from the 17,000,000 or 18,000,000 taels given by the Board of Revenue, and this leaves from 9,000,000 to 10,000,000 taels collected on miscellaneous goods.

MISCELLANEOUS TAXES.

These taxes are levied (1) on sales of land and houses, at the rate of three per cent on the amounts involved; (2) on marshy lands along the Yang-tse River which are too low to be cultivated, but yield enormous quantities of reeds, used for fuel and thatching houses; (3) on mines, of which there are but few; (4) on merchandise at the place of consumption or upon produce at the place of production, including tea and silk in some districts; (5) for licenses to brokers, merchants, and pawnbrokers; and, finally (6), on the sales of honors and titles. These various taxes, properly levied, collected, and accounted for, should yield a large sum, perhaps ten times as much as they do now. The actual yield is placed at only 1,500,-000 taels, but this is a mere guess.

MARITIME CUSTOMS DUTIES.

Prior to the coming of foreigners and modern trade, the duties levied at the various custom-houses situated at the principal seaports and at a few important inland stations did not amount to much, but since then they have grown into great importance. They are collected under the immediate orders of the Imperial Government and sent direct to Peking, and constitute one of the largest items in the imperial revenues.

The maritime customs, as is well known, are collected under foreign supervision, with Sir Robert Hart as inspector-general. He has organized a corps of customs officials composed of nearly all nationalities, and has brought the service to a high state of efficiency. Under his management the receipts have grown from about 4,000,000 taels to an average of something over 13,000,000 taels net, after paying all costs of collection. Besides this, a further sum, estimated at 5,000,000 taels, is collected at native maritime and inland custom-houses, a large part of which is from foreign opium.

SUMMARY OF REVENUES.

1. Land-tax, payable in silver, taels..............	20,000,000
2. Land-tax, payable in rice-tribute, sent to Peking at taels, 1.50 per picul, and rice-levy commuted in silver............................	7,000,000
3. Salt-tax and likin on salt....................	9,500,000
4. Likin on miscellaneous goods and opium......	9,500,000
5. Miscellaneous...............................	1,500,000
6. Maritime customs under foreign supervision...	13,000,000
7. Native maritime and inland customs..........	5,000,000
Total taels.............................	65,500,000
Or.....................................	$87,333,300

This money does not all go directly to the imperial treasury at Peking, but an arbitrary part, according to the budget drawn up by the Board of Revenue for the whole empire, is assigned and set apart for provincial uses, and goes into or is retained in the provincial treasuries, and drawn out as required. With the increase of importations which is steadily going on, it is probable that the net revenue derived from the maritime customs will reach 15,000,000 taels, or $20,000,000 (Mexican), for the fiscal year 1886, which, with no diminution in the other items as given above, would bring the entire imperial revenue up to about $90,000,000. Without going further into details, it is safe to assert that the entire system of Chinese finance, except the maritime customs, is antiquated, cumbrous, and inelastic, and therefore poorly adapted to meet the emergencies of war, famine, and flood, as they arise. It is also abundantly evident that, bad as the system is, its administration is worse. It is apparent to the most casual observer that there is here a vast field for revenue reform, and the possibilities in that direction are suggested by comparing the Chinese revenue with that of British India on the following taxes :

India, land-tax	£21,000,000	China, taels	20,000,000
India, salt	7,000,000	China, taels	9,500,000
India, opium	10,000,000	China, taels	5,000,000
Total	£38,000,000	China, taels	34,500,000

China has a larger population, a greater area, and a better soil, and also a great advantage in the export of tea and silk ; and yet, if the foregoing figures are correct, the Chinese revenue is not above one fourth of the Indian.

It is not infrequently the case that the provinces are compelled to borrow money to tide them over till the new taxes come in, and this is done by the governor-general, usually on the credit of his province and the faith which the lender has in his character, and sometimes such loans are approved by an imperial edict. They have always been repaid, both principal and interest, promptly on time, and it is quite certain that either the Imperial or Provincial Governments are good for any reasonable sum they will consent to borrow.

As the Imperial Government does not publish the budget prepared by the Board of Revenue, there is, of course, no sufficient data of any kind upon which to base a complete statement of its receipts and disbursements. The statement of revenue given herein is as nearly correct as it can be made, and yet it is merely an approximation which may be $10,000,000 out of the way.

In connection with this subject, the following estimates, made at various times and by various persons, are interesting. Besides, they show in a most striking manner in what great uncertainty the whole subject is involved. For convenience of comparison, those given originally in taels are now stated in dollars:

1587, Trigault, a French missionary............	$26,600,000
1655, Ninhoff...............................	144,000,000
1667, Magalhaens...........................	50,423,962
1667, Le Comte.............................	52,000,000
1777, De Guignes...........................	119,617,360
1796, Barrow..............................	264,000,000
1796 (?), Staunton..........................	330,000,000
1838 (?), Medhurst..........................	200,958,694
1823, a Chinese graduate, estimate translated by P. P. Thomas..........................	98,482,544
1840, Chinese Red-Book.....................	77,462,000
1883, Chinese customs service................	106,000,000
1886, "China Mail" and other sources.........	87,333,000

EXPENDITURES.

No correct account can be given of the expenditures of the Chinese Government, or, at least, none is within reach. It is known, however, that considerable sums have lately been spent on ironclads, fortifications, heavy guns, and dock-yards, and also upon small-arms for the army, and that nearly every year extraordinary floods and disasters on the Yellow River entail heavy expenses, not only upon the provincial, but upon the imperial treasury. It is, however, certain that the Imperial Government generally pays as it goes, and even in the hardest times has succeeded in avoiding the luxury of any considerable public debt. It has, of course, borrowed money, both at home and abroad, but in comparatively small amounts, for short periods, and usually at pretty high rates. But having always met its money obligations with promptitude and in scrupulously good faith, it is now able to borrow under much more favorable terms.

It is said that the expenditures frequently exceed the revenue, but how the deficit is made up is by no means clear. It is probable, however, that this has been done at times by debasing the currency, by the sale of offices and titles, by the reduction of salaries, and by assessments, subscriptions, and contributions, all in the nature of forced loans.

At present, although trade is dull, and great loss has been incurred by all Oriental countries, through the fall in the price of silver, it is believed that the revenues are equal to the expenditures, and that the Imperial Government has fully adopted the policy of making no foreign loans, beyond what may be necessary, from time to time, to pay off such part of its maturing debt as it may not be able to meet from current receipts.

The following tabulated statement, prepared some years ago by De Guignes, and published in the new edition of the "Middle Kingdom" in 1883, gives an approximation to the average annual expense for the various items specified :

SUMMARY OF EXPENDITURES.

Salary of civil and military officers	$10,364,600
Pay of 600,000 infantry, at $4 per month	24,000,000
Pay of 242,000 cavalry, at $5.33 per month	12,900,000
Remounts for cavalry, at $26.66 each	5,853,000
Uniforms for cavalry and infantry, at $5.33 each	4,490,600
Small-arms and ammunition	1,122,000
Fortifications, artillery, and ammunition	5,066,600
Ships-of-war and revenue-cutters	18,000,000
Canals and transportation	5,330,000
Total	$87,125,800

It will be observed that these figures are slightly under the latest estimates of revenue, but this is a coincidence of no great value, and, as they do not include interest on the funded debt, an addition of about $2,000,000 should be made for that item, which would increase the average annual expense to $89,125,000.

FUNDED DEBT.

The funded debt of China, which is held nearly altogether in England, is stated at £5,470,000—equal, say, to $26,000,000. The bonds are for short terms, and the average rate of interest, owing to the fact that the money was borrowed mostly during the late Franco-Chinese War, is about eight per cent. The last bonds bear interest, however, at six per cent, and were quoted during the last year at about ten per cent premium in London. It is said, upon what seems to be good authority, that money has been lately offered by European bankers to the Imperial Government at five per cent, but so far it has declined to borrow even at that rate, and it is understood that it does not wish to borrow foreign money for any purpose at present, and least of all to pay for railroads or railroad materials.

It is apparent to all who have conversed with Chinese

CREDIT OF THE IMPERIAL GOVERNMENT. 213

statesmen, and are familiar with their feeling toward foreign nations, that the one fear in which they are all united is, that any great money obligation on the part of the Imperial Government toward foreign bankers would be the sure precursor of foreign interference in the internal affairs of China. Whether this fear be well or ill founded, it is hardly worth while to consider. It is deep-rooted and wide-spread, and must be considered as an important factor in all questions connected with progress in that country.

In view of the evident conservatism of the Chinese Government, and also of its promptitude and good faith in meeting its agreements, it is the opinion of those who are best acquainted with its resources and claims to public credit, that its obligations would be good and readily negotiable for $100,000,000. Under good management, that sum would supply it with the framework of a railroad system which would be invaluable in case of war, and which would earn enough net from the start to pay interest upon its cost, and leave a handsome surplus for the public treasury. I have no doubt that this opinion is well-founded but of course it depends upon the cost of the railroads. If that should, for any reason, reach such a sum per mile as the railroads built in Japan under English auspices, in the construction of which pounds were spent where dollars would now do the work, the opinion would not only prove to be erroneous, but the railroads produced would be insufficient in length, and could not, for years to come, except in a few special cases, pay their working expenses and interest.

In connection with this subject, the amount of accumulated capital in the hands of private individuals is a matter of great interest, but unfortunately there are no statistics whatever bearing upon it. Generally speaking, China is a poor country, and there is but little wealth per capita among the people at large; but in the aggregate, the wealth of the country, if it could only be got at, or induced to seek investment in railroads, mines, furnaces, and manufactories, is doubtless sufficient for all present needs. The enterprise, shrewdness, and frugality of the Chinese mercantile class are proverbial throughout the East, and it is well known that many of that class in the maritime provinces, and especially in the treaty ports, have amassed large fortunes. It is estimated that $100,000,000 could easily be raised as fast as required, for such purposes, if proper legal protection could be given to the undertakings, and to those who may invest their money in them.

The Chinese are naturally suspicious, and especially so of one another, and it is likely that they will be slow to lend money in large amounts to their own Government, or to invest it in joint-stock companies under the exclusive management of their own countrymen. Education and confidence in such matters are of slow growth at best, and it is of prime importance to the world at large as well as to China that the measures which are resorted to for their promotion shall be carefully considered and matured before they are adopted.

CHAPTER XIV.

Visit to the Great Wall—Decay of the ancient road through the Nankou Pass—Mongolian caravans—Origin, uses, and description of the wall—the return to Nankou—The ride to the Ming tombs—Description of the inclosures and buildings—The Avenue of Statuary—The return to Peking.

As Peking is the capital and therefore the best place to study the Government of China, so the Great Wall, which was for over two thousand years its chief defense, and to this day the greatest work ever raised by Chinese hands, is the best place to get an idea of their capacity to overcome physical difficulties and to study what they may do when once they have begun the march of modern progress. Accordingly, I resolved to see it; and, although winter was rapidly approaching, Mr. Rockhill, First Secretary of Legation, and Mr. Cheshire, Chinese Secretary and interpreter, kindly consented to accompany me. The former, in addition to being a gentleman of excellent education and literary tastes, although still a young man, is an old Algerian campaigner. Having graduated at the Military School of St. Cyr, he entered the French army and served several years in Africa. He has a great gift for languages, and as much of a frenzy for traveling as an Englishman. Mr. Cheshire is an "old China hand" of long experience, though yet on the sunny side of middle age. He has traveled much, and speaks Chinese like a native. Cheerful, bright, sparkling, and musical, he is a delightful companion, and a treasure to any expedition he consents to take under his charge as commissary-general.

With a cook, an assistant, and two horse-boys or *mafoos*, two carts, each drawn by two stout mules, and a liberal outfit of bedding, provisions, and cooking-utensils, we started on a bright but blustering Monday morning, by the road leading through the north gate of the city to the Nankou, or South Pass in the Northern Hills. The north wind was blowing a gale, and, in addition to raising a blinding cloud of dust, it cut our faces like a razor. As such gales rarely last longer than a day, we pushed on through the sear and treeless plain by a broad road, the surface of which was sunken twelve or fifteen feet below the level of the surrounding country, and looked as though it might have been the bottom of an old canal, but it had really been excavated by the combined action of centuries of travel along it, pulverizing the soil into dust for the high winter wind to blow away. The country and villages through which we passed were cheerless and univiting. Here, as everywhere else in the Great Plain, there are no hedge-rows, no fences, no farm-houses, and but few straggling and wind-wrenched trees; the villages are built mostly of sun-dried bricks, and seem the very home of dirt, dilapidation, and discomfort. The prospect was enlivened, however, by the distant hills, rising bare and ragged from the edge of the plain, and sweeping around us in a great circle as far as the eye could reach. It was made still more interesting by the many Mongolian caravans with from twenty to a hundred and twenty camels in each, all laden with grain, sheep-skins, peltries, honey, or game, going to Peking, and returning laden with brick-tea for Kalgan, Mongolia, and Russia. The Mongolian men and women, mounted on the tops of their packs, riding astride, and clad alike in sheep-skin cloaks and hoods, looked as dirty and bronzed as our wild Indians, of which their race are no doubt the progenitors; but they were exceedingly good-natured, and it was amusing to witness their amazed but gratified looks as they heard themselves saluted by our little party of foreigners with "Mundo!" which means in their native dialect, "How do you do?" As soon as they realized that they had been politely accosted, they replied one after the other down the line, "Mundo"—"Mundo-o"—"Mundo-o-o-o!"

We camped the first night at Sha-ho or Sandy River a poor but considerable walled town of the usual description about twenty-five miles north of Peking, on the banks of the only stream of clear running water I had yet seen in China. Our cook soon had dinner for us, and almost immediately after we went to bed to keep warm. At five o'clock, next morning, we were up, and at six we were mounted and off for Nankou, a very dilapidated village, at the entrance to the pass leading to the Great Wall. Leaving the carts and servants at an inn, we exchanged our ponies for donkeys, and by half-past nine were again on the way through the pass. Our donkeys were small but agile, and would have carried us well enough, but for the fact that they were provided with rope halters without bits, instead of bridles, and bags of millet instead of saddles. A pair of iron stirrups, tied together at the opposite ends of a rotten old rope, were thrown across each donkey, and as they were not fastened in any way to the bag which served as a saddle, the riding soon became more difficult and painful than walking. In fact, it required about as much skill to keep one's seat on the back of one of those donkeys and his archaic trappings as to walk a tight-rope without a balancing-pole, and as the road was nothing but a very rugged ravine for much of the distance, the bed of a torrent, filled by bowlders of granite and porphyry worn smooth as glass by the pad-like feet of camels which have been going through that pass in countless numbers since the days of Adam, we soon found it much safer and more comfortable to walk than to ride.

I never saw a worse or harder road to travel, and, whether riding or walking, it was equally dangerous. Each of us got a fall, but fortunately none of us was seriously hurt. Originally the gorge had been occupied by a grand highway twenty-five feet wide, paved with granite slabs six feet long, three feet wide, and a foot thick; but nearly every vestige of this road has long since been swept away by the torrents of the rainy season, or worn out by the ceaseless travel of caravans along it.

About two thirds of the way through the pass we caught sight of the Great Wall on the hill-tops, a thousand or fifteen hundred feet above us. Once seen, it can never be forgotten. Here we passed through a curious arched gateway, which spans the road, and carries a loop of the main wall—a sort of inner defense, as it were—which crosses the valley at this place. This arch was erected in 1345, and on its interior face is a curious Buddhist inscription in six different languages—Chinese, Mongolian, Oigour, Devanagari, Niu-Chih, and Thibetan. It is, of course, hoary with age, and, like everything else, whether new or old, in China, seems hastening toward ruin and decay. From this point to the Great Wall itself the gorge rises rapidly, becomes rougher and rougher, and is overlooked on either side by tablets and shrines, erected by travelers in years gone by to commemorate their piety or the safe arrival at the gateway of Cambaluc — the capital and Mecca of all Eastern Asia.

After much hard scrambling, during which we could scarcely realize that we had not lost our way, but were on a national highway—one of the great historic roads of the

THE GREAT WALL.

world, by which primeval tribes had descended into the Great Plain, and an almost boundless empire had been conquered—we reached the summit of the pass and the portal of the wall shortly after noon; but we were amply repaid for all the trouble we had gone through in getting there by the wonderful work before us.

The Great Wall was evidently an effective national barrier, built at a time when the wild tribes of Northeastern Asia were pressing forward into the richer lowlands, whither their kinsmen had gone centuries before; but it may well be doubted that it was conceived and completed, as it is now, by a single mind, or as a single undertaking. It most probably consisted originally of a line of detached earthworks, which some able ruler or captain strengthened and connected so as to present an unbroken line to the public enemy.

It is said to have been finished two hundred and five years before Christ by Tsin Chi-Hwangti, and to be nearly 1,600 miles long. The Chinese call it the "Ten-thousand-*li* wall"; and, if it really had any such length, it would be something over 3,350 miles long. That part of it which we visited has evidently been rebuilt within the last three or four hundred years, and, while it looks old and at places is in ruins, it has something of a modern appearance. It is from twenty-five to thirty feet high, fifteen to twenty feet thick, and revetted, outside and in, with cut-granite masonry laid in regular courses with an excellent mortar of lime and sand. It is surmounted by a parapet or battlement of gray burned brick eighteen or twenty inches thick, covered with moss, and pierced with crenelated openings for the defenders, whether archers or matchlock-men, to fire through. The rear or inner revetment wall is also furnished with a lower parapet, but it is not crenelated. The top is paved with a double layer of brick about a foot square. The inside of the wall is made of earth and loose stone well rammed in. Every two or three hundred yards there is a flanking turret thirty-five or forty feet high, projecting beyond and overlooking the face of the wall in both directions, and near each turret is a stone staircase leading down between the walls to a door opening upon the ground to the rear.

The most astonishing thing about it is, however, that it climbs straight up the steepest and most rugged mountain-sides, courses along their summits, descends into gorges and ravines, and, rising again, skirts the face of almost inaccessible crags, crosses rivers, valleys, and plains in endless succession from one end of the empire to the other—from the sea-shore on the Gulf of Pechile to the desert wastes of Turkistan. No spot is left unguarded or uncovered, and, no matter how fierce and active were the wild tribesmen who assailed it, or how innumerable were their armies, it is evident that it could, if well defended, even by men armed with nothing better than stones, defy the world up to the day of gunpowder and artillery. Indeed, it is almost impossible to conceive of its capture except through treachery or gross neglect on the part of those whose duty it should be to defend it. It is laid out in total defiance of the rules of military engineering, and yet the walls are so solid and inaccessible, and the gates so well arranged and defended, that it would puzzle a modern army with a first-class siege-train to get through it if any effort whatever were made for its defense.

One can form no adequate idea of the amount of labor or materials expended upon this great work unless he has seen and measured it. The simple problem of cutting the stone, making the brick, and transporting them to the wall, must have been a sore puzzle to those who had it in hand, and it is almost impossible to conceive the means by which the water used in making mortar could be carried to the mountain-tops across such a rough and arid country.

It is of course known that the movement which crystallized itself in that way was a national if not a popular one, and that it was carried through by contingents of men from the various provinces, the men being paid and subsisted by the province to which they belonged till they had finished the task assigned them. The road from Mongolia, which lies just outside the wall, enters it by an immense postern-gate, which is defended by a sort of square bastion and turrets so arranged as to command and bar all approaches. At the point where we climbed to the top of the wall, and sheltered ourselves from the wind in a corner between a turret and the parapet, the elevation above Peking, as shown by my aneroid, is 2,150 feet, but within half a mile it is at least 600 feet higher. There is a strange fascination in the grandeur and barbaric strength of this wall, as well as in the wild and desolate scenery surrounding it, which holds the most prosaic traveler firmly in its grasp. We lingered till our guides said we must go, or it would be impossible to rejoin our carts and servants that night. So, with our faces once turned toward Nankou, we hurried on as fast as the execrable road, or rather the wild, bowlder-strewn gorge, would allow; but, with all we could do, riding and walking in turn, darkness overtook us, and it was eight o'clock before we reached our inn. Here the scene changed. Our sitting-room was well lighted, and the table was spread for dinner, which was ready. It consisted of pea-soup, broiled beefsteaks, and excellent chops of Mongolian fat-tailed mutton, Boston baked beans, canned corn, and pancakes, with claret, port, tea, and coffee; and it was all just as good as if it had been served at Delmonico's.

As soon as dinner was over, we went to bed, and almost immediately to sleep. We had done about forty miles that day, thirty of them over the worst road I ever saw, and were consequently tired. Recollecting the experiences of my campaigning days, I had furnished myself with an India-rubber air-mattress before leaving home, and I found it upon this occasion, and during all my subsequent travels in China, a source of unalloyed comfort.

The next day, we were up and off before dawn. Our route lay to the eastward along the foot-hills, which were as bare, sharp, and clear in the brilliant light of the full moon as the hills of New Mexico in the transparent atmosphere of that distant region. The morning was sparkling with frost, but not a breath of air was stirring. The country was everywhere still and deserted; no travelers were abroad, no lowing herds were heard, and no sounds arose, except the music of our ponies' feet as they clinked against the gravel of the stony hill-sides and ravines, to break the solemn stillness of the invigorating air. After an hour's sharp trot, the faint gray light of dawn appeared in the distant east. The edge of the horizon shone with a deep pearly blue, shading off into gray, and that again into a beautiful glow of pink upper lights, which covered the awakening landscape with an indescribable charm. In another half-hour the sun rose clear and red in a cloudless sky, and the day was glorious with sunshine and beautiful scenery. Our route lay still along the foot-hills, with persimmon-groves to the right and left of us, but no other trees anywhere to be seen. In another hour we had arrived at the edge of a broad, park-like amphitheatre, formed by the main ridge of mountains and a line of detached isolated hills rising from the plain. This charming spot had been selected several hundred years before by the Ming Emperor Yungloh for the burial-place of the dynasty (1318–1644), and here their celebrated tombs are placed at intervals around the amphitheatre, which is from three and a half to four miles across.

Standing at the entrance to the park, it seemed to be perfectly level. The hills themselves were bare, but beautiful in outline and the color of their stratified rocks. Here and there on the foot-hills were clumps of evergreens and deciduous trees inclosing a compound, above the walls of which could be seen the red eaves and yellow-tiled roofs which betoken an imperial burial-place. Selecting what seemed to be the largest one, we rode straight across-country toward it; but, instead of finding a plain all the way, we soon came to a deep, wide ravine, across which at one time there had been a broad paved road and two splendid gray-marble bridges of six or seven arches each. One of these had been partly carried away by a torrent, which was now dry, but the other was standing solitary and alone, and looked as though it had not been used for centuries, which is probably the case, for the Mings were pure Chinese, and their descendants have entirely disappeared. The present dynasty, it must be remembered, are Manchus, and, while they publicly reverence their predecessors, although of another race, they really never worship at their tombs. There is a public keeper appointed, and a small allowance made for their maintenance; but, so far as I could see, no evidence whatever of care or attention. We soon reached the first tomb, which we found in a grove surrounded by a high brick wall, the gates of which were barred and locked. After calling loudly, but in vain, for the gate-keeper, we turned to the left, and went on about a mile to a still larger inclosure. It was embowered in a grove of stately arbor-vitæ, built like the other of bricks, faced with red stucco, and entered from the front by a splendid *pailow*-like gate, covered with green and yellow imperial tiles of perfect glaze and workmanship. Here we soon found the gate-keeper, and for a Mexican dollar induced him to open the ponderous wooden doors and act as our guide. The first building we passed through was a great open shed, with the peculiar Chinese ridge-pole, eaves, and roof covered with yellow tiles. A hundred and fifty feet farther on we came to a stately pavilion on a raised platform, surrounded by three low, narrow terraces, overgrown with bushes, and divided from each other by beautiful white-marble balustrades. The whole floor of the pavilion is occupied by a hall two hundred feet long by eighty feet wide, the vaulted ceiling of which is supported upon lofty wooden columns, which are unvarnished and perfectly plain. It is entirely empty, except that it has in the center a wooden cabinet containing a small painted tablet, on which are inscribed the name of the Great Yungloh, in whose memory it was erected. Near the cabinet is an altar, or rather a large table, on which the faithful are supposed to burn incense and in front of which they offer their prayers to the spirit of the dead Emperor. The place is certainly not used as a sanctuary at present, for every nook and cranny of it is covered with dust, and all its surroundings indicate that it has been absolutely deserted and neglected for cycles, if not for centuries. Back of this hall, two hundred feet farther, is a brick pagoda of two stories, about thirty feet square and forty feet high, in the base of which Yungloh lies buried. It is a solid structure, and abuts against the hill-side, which is covered by arbor-vitæ, young oaks, and underbrush, all entirely neglected. Vigorous saplings are growing out of the walls at several places, and gradually pushing them over.

These buildings, which might well have been called splendid in their day, are over three hundred years old, and going rapidly to wreck and ruin. The roof-timbers are rotting, the beautiful tiles are dropping to the ground, the balustrades are tumbling over, and in a few years more the place will surely become only a study for antiquarians. No one can see it without being impressed with the reflection that the worship of parents and emperors alike is no longer an active cult in China; and even to the tombs of monarchs, who claim to be sons of Heaven, there comes a time when no human soul is left to offer its prayers before it, nor any human hands to preserve it from ruin and desolation.

After wandering about the place for a couple of hours, we started on our return trip to Peking. Within four miles we came to the Avenue of Statuary, a mile long, and ending at a marble gate, or *pailow*, which is by far the most stately and beautiful structure of the kind in China. The statuary is herculean, and consists of four pairs of civilians, two pairs of warriors, a pair of horses standing, a pair lying down, a pair of elephants standing and a pair lying down; and also of camels, lions, and tigers in pairs, all arranged at intervals on opposite sides of the paved but untraveled and grass-grown road, leading from the gate toward the tombs. The effect of these stately and solemn monoliths standing in the edge of the cultivated fields is exceedingly impressive. They bear witness to the glory of a great dynasty, as well as to a period when China seems to have been more prosperous than it is at present. They are well worth visiting even in the wintertime. We reached the city before sundown, having enjoyed every minute of our absence. The cold, exposure, and hardship which we underwent were just enough to give value to what we saw, and heighten the pleasure of our trip.

CHAPTER XV.

The Kai-ping coal-mines and railway—The first locomotive-engine built in China—Extension of the railway to Lutai—The Kai-ping coal-measures—Output of the mines.

SHORTLY after returning to Tientsin I made a horseback trip of seventy-five miles across the country to the Kai-ping coal-mines, which are situated at the northeastern edge of the Great Plain. They are worked by an excellent but costly European plant, and use the only railroad in China for carrying their output to the canal, seven miles away. It is commonly supposed that there is not a mile of railroad in the country, and this belief has been spread throughout the world since the Imperial Government bought and took up the experimental line of ten miles, built by Messrs. Jardine, Mathison & Co., in 1874, from Shanghai to Wusung. Although this road did not run to a place of any commercial significance, and was a hastily constructed, narrow-gauge affair, it paid from the start. Its principal business was in carrying Chinese passengers, who traveled on it merely to gratify their curiosity. It was built, however, without any guarantee that it should become a permanent road ; and, inasmuch as it could never become a link in any great line, and the country was not ready for the general introduction of railways, the Chinese Government bought the road at a fair advance on its cost, tore it up, and stored the rails and fixtures.

THE KAI-PING RAILWAY. 227

The original intention of the Chinese Engineering and Mining Company, which built the Kai-ping road, was to connect the colliery with the town of Peh-tang, near the mouth of the Peh-tang River; and this would have required a line forty miles long. English engineers were employed, instruments for the surveys were ordered in August, 1878, and work was commenced shortly afterward; but in October the Chinese authorities notified the directors that no railway construction would be permitted.

The management then ordered the survey of the Ciangho, a small stream running past the mines to the sea, but it was found quite impassable for boats carrying over three tons.

In November, 1879, surveying for a canal system was begun, and in October of the following year the work of excavating a canal to connect the colliery with the nearest point on the Peh-tang River was started; but it was found that it would be impossible to bring the canal nearer than seven miles of the colliery, so the directors told the Provincial Government that, unless permission were granted to build a line to connect the colliery with the head of the canal, the company would be forced to stop work. But not till April, 1881, would the Government listen to any appeal, and then permission was given to put down a line from the colliery to the head of the canal on condition that only horses or mules should be used as the motive-power, and that it should be called a tramway.

In the mean time the engineers had been quietly constructing a locomotive in the shops, out of such odds and ends as were obtainable, and the use of the men and materials for this purpose was kept a secret, for fear that it would become known to the Government that they were building a "locomotive." The machine was tested, with twenty pounds of steam, on the 24th of March,

1881, and worked well; but on the 7th of April, all further work on it was stopped by order of the managing director, and on the 9th all the rails on which it had been run in the yard were pulled up, and on the 5th of May it was shunted into a shed, presumably to let it rust out.

Work was, however, again begun on it, and at last, in spite of all obstacles, the engine was finally completed, at small expense, though in the roughest manner, owing to want of facilities in the shops, and was run in the yard on the centenary of George Stephenson's birth for the first time; whence it was not inappropriately christened "The Rocket of China."

The first trial on the main line was made on the 8th of November of the same year, and since then the engine has done good service, running over 12,000 miles, and supplying all requirements till locomotives could be got out from England.

This engine, in all its details, and indeed most of the railroad, was planned and built by Claude W. Kinder, a young English civil engineer, who was at the time assistant to Mr. Burnet, chief-engineer of the mining company. The boiler is a second-hand portable one of English make. The cylinders, 8 by 15½ inches, belonged to an old winding-engine from England.

The wheels, 30 inches in diameter, were bought as scrap; they are of chilled-iron, from Whitney & Son, Philadelphia.

The frame is of channel-iron, from head-gear of No. 1 shaft.

The axle-guards are of angle-iron, riveted to the same.

The springs, and all other work, were made at the colliery.

The wheel base is 8 feet 4 inches (six wheels, four coupled).

The weight on drivers is six tons; on leading-wheels, three and a half tons.

It has side-tanks; end coal-bunkers.

One motion-pump and one donkey-pump.

Stephenson's link-motion. Cost of construction, about $650 for labor and new materials.

The railway has a total fall of 70 feet between termini; maximum gradient, 1 in 100; sharpest curve radius, 1,500 feet, except in yard, where there are curves of 600 feet radius.

The rails are steel, 30 pounds to the yard, Vignole's pattern.

The line is single, the sleepers are of native elm, rough-hewed, and laid on an excellent road-bed, well ballasted with broken limestone, and the gauge is 4 feet 8½ inches.

On the first section of the road there is one tunnel of 300 feet, one arch of 20 feet span, one open-top iron-girder bridge, 10 feet span, one iron Warren girder bridge, 30 feet span, besides several culverts. There is one half-way station at Liu Ying-Chong.

The imported rolling stock is two locomotives, 11-inch tank-engines, 18-inch stroke, six wheels coupled, from Stephenson & Co., England; three third-class passenger carriages; thirty-five 10-ton coal-wagons; seventeen, 5-ton wagons, and one brake-van. There is also one saloon-carriage, built at the company's works.

There are seventeen grade crossings on the first seven miles of line.

The traffic is daily about 600 tons of coal, 100 tons of limestone, besides pottery and sundries, and about 160 passengers, who pay five cents for the seven miles.

The tunnel above mentioned takes a branch line to the company's quarries, and all bridges are made for a double line of rails.

Flag-signals are used, and there is a gate-keeper at each crossing.

Notwithstanding the fact that this road is in daily operation, runs smoothly, and is a beautiful model of what a light railroad should be, its existence until lately has been ignored by the Government. So far as known, it has never been seen by any member of the Board of Public Works, nor, indeed, by any other considerable person connected with the Government at Peking, or of the province in which it is situated, although it has a state carriage and a fine house for the accommodation of such visitors.

It is situated in an out-of-the-way region, has no general traffic, and can never become a part of one of the great lines of the country, although it may be used as part of the line from Tientsin to the province of Shinking, and the northeastern corner of the empire. The canal at which it terminates has already proved to be insufficient to accommodate the business of the mines, and inasmuch as it freezes up for three or four months every year, it is thought to be absolutely necessary to close the mines for the same period, or to extend the road to the Peh-tang, and ultimately to the Pei-ho. As these rivers freeze up also, the extension will give only partial relief, unless it is carried to Tientsin, where a large market is already open for the coal.

The Government has recently authorized the extension to Lutai, on the Peh-tang, twenty-one miles from the present terminus; the rails have been bought in Germany, new locomotives in the United States, and the contracts have been let for the grading, and also for the cross-ties and other materials required. It is supposed that the extension will be completed and opened this spring.

The company having this undertaking in hand, as explained elsewhere, is purely a Chinese organization, and while it has had the assistance of able foreign experts, and the *quasi*-support of the Government, owing to the fact that it must have coal for the naval fleet which it is now organizing, it has not yet proved a financial success. The fact is, that it is over-capitalized, and compelled to support too many people besides; hence it is difficult to see how the extension already authorized can save it from bankruptcy, or enable it to pay working expenses and interest on its old and new capital, which, together can not be far from $2,500,000, and may even overrun these figures. It mined and sold last year nearly 136,000 tons of coal, about one third of which was taken at the pit-shaft by the natives of the neighboring country. The rest was sent to the Pei-ho and Tientsin, where it was taken by steamships or sold for domestic use, the selling price being about five dollars (Mexican) per ton. The coal is bituminous, of fair quality, but it has to compete even on the Pei-ho with Japanese coal from the Takasima mines near Nagasaki, and therefore the selling price can not be raised, but is more likely to be reduced.

The country surrounding the Kai-ping mines is highly cultivated, but there is much waste land which could be reclaimed along the road to the Pei-ho and Tientsin. The country is perfectly flat, shallow ponds abound, the villages are poor and widely separated, and nearly every house is built of sun-dried brick. There are but few domestic animals and fewer trees, and altogether the region is a cheerless and uninteresting one.

The coal-measures of this region are supposed to be of considerable extent, but Baron Richthofen's map on which they are delineated, shows them to be only ten or twelve miles long. They pitch sharply to the southeast, and hence can not be worked for a greater width than two thousand feet. A few native mines are worked in the same field, and a more careful survey may show that the measures extend much farther than Richthofen has indicated. Be this as it may, there is sufficient coal already within reach to supply every possible demand for the Government, as well as for commercial and domestic purposes, for many years. In the future development of railroads in Northern China, the first coal will necessarily have to come from the Kai-ping mines, and this fact gives additional importance to them as well as to the railroad connected with them.

This road was subsequently and by successive stages extended to Tongku, near Taku, at the mouth of the Pei-ho, and also westward to Tientsin. Still later it was extended northeastward to Shan-hai-Quan, at which place the Great Wall leaves the sea. The entire length of road now in operation is about two hundred miles. It is nowhere more than one or two days' march from the seacoast, and could be easily seized or broken by an invading army. The necessary money for its construction was furnished entirely from the treasury of the province of Chihli, aided by a few leading officials, the Chinese merchants and capitalists being unwilling to go into partnership with the Government.

CHAPTER XVI.

Trip to the Yellow River—"China's Sorrow"—Organization of the party—The route—The roads—The winter climate—The inns and innkeepers—The old towns—The Grand Canal and its embankments—The sluices—Impracticability of keeping the canal open by Chinese methods—Necessity for a railway—The Yellow River and its embankments—Worship of the river-god—Change of channel at Lungmun-Kou in 1853—Views of Dr. Williams and Ney Elias—Error of Abbé Huc—Probable cause of change—Embankments can be maintained—The river can be regulated and controlled by the resources of modern engineering—Railways can be built and maintained in the delta.

HAVING seen everything of interest in the region between Taku, Tientsin, Peking, and the Great Wall, I determined now in pursuance of the suggestions of the Viceroy Li to visit the country to the southward, along the Grand Canal and the Yellow River.* I had often read of the canal as "the great internal highway" of Chinese commerce, and of the Yellow River—the "Hoang-ho" of our earlier geographies—as the cause of unnumbered woes to the inhabitants of the Great Plain, and hence known to the natives as "China's Sorrow"; but, curiously enough, notwithstanding I had been in China for three months, I could find no one who could give me any definite information about them. The books

---

*Parts of this, and also of the seventeenth and eighteenth chapters, are reprinted from letters which appeared in the "New York Sun."

are vague and uncertain in what they say. The "Peking Gazette" mentions both the canal and the river frequently, but the former generally in connection with the difficulty of keeping it open long enough to bring the "tribute-rice" of the southern provinces through it to Peking; and the latter in connection with the futility of all efforts heretofore made to protect the adjacent country from its devastating floods. In order to understand the reason for all this, I resolved to see both the canal and river, and to study them from my own observations, in spite of the fact that it would require a journey in midwinter of about fifteen hundred miles through remote and unfrequented regions.

My party consisted of Lieutenant F. W. Nichols, of the United States Navy, who was kindly permitted by Captain Higginson, of the gunboat Monocacy, to accompany me; Wang Fuyeh, a mandarin of the sixth rank; Li Chung-Ting, Chinese interpreter; Hsieh Sz, an intelligent mechanic from the Tientsin arsenal; a cook, two boys, a servant, two *mafoos*, or horse-boys, and six carters, making, with myself, sixteen persons in all. In addition, we had six Chinese carts, two mules to each, and six saddle-ponies, together with the necessary supplies of flour, biscuits, sugar, tinned soups, fish, meats, and vegetables, for a sixty days' absence, it being understood that the Chinese members of the party would get their daily meals at the inns by the wayside.

Our route lay along the general course of the canal and Yellow River to Kai-fung-fu, the capital of the province of Honan; thence eastward to Lung-mun-Kou, the point at which the river left its old bed in 1853–'54, and thence to Tung Ming, where a disastrous breach occurred in its southern embankment last year. From this point, there being no inns near the river, we struck across the country to Chining-Chou on the canal, and from there made a visit to Chü-fu, the home and burial-place of Confucius, and also to Tai-Shan, the sacred mountain of China. Retracing our path, we returned to the canal at Nan-Shan, and turning north followed it back to the Yellow River at Shih-li-pu. From this point we skirted the river as closely as possible, going northeastward through Ping-yin and Chang-Ching to Chi-nan-fu, the capital of Shantung. After examining the embankments near the city, we recrossed the river at Chi-ho, and returned through Ter-Chou (at which place we intersected our route to the southward) to Tientsin, having been gone forty-five days, and traveled something over fourteen hundred miles.

The roads were found to be in excellent condition for China, dry, hard, and dusty, but very crooked, as is generally the case throughout this country. There being no fences, no hedge-rows, or ditches to mark the boundaries of farms or gardens, and apparently no work done upon the roads either in their original construction or for their maintenance, every traveler feels at liberty to mark out a road for himself, and this is a liberty of which every one is compelled to avail himself in the rainy season, when the alluvial soil of the plains becomes a sea of mud. The consequence is, that it is no infrequent occurrence to see a road go around three sides of a field instead of along the fourth side, or run zigzag like a ship tacking against a head-wind. Even the roads laid down on the maps as imperial highways are unnecessarily crooked. They are neither paved nor graveled, even where the materials can be had, and macadamizing seems to be entirely unknown. Indeed, it is not too much to say that roads in China are never worked, and could be hardly worse in the rainy season.

During our entire journey we saw only one stretch of road, about ten miles long, which showed that it had been laid out, heaped up in the middle and ditched, and that was through an unusually low and desolate portion of the plains, which would have been otherwise impassable for most of the year. Judging from the crookedness of the canal embankments, as well as of the roads, it is difficult to believe that the Chinese who laid them out ever had the slightest conception of the fact that a right line is the shortest distance between two points. There are few running streams, and no mud in winter, and, as the plains are everywhere as flat and smooth as any floor, wheeled vehicles can drive indefinitely in any direction. It is curious that the Chinese never put springs in their carts, and, in fact, seem to be ignorant of their existence or of the use which is made of them in other countries.

The winter climate of this region is quite remarkable. Throughout our journey we had only three days when we did not see the sun, and most of the time it shone clearly and brightly from morning till evening. The nights were also clear and bright, but generally very cold. One day we had a slight fall of frozen mist, and the next morning the neighboring hills were barely covered with snow or heavy frost, which was all gone long before noon. The only interruption to the most perfect weather is an occasional dust-storm from the north, which blows with fury for several hours, sometimes a whole day, or even longer. It never rains here in winter, but makes up for it in June, July, and August, when the winds blow steadily from the south and southeast, and are heavily laden with moisture. It is these winds, therefore, which cause the floods of the Yellow River; the clouds which are brought in by them break over the land in torrents as far as the Desert of Gobi; the streams are taxed to their fullest capacity; the Yellow River becomes charged to its brink, and, when it reaches the plain, its flood is piled up and frequently augmented by a downfall of rain to the depth of many inches in a single day.

Our journey was made in stages of from seventy-five to one hundred and twenty *li*, or from twenty-five to forty miles per day, and in several instances to forty-five miles per day, our practice being to start at dawn, or shortly after, and travel fifteen or twenty miles at the rate of three and a half or four miles per hour, according to the roads, after which we halted for an hour and a half to feed the animals and take luncheon. This done, we resumed our march, and, after making a similar stage, selected an inn, if we could find one, and put up for the night.

The inns are generally found at the larger towns, and are of various grades, but all constructed on the same plan. They consist of a compound wall of sun-dried brick—rarely of fire-burned brick—the entrance to which is through a pair of large doors, which may be closed and barred. Sometimes there is an inner yard or court. The principal guest-rooms are in a low, single-storied house opposite the entrance. We saw one, and only one, two-storied guest-house on the trip. The house is divided in the better inns into two and sometimes three rooms, the middle one containing a square table and two chairs, or benches, and the end ones containing a *kang*, or two trestles, covered with coarse mats, upon which the guest's own bedding is spread by his own servants. The smaller houses have only a single room, in one end of which is the *kang*, or trestle, and in the other the table and chairs. The rooms are lighted from the front by square windows, with paper panes, and heated, if heat is required, by a pan of charcoal burning in the middle of the floor, which is sometimes of brick, but generally of clay.

The kang is a raised platform across the end of the room, of the same kind of material that the house itself is built of, which as before stated is generally of sun-dried brick. In theory, it is supposed to be provided with a furnace and a flue connecting with the open air, for the purpose of burning millet-stalks or grass, and thus heating the body of the kang; but, in practice, the furnace is rarely found, and when found it is generally impossible to use it. During all our travels south of the Yellow River we saw only one kang, trestles being used instead.

On either side of the compound are the rooms for servants and carters, and also for guests who do not absolutely require the best. The carts are placed in front of the rooms, and the mules and horses are fed in movable troughs which stand in the open court, or under the sheds which are sometimes provided for shelter. The innkeeper furnishes hot water, charcoal, and Chinese meals for such guests as want them, and provides for the animals, and all at reasonable rates. During the night a watchman goes around the premises frequently, beating a piece of hollow wood with a small stick in a peculiar rhythmical manner, which is everywhere the same, and is sometimes quite annoying.

The scene presented by an inn-yard full of carts, horses, and mules is quite animated, but by no means suggestive of extraordinary comfort or cleanliness. The inns themselves in the winter are generally dirty and cheerless, and always cold and damp, so that the traveler's only refuge is to go to bed as soon as he gets his supper. The best and neatest inns are everywhere kept by the Mohammedans; but, as they do not serve pork in any form, the Chinese carters and *mafoos* will not patronize them if they can find any other inns open. As we had our own cook along, and ate no Chinese food, except mutton, poultry, eggs, and vegetables, it made but little difference to us whether the inns at which we stopped were Mohammedan or Buddhist. We, however, had the good fortune to stop at a Mohammedan inn, on Christmas-day, at the town of Chieh-ti, nearly one hundred miles south of Tientsin, and had a most excellent Christmas dinner, the principal articles of which had been furnished by kind friends before we started.

The next point of importance on our route was Ter-chou, an old, dilapidated city, surrounded by a crenelated brick wall, which looked as though it had defied the storms of a thousand winters. Its turrets and buttresses were crumbling, its gates were rotting down, its moats were filled with broken bricks which had slipped from the walls and foundations, and everything about it, both inside and out, was fast falling into decay.

This city is situated on the bank of the Grand Canal, which once doubtless brought a large business to it, but its glory has departed along with that of the canal. Its only significance now is that it is the first station on the imperial telegraph-line south of Tien-tsin.

After tarrying there only long enough to send a message to our friends, we crossed to the west side of the canal, which here follows the bed of the river, and pushed on toward Lin-ching, where we arrived the next night after a ride of almost interminable length. This city is much larger than Ter-chou, and, although it presents by no means a flourishing exterior, it appears to be a place of some business importance.

The Grand Canal at this point leaves the bed of the Wei-ho (the main southern affluent of the Pei-ho), which it follows from Tientsin, and winds its way by a very devious course across the plains to Jung-chang-fu and the Yellow River, a distance of about seventy miles by the road, but over a hundred by the canal. From the great amount of curvature there is no doubt it follows the beds of one or more old creeks or rivers in this part of its course also.

We rode along the embankment, and found it to be of very irregular section, of varying height and thickness, sometimes very wide and strong, in some places in excellent repair, and in others greatly decayed, or totally missing. The telegraph-line follows its general direction, and it is said that the Chinese officials have proposed to lay a railroad upon it. This is possible, by adding to it where it is not wide enough, and by cutting off the corners and bends where they are too sharp, but the road would still be very crooked, and it would be unnecessarily expensive to construct and operate.

Lin-ching is stated by some writers to be at the summit of the canal, but this is not the case ; the real summit is at Lung-Wang Miao, the junction of the canal with the Ta-Wen-ho, a river which rises in the hills of Shantung, and after flowing westward for many miles divides into two branches, one of which, bringing with it an abundant supply of sand, which is very scarce in the Great Plain, falls into the canal, and the other into the Yellow River opposite Yu-Shan.

Before the latter river left its old bed, the canal crossed it at Chin-Chiang-pu, about one hundred miles north of the Yang-tse-kiang, leaving a reach of over four hundred miles of canal north of the crossing, which was supplied with water mainly from the Ta-Wen-ho, and although this water was not and could not be properly utilized, because the canal was not furnished with locks, it afforded fair navigation, except when interfered with by excessive drought or floods from Chin-kiang to the Wei-ho, or rather from the Yang-tse to Peking.

It would give a false impression to leave the subject without further reference to the regulation of the flow of water in the canal, the necessity for which was apparent even to the Chinese ; and to accomplish this they constructed sluices at many places along the canal, so as to divide it up into reaches or sections varying from a mile to ten and twenty miles in length. These sluices have vertical walls, built parallel with and facing each other, about twenty feet apart in the bed of the canal, and connected with the shores and embankments by wing-walls of the same kind of masonry. The faces of the wall are slotted vertically, so as to permit the ends of cross-timbers to slip or drop into them, and thus form a bulkhead across the twenty-feet opening left between the walls. Stone davits and snubbing-posts are provided to facilitate the lowering or raising of the timbers and the passage of boats, which, against a strong head of water, is, of course, more or less difficult. The masonry of these sluices is excellent, and is still in good condition.

After the change of the Yellow River to its new bed the canal was practically cut in the middle, and the new river, carrying for the time a much larger volume of water to sea-level, not only excavated a channel for itself much deeper than the canal, but swept away the canal embankments and filled up its bed, completely obliterating it for three or four miles on the north, and nearly as many on the south side of the crossing. As the river-bed gradually deepened, the surface of the water also subsided, until now at low water it is about ten feet below the bottom of the canal; and, as there are no locks on either side, but a simple embankment or sluice thrown across the canal, it is impossible for boats to pass from the river to the canal, or from the canal to the river, except during high-water, and even then only after the embankment has been cut, the sluice opened, and the canal-bed cleaned out and deepened.

Notwithstanding this state of affairs, and the danger of flooding the entire country in the vicinity, the Chinese Government, in pursuance of a custom as old as the canal itself, has made the most strenuous efforts every year to clean it out and bring the tribute-rice from the southern provinces through it to Peking. The junks necessary to carry that part of the rice sent by this route number six or seven hundred. Some seasons they all get through, some seasons only a part of them, and occasionally none; but it is apparent that the money expended in opening the canal, crossing the river, and paying the freight, which De Guignes estimates at four million dollars, must amount to considerably more every year than the value of the rice.

The use of this canal has been considered by Chinese statesmen as a matter of national importance at all times, but especially so in case of war with foreign powers. During the last war with France every effort was made to put it into efficient condition, but, as usual, with but little success. It should be remembered that the canal really extends from the moats of Peking to the Yang-tse-kiang, and that if it were in good condition it would afford a most valuable line of internal communication for food and military supplies between the capital, the southern, and the central provinces. The Imperial Government has frequently called upon its ablest statesmen and military commanders to take it in hand, but never yet upon competent foreign engineers. It is, of course, fully within the resources of modern science and skill to open and keep it open at all times except when frozen, but the cost would doubtless be large; and, even after the work had been done, the canal would be useless for purposes of national defense, and would necessarily be frozen during the winter.

At Lin-ching there is about three feet of water in the canal at present, but it gradually shoals till the Yellow River is reached, where its bed is entirely dry. Its width at water-surface is from twenty-five to forty feet, and it is badly silted up at several points both north and south of the river. We had considerable difficulty in getting at the condition of the canal and the relative location of the towns near the crossing, until we had made a sketch-map from our own observations. After riding all one day and part of the next, we found that the canal south of Pa-li-Miao (eight-li temple) to the river-bank had been entirely obliterated, and that the plain through which the river runs had been raised by the deposit of silt from the flood four, five, and in places as much as six feet. One sluice of the Chang-Wang Canal, also obliterated, had been buried, and nothing was left to mark its site, except the tops of the stone davits, which were sticking out of the ground about two feet. Even the miao, a small temple, one of which is always erected at or near a canal-sluice, was in ruins, and more than half buried in the silt. Owing to this fact, and the impossibility of making a straight crossing of the river, a new canal, seven miles long, has been constructed from Ur-Cheng-Cha, ten miles north of the old river-crossing, to a point farther down the river. There is a good landing at the last-mentioned point, and the river has there a deep, well-defined bed skirting the foot-hills of Shantung at a distance of three or four miles from them, all the way from the vicinity of Shih-li pu to the vicinity of Chi-nan-fu.

Chang-Chin-Chun was once a place of large population and great wealth, abounding in fine temples and buildings, and surrounded by a wall, all of fire-burned brick ; but its glory has also departed. It is now by all odds the most dilapidated-looking place visited by us in all the delta country. This is doubtless due to the fact that it is situated south of the junction of the new canal, and is left high and dry by what little commerce there is yet remaining on the canal. Pa-li Miao and Shih-li-pu are also in a state of utter desolation and ruin, and tell the story of the decay of commerce on the canal and the devastating effect of the Yellow River floods more eloquently than any description can possibly do it.

Li Hung-Chang, in a memorial to the Throne, says it

is clear that, so long as the Yellow River follows its present course to the sea, navigation can be had through the canal, accompanied by constant danger of inundations from the river; while, if the river were restored to its old channel, emptying into the sea south of the Shantung province, comparative security from floods would be had, but the navigation of the canal would become still more difficult. He adds that the suggestion which has been "made in regard to turning the river back into its old bed is but a figment of the mind," as he regards such a feat as impossible. He may be right in the first conclusion, as he certainly is in the last, but, as the last can not be accomplished, the great problem still remains of how to regulate and control the Yellow River, and maintain a line of internal communication between the imperial capital and the Yang-tse provinces.

The solution of these problems is clearly within the resources of modern engineering; but it is a matter of doubt whether the imperial authorities are yet ready to call in foreign help, or to adopt the conclusions which may be arrived at by a proper consideration of the facts pertaining to each case. There is no doubt that, for the present, and under the plans now existing and the system of administration now practiced by the Chinese, every dollar expended upon the Grand Canal, except for strictly local purposes, is wasted.*

On the other hand, it is certain that the only way in which they can secure a line of internal communication, equal at the same time to the demands of the enormous commerce which would be secured by it and to the re-

---

* Since the above was written, it is understood that both French and German engineers have submitted propositions for the repair of the embankments and the regulation of the river, but these propositions have been rejected, and it is given out that Chinese methods are to be adhered to, at least for the present.—J. H. W.

NECESSITY FOR A RAILROAD.   245

quirements of the national defense, is by building a first-class railroad from Peking to the Yang-tse-kiang, and from Kiu-Kiang a point farther up the Yang-tse to Canton, with branches to certain important mining, commercial, and political centers more or less remote from the trunk line. Such a railroad, including a bridge over the Yellow River, can be built at a reasonable cost; and, what is more, it can be maintained against the floods of the Yellow River, and under foreign management will pay the interest upon its proper cost and a reasonable profit besides, from the day that it is opened for traffic.

From Chang-Chin-Chun we rode along the embankment on the north side of the Yellow River for a distance of about eighty miles to a point in the plain a short distance beyond the village of S'zma, where the embankment abruptly came to an end. Thinking that there might be some mistake about this, or that there were some local features which rendered an embankment unnecessary, we rode at once to the river, some three miles south; but we found the latter here, as elsewhere, occupying a well-defined bed, in a perfectly level plain, the surface of which was, by actual measurement, only an average of five feet above the surface of the water. We also ascertained, by carefully questioning both boatmen and natives, that the water was from eight to ten feet deep in the channel, and had frequently risen as much as ten or more feet, overflowing the plain and spreading through the country to the Grand Canal, to a depth varying from two to six feet.

We then found, by riding straight back into the country twenty miles, that there never had been any embankment to this part of the river since it had left its old bed over thirty years ago; but all our efforts to obtain a satisfactory reason, or even an unsatisfactory one, for the omission, have been so far unavailing.

The embankment along which we had ridden was

found by frequent measurement to be from twelve to fourteen feet high, from twenty to thirty feet wide on top, and to have outside and inside slopes of two base to one perpendicular. In many places and for considerable stretches it was well laid out, admirably constructed, and in excellent condition, but at others it was not only crooked, but of insufficient height and width, and was in bad condition generally. It was frequently cultivated on the top and sides, cut through by road-crossings, and burrowed into by animals, and of course all these are points of danger during floods. The same thing may be said of the embankments wherever we came to them.

Between Tao-chung-fu, at the junction of the present canal with the Yellow River, and Chang-Chin-Chun there is an excellent embankment; but at the latter place it joins an embankment of the old canal, which is in a state of dilapidation; and, while the river embankment turned the water last year admirably, the canal embankment was overflowed, and all the country between the two flooded to a depth of from four to six feet.

From the end of the embankment above referred to, we proceeded through several old walled towns in the interior to Kai-fung-fu, the capital of the province of Honan, about six miles south of the Yellow River. Before reaching the latter, we came to an enormous embankment, about four miles from the ferry, which was built by the Emperor Kien-lung over a hundred years ago. We saw it from a great distance across the plain, looming upon the edge of the horizon like a well-defined hill of considerable height. On a nearer approach it grew in size, and was seen to be surmounted by crenelated walls and city-gates. On measuring it, we found it to be forty feet high and fifty feet wide on top, with the usual slopes of one on two, and to contain about a million cubic yards of earth for each mile in length.

Doubtless it was built by that magnificent monarch to show how, according to his ideas, a wall should be built, and was left to take care of itself, with the firm conviction that it would restrain the floods of the river forever. How far it extends, we could not ascertain; but were informed that it runs to the westward or up the valley of the river only a few miles, but eastward along the bed of the old river indefinitely. We afterward ascertained that it was an extension of this enormous embankment through which the river broke when it changed its bed the last time.

Before crossing the river, we made observations and measurements with sextant and tape-line, from which it was found to be fifteen hundred feet wide and six or seven feet deep on the north side, but quite shoal on the other side, till a reverse bend three or four miles farther down was reached.

Before going on the boat, our attendants and servants offered their devotions to the "river-god," lighting candles, burning incense and gilt and silver paper supposed to represent gold and silver money, prostrating themselves, and knocking their heads reverently and solemnly against the ground three times.

Having done all that was required by custom to secure the smiles of the god and dispose him to vouchsafe us a safe passage, we crowded our whole party—carts, horses, mules, and servants—into a junk about fifty feet long and fifteen or sixteen feet wide, and, casting loose from the north shore, the top of which was then only five feet above the surface of the water, in an hour and a quarter we were safely landed against the southern bank, which was found to be fourteen feet high. In the passage we simply floated with the current, which was of moderate velocity, the boatmen guiding the junk by poles and by dropping their anchor and "clubbing" whenever necessary. Our junk struck against sand-bars several times, but by skillful use of the poles and anchor she was guided safely along without stopping.

Williams, in the "Middle Kingdom," states that the bed of the river near Kai-fung-fu is so silted up, that the surface of the water is higher than the country outside; but this can hardly be the case, for, if it were, we should have probably found back-water or marshes between the river-brinks and the embankments and possibly outside of them also; but no such marshes were seen or crossed by us. Nor were there any other indications that either the bed of the river or the water in it is now or ever has been, except during freshets, higher than the surrounding country. Of course, it would require a careful set of cross-sections, made with good levels by competent engineers, at this and other places, to ascertain the exact facts, but there is no evidence which we could discover going to show that they are as stated by Dr. Williams. To the contrary, so far as any one could see, the ground from the northern embankment to the river was level, and that from the river to the southern embankments, of which there are two, gradually rises on the road to the city walls.

At Lung-mun-Kou, about twenty miles east of Kai-fung-fu, the river burst through its southern embankment in 1853. It was, according to tradition, higher then than ever known before or since; but just how or why this disaster occurred has never been satisfactorily explained.

The most commonly received theory is that the bed of the river was here silted up to a higher level than that of the adjacent plains outside the embankments, which were found to be of enormous dimensions, as at Kai-fung-fu, but this is by no means proved. Careful observations made by us show that while the river has here turned abruptly to the north, leaving the old bed along which we rode for about ten miles, and all of which, including the sides and tops of the old embankments, is now under a high state of cultivation, at a considerably higher level than the new bed, they failed to show that the old bed is higher than the country outside of it. We found from actual measurements that the bottom of the old river-bed was on the 10th of January, 1866, nearly eleven feet ten inches above the surface of the water in the new river-bed, just abreast of it, and only a short distance away; that the top of the old river bank or plain inside of the old embankments, was twenty-two feet six inches above the water-surface, and that the top of the old embankment, now covered by the town of Lung-mun-Kou, has been somewhat changed, but where it is cut squarely through by the river in its new course it is fifty-five feet six inches above the water-surface.

On their face these figures seem to suggest a probability that the river had silted up its bed to a higher level than the country near by, but the appearances of the country, inside and outside, indicate more strongly that this is not the case. Nothing but a careful set of sections made at frequent intervals across and along the old and the new river-beds, both above and below the breach, at points where the condition of the surfaces has not undergone material change since the disaster occurred can set this question satisfactorily at rest.

Mr. Ney Elias, Jr., F. R. G. S., an English merchant of scientific education, then living at Shanghai, visited this point in the fall of 1868, and a full report of his observations is found in the "Journal" of the North China Branch of the Royal Asiatic Society for that year. He states that the course of the low-water channel "was not always parallel to the flood-banks, but made a winding, tortuous line between them, apparently like a natural river, and the point where the breach now is was one where the current impinged upon the north bank." He also states that "the river had so diminished the capacity of its bed (which, by-the-way, was always an artificial one), by depositing the alluvium with which its waters were charged, that the main pressure during the flood-season had come to bear on the upper or weaker part of the embankments, and, no measures having been taken to strengthen these or deepen the channel, the great catastrophe happened, which, with its consequences, had been predicted by Abbé Huc some years before," but he gives no proof except that of "mere cursory inspection" that the bed of the river at the point under consideration had come to be higher than the "general level of the neighboring country."

Abbé Huc distinctly states that "the actual bed of the Yellow River in the provinces of Honan and Kiangsu, for more than two hundred leagues, is higher than nearly all the immense plain which forms its valley," but he also fails to say that he carried surveying-instruments with him, or to give the observations and facts upon which this statement is made. I therefore take the liberty of suggesting that its truth must not be taken for granted. It seems to be more likely that, then as now, the river-embankments were sadly neglected, that the enormous one in which the breach occurred was regarded as so safe that it need not be looked after, and that roads were cut through it, or animals had burrowed in it, or that, where "the water impinged upon it," it had perhaps for years been cutting its way at low stages through the plain to the foot of the embankment, so that the full volume of the great flood had nothing to do at that point but to continue the undercutting till the whole embankment was so undermined and weakened as to make it yield readily to the pressure. It is certain, at all events, that if the bank had been undermined here, as described, it would have broken then or at some other time, whether the river-bed was or was not higher than the neighboring country. In other words, it is not necessary to assume that the river-bed had silted up, as claimed by Ney Elias and Abbé Huc, to account for the breach.

It may be naturally asked, if this assumption is not proved, why the river did not return to its old bed after the flood subsided, but, on the contrary, continued to pour through the breach, and made a new bed for itself on its way to the sea. The answer to this is obvious. As the great volume of water poured through the breach from the top of the flood to the level of the plains below, it acquired a high velocity due to the difference of level, probably as much as fifteen or even twenty feet, and rapidly cut out a new channel, deepest where the velocity was greatest. As Confucius might have said, it is the nature of water to flow in devious lines, and also to run down-hill, and hence, once outside of the great embankment, on a plain sloping gently down to sea-level, it was impossible for it to turn back into its old bed till after the flood had subsided; on the contrary, all that had got outside was forced to flow onward, and in doing so to find the line of steepest declivity open to it. As might naturally have been supposed, in doing this it also found the shortest line from the breach to sea-level, which chanced to be at the mouth of the Ta-Ching-ho, on the Gulf of Pechili, two hundred and forty miles north by west in a right line from the old mouth, and six hundred miles by the coast-line.

The distance by the new course of the river to the sea is about two hundred and fifty miles, while by the old bed it is about three hundred miles. It is also obvious that the water pouring out through the breach, found the deepest natural depression in the surface covered by it, and this depression, also having a steeper decline toward the river, induced a more rapid current not only throughout its course, but also in that part of the old river just above and next to the breach, and consequently eroded that part of its bed to a greater depth than it had ever had before. When the water subsided to its low-water stage, its surface was found to be lower than the bottom of the old bed below or east of the breach. After that it was obviously impossible for it to resume its old channel.

The river at the breach is wider and more filled with sand-bars than anywhere else we saw it. It was a misty, dusty morning the day we were there, and hence we could neither see across nor measure it, but an intelligent citizen told us that the old embankment had been carried away for a distance of 16,960 Chinese feet, or about three and a half miles, English. There is no doubt that the water could be easily concentrated into one channel, or that such concentration would so deepen it as to make good navigation for light-draught steamers of the class used on the Western rivers of the United States. Indeed, the Yellow River is very much such a stream as our upper Missouri, only not generally so wide, and perhaps not carrying so large a volume of water to the sea. Its water has about the same color, and it seems to hold for the same velocities about the same amount of sediment, but the sediment is more muddy or less sandy than that of the Missouri.

Our measurements showed the river to be only 983 feet at Shih-li-pu, 1,656 feet at Yu-shan, and 1,092 at Chi-ho, or counting the measurement at Kai-fung-fu, an average of say 1,400 feet, or 466 yards. It should also be mentioned that for six or eight miles from Lung-mun-Kou, and, indeed, nearly all the way back to Kai-fung-fu, or about thirty miles, there is a marked tendency, not observed by us anywhere else in the delta plains, for the dust or fine sand to gather into sand-dunes, those next to the city reaching almost to the top of the city walls, or from twenty-five to thirty feet high. There was no reason which we could discover why this tendency should show itself here rather than at other places, but the fact is as stated. It is also barely possible that the soil in this particular region is somewhat more arenaceous than elsewhere, and that the embankments built out of it are not quite so solid as they are on other sections of the river; but we could not discern that the soil actually used was in any way different from that used above or below, nor do I believe that such was the case.

After careful consideration of all the facts observed there and elsewhere, and especially the lack of intelligent and responsible supervision of the embankments, the neglect of all ordinary precautions for their maintenance, the reckless manner in which they are cut through by roads, the persistency with which they are cultivated, and with which every vestige of grass and herbage and osier-twig is raked and cut from their top and slopes, there is no need to look further for an explanation of the great breach of Lung-mun-Kou, or of those which have occurred at other points year after year, both before and since the river changed its course to the sea.

A great deal of excellent embankment has been built, and also much which is badly located and in bad condition; but with a watchful supervision and honest administration under one responsible head, together with the construction of such new embankment and such additions to the old, as any fairly intelligent man could point out as being necessary, it is quite certain that comparative immunity from devastating floods could be obtained at least till the whole question of regulation and control could be studied from data obtained by careful surveys and a general system devised in compliance with the requirements of the vast interests involved, and in harmony with the principles of modern engineering.

It may be safely said of a river embankment, as of a chain, that it is no stronger than its weakest link, and hence special and immediate attention should be directed to the discovery of all such points, and to the application of the necessary remedy. It is a truism which none will dispute, in this case at least, that an ounce of prevention is worth many pounds of cure. But whether this ounce of prevention will be applied, or the great river, which is so appropriately called "China's Sorrow," be allowed to break its embankments through criminal neglect or official incompetence and peculation, and sweep off hundreds and even thousands of lives hereafter, as it has done so frequently in the past, it is, of course, impossible to tell. There are some indications that the Board of Public Works and various officials of importance in Peking are giving the question careful consideration. Acting on a petition from a member of the Board of Sacrificial Worship, the Government has recently detailed a general, who has distinguished himself by compelling his idle soldiers to clean out the filthy moats of Peking, to make a complete inspection and report of the river and its embankments. It is understood that this officer protests most earnestly against the order, and declares, perhaps truthfully enough, that he knows absolutely nothing in regard to river-works or any other kind of engineering. The probabilities are that he is perfectly honest in this, though it is also possible that his merit may be even greater than his modesty. Be this as it may, this is a move in the right direction, since it sends one man to take a comprehensive view of the whole situation, the result of which must be in some degree better than what has gone before.*

---

* See note, p. 244.

THE YELLOW RIVER CAN BE BRIDGED.

At the time of my visit to the river, which was during the season of the lowest water, instead of finding it spread out over the plains, and having no well-defined bed between Lung-mun-Kou and Yu-shan, as was reported to be the case by Mr. Ney Elias, and as has been shown for many years on all the principal maps, I found that it had gradually made for itself a new channel with shores from five to ten feet in height, and that it was otherwise assuming the characteristics throughout that portion of its course which it has above and below.

I have not seen the river during flood, but can well imagine that it appears altogether different at such times, and yet I do not doubt that it can be bridged and crossed by a railroad at almost any point, or that the railroad can be maintained without any extraordinary trouble or expense. There are several places in the province of Shantung where natural abutments may be had, and which are otherwise favorable for bridging, and also for obtaining an abundant supply of stone for riprapping or paving the approaches, so as to protect them from the action of the water.

A great flood, devastating a wide extent of country near Kaifung fu, in the province of Honan, took place during the rainy season of 1887. It resulted in another change of the river from its old bed, but this time to the southward. The breach in its embankment was repaired after incredible effort and expense, and the river was thus compelled to resume its former bed to the sea.

CHAPTER XVII.

Visit to the city of Kai-fung-fu—The immense number of wheelbarrows on the road—The curiosity of the citizens—Difficulty of securing an inn—Inn-yard invaded by the mob—Visit of the officials from the yamen—Mob finally driven out—Respectable merchant compelled to crawl out under the gate—Call of two young officials from the governor's yamen—Tung-ming district—Approach to the Shantung hills—Cross the Grand Canal at Chi-ning-Chou—Visit to Chü-fu, the home and burial-place of Confucius—The "Ever-Sacred Duke" and his descendants—The Grand Pavilion and grounds—The avenue—The Confucian cemetery—The tomb of the sage—Burning of the Confucian residence—Singular superstition in regard to it—Visit to Taishan, the sacred mountain of China—Ascent of the mountain—Beautiful scenery — Temples and shrines — Return to the Grand Canal and journey to Chi-nan-fu—American Presbyterian mission—But few Christian converts—Superiority of technical instruction—Influence of war, commerce, and the missionaries—The city of Chi-nan-fu—The Yellow River again—Navigable from Chi-nan-fu to the sea—Chinese are ignorant of science in the work of controlling the floods—Journey back to Tientsin—Old embankments—The country—Mission at Pang-Chia-Chwang—Case of first convert—Chinese New-Year—Ancestral worship—New-Year's dinner—Lost in a dust-storm—Dreariness of the Great Plain—Not over-populated—Condition of the people—The Yellow River can be crossed by railroads—Return to Peking—Received by the Tsung-li Yamen.

OUR visit to Kai-fung-fu was the first one made by foreigners for many years; as a consequence, we attracted great attention—far too much, in fact, for our own comfort. The city covers a large area, is surrounded by the usual high brick wall surmounted by a crenelated parapet, and furnished with buttresses, turrets, ponderous gates, moats, and all the appliances of the Chinese middle ages. It also has a thirteen-storied pagoda, built of brown brick, and presents a grand but somewhat barbaric appearance from a distance. On a closer approach, it is seen to be, like other interior Chinese cities, dirty, dilapidated, and decaying, and yet it is, perhaps justly, regarded as a place of great importance. It contains a population estimated at five hundred thousand souls, and is the capital of the province of Honan, which is noted for the roughness of its people and its hostility to everything foreign.

As we approached it we were struck by the immense number of wheelbarrows we passed on the road carrying coal from the river. Each one of these curious vehicles was drawn by a donkey and pushed by a man, who held the handles and balanced the barrow and its load of three or four hundred pounds by means of a strap passing over his shoulders. We must have seen over a thousand, and all were screeching like a high-pressure steam gauge-cock. It is said that no barrow-man will have or use one of this particular class unless it screeches, and the more unearthly the sound the better it is liked, as it is supposed to be good fung-shuy.

We entered the main gate on the north side at noon of January 8, 1886, but were promptly stopped at the custom- or guard-house, just inside the wall. Our mandarin, however, dismounted, and, after making the proper explanation and exhibiting our Chinese passports, during which a crowd began to gather and gaze at us, we were permitted to pass on.

Our route at first lay through a rather thinly settled suburb, if any part of a city within the walls can be called a suburb, but soon led us into one of the principal streets, straight and broad, through which we made our way, somewhat after the manner of the grand entry of a circus into an American town. Our mandarin, wearing his official hat, and accompanied by the interpreter, rode ahead, followed by Mr. Nichols and myself abreast. Behind us came Hsieh-S'z (Aleck) and two mounted *mafoos*, and then the six carts well closed up; but no circus ever had a larger or more curious audience than we soon had. How the news spread it is impossible to say, but spread it certainly did, for in an incredibly short time we had hundreds of men and boys in our train, and the shop-fronts, sidewalks, and door-steps were crowded by people staring at us as we passed. In this manner we threaded our way for over a mile, when we came to an inn, which we turned into; but the landlord, seeing the crowd following us, and perhaps fearing annoyance, at once told our mandarin that his house was full, and he could not accommodate us. Solicitation was in vain, and there was nothing left for us but to go farther. At the next inn, which was only a short distance beyond, we received the same answer; but we resolved to stay in the court-yard till our people had found an inn for us, and this we did, the center of a gaping but respectful crowd. Men and boys closed in around our horses and gazed at our boots, trousers, coats, and caps, our gloves, whips, and saddles, one after the other, but all in silent admiration, which we submitted to with pretty nearly as much interest as our visitors.

In the course of ten minutes, our "Number One" *mafoo* returned with the gratifying intelligence that Li (the interpreter) had found an inn which was at our disposal. We therefore resumed our procession through the street, and after a short time entered a cross-street, where, within a square, we found our quarters; and, turning hastily into them, had the gates closed in the hope that we should thus get rid of the crowd. In this we were partly successful at first, but, as it was necessary to open the gates for the carts, the crowd, which had now gathered in strength, rushed in, and before the carts could be unloaded the outer court-yard was filled to overflowing. Li and the servants made an effort to expel the intruders, and succeeded in doing so and closing the gates; but shortly afterward the carters opened the gates again to turn the mules into the street for water and to roll, and as the mules returned the crowd came in with them. Seeing the futility of trying to keep them out of the outer court, the servants retreated to the door of the inner court, and made a determined effort to hold it. In this they were successful for a half-hour. Meanwhile we had sent Wang-Fuyeh with our passports to the governor-general's yamen, with instructions to say that, if agreeable to him, we should call and pay our respects, and, so far as might be necessary, explain the object of our traveling in that part of Honan.

We had already been informed by a young mandarin connected with the yamen, who had crossed the river with us, that the governor-general was only temporarily holding the office, that he was not well, and that a new governor-general was expected soon; hence we anticipated that it might not be convenient for him to receive us, and instructed Wang-Fuyeh to say, in that case, that we were examining the Yellow River and its embankments, and would like to have a safeguard through Honan into the province of Shantung, together with a detachment of policemen or soldiers to protect our inn and relieve us of the unwelcome attentions of the crowd of men and boys who were gathering there.

During the absence of our messenger they continued to collect in the outer court, which was now densely packed, and to press upon the inner gateway. Finally, through the persistency and activity of the boys in front, and of the pressure of the men behind, and perhaps also through the relaxed vigilance of our servants, they succeeded in unhinging the gate and gained admission into the inner court, around the farther end of which ourselves and servants had been assigned to rooms. The first thing which attracted their attention, and seemed in some degree to satisfy their curiosity, was "Ferguson," our big Chinese cook, with his charcoal-fire and his pots and pans, preparing dinner. This was evidently a rare treat to them, and enabled our men to hold them in check opposite the kitchen-door, about twelve feet from our own, for perhaps twenty minutes; but during this time the pressure from behind increased, and the inner court-yard, which was only thirty-six feet long by twelve wide, became crowded to suffocation. Li, Hsieh-S'z (Aleck), and the three "boys," aided at times by Ferguson, screamed themselves hoarse and exhausted all their strength in their efforts to expel the intruders without doing them bodily harm. Our visitors had but little to say, but with wide-open eyes and gaping mouths they pressed each other steadily forward, recoiling whenever the servants made a threatening rush at them, and then, as the servants retreated, edging a little farther into the open space just outside of our door, which was closed and covered by a cotton-cloth *portière*. At this juncture one of the servants, seeing that they would reach the door and break their way in unless they were turned away, came inside and said that the crowd, who had never seen a foreigner before, simply wanted to look at us, and that if we would go outside and show ourselves, perhaps they would scatter and go home; whereupon we walked out among them, and, after standing a minute or two to be gazed at, went forward, and by motions and gesticulations, aided by the servants, cleared the inner court-yard and half the outer one. There is no doubt that we should have got them entirely outside, but, just as Mr. Nichols had pressed his way through to the street, Wang-Fuyeh returned from the yamen, and we both went back with him to our room to hear his report. The servants, seeing that we had gone in, gave up the struggle, and the crowd surged in after them.

The governor-general received our messenger very politely, but said it would not be necessary for us to call, unless we had something important to communicate, and he would not call on us because he had sore eyes, but would send one of his mandarins to give us such assistance as we might require. He also said he would send a guard at once. Wang-Fuyeh had scarcely finished his report, when a mandarin, wearing the crystal button and peacock's feather, and clad in silk and furs, made his appearance, accompanied by his chairmen and retainers, bearing high umbrellas and spears, and wearing official hats, and all this state was to bring the governor-general's return cards. After leaving them he departed hastily, and the multitude lost no time in pressing into the inner court and up to our door again. We gathered our servants once more and drove the crowd back, nearly to the street, when we were again stopped in the full tide of victory by the coming of a still more stately mandarin, with banners and umbrellas, and a larger and more showy retinue. It would not comport with Chinese etiquette to be caught out of our quarters or engaged in such an occupation by a distinguished visitor, so we returned to our room and received him with all the state we could assume. On entering he bowed and saluted us politely, in the usual Chinese way, by clasping his hands and raising them to his face, and we returned his greeting in the same manner, after which we showed him to a seat, and a short conversation followed. He told us he had been sent by the governor-general, to ask us what assistance we required. Being a bright and intelligent man, he took in the situation at once, apologized for the roughness of the people of Kai-fung-fu, and said he would explain to them that we meant them no harm, but had come on a friendly mission. He intimated, perhaps by direction of the governor-general, that as soon as we were rested and had got such supplies as we desired, we had better resume our journey. Before taking his leave he directed one of his own attendants to remain with us, and said he would send a guard without delay to drive out our unwelcome visitors and keep order. The single man left with us did his level best to hold the inner gate against the increasing pressure from without, but he was overpowered and pressed back like the rest, and finally folded his hands in despair. Our servants still stood their ground as best they could, but were at last pressed back against our door. It was now nearly half-past five, and no policemen had yet made their appearance.

The most venturesome of the crowd had gained our windows, and begun poking holes through the paper panes for the purpose of looking in, and thereupon, having lost all patience, we sallied out for the last time, and went for the "heathen Chinee" in a way they were not slow to understand. Our servants and carters came to our assistance manfully, and even the solitary policeman plucked up courage to pitch in. By dint of pushing, yelling, and gesticulating, aided perhaps by fear on the part of the crowd, we gradually pushed those in front back upon those in the rear so vigorously that, in the course of ten minutes, we had got the court-yards nearly clear. In the midst of our most vigorous onset, we found ourselves suddenly re-enforced by a detachment of six or eight policemen, with the chief of police at their head, and this re-enforcement was less gentle in its treatment of the intruders than we had been; but it was quite noticeable that there was no clubbing, as would have been the case with an American mob that would not "move on." In a few minutes afterward we had the court-yard cleared and the gates barred ; but the crowd still remained in the street and made one or two efforts to regain its lost ground, but in vain. In this bloodless contest men lost their hats and shoes, and the boys were knocked over and trampled upon. Several of them cried most lustily, and there was a babel of yelling and shouting, as is generally the case with a Chinese crowd, but, so far as we could make out, nobody was angry, or inspired by any other motive than that of gratifying an insatiable and ravenous curiosity.

There seemed to be all sorts and conditions of men in the crowd. Many of them were well-dressed and intelligent in appearance, and all appeared to be good-natured and amiable. The last out was evidently a respectable merchant or shopkeeper, wearing his best hat and new silk gown ; but when he got to the gate it was closed and barred, so the chief of police, instead of opening it, made him get down into the dust and crawl under it, much to his disgust, but to the great delight of the crowd outside.

It was now about six o'clock, and quiet and order reigned at last in our court-yard. The chief of police and his men fraternized at once with our attendants, and assured us we should have no more unbidden visitors. Later in the evening, after we had received cards and a friendly message from the local prefect or magistrate, and all the members of our guard had duly inspected us and our belongings while at dinner, two sub-officials were brought in, bearing with them the paper-seals, half as big as an ordinary newspaper, which they said they were going to paste on our outer gates, as a sure protection from all further annoyance. These two young men were very nicely dressed, and seemed to be quite civil and obliging, but, like the rest, they lingered as long as possible, evidently for the purpose of gratifying their own curiosity. We finally got rid of them by giving them all the lumps of cut-loaf sugar we had left on our dinner-table. We had a quiet night, but not caring to repeat the experiences we had gone through, and fearing that the indiscretion of a servant might turn the current of curiosity into one of anger, and thus lead to a real mob, we left at daylight the next morning, with the chief of police as our guide, before the crowd had time to gather again. It would have been impossible for us to go in or out of our inn, or for shopkeepers and curio-dealers to bring their wares to us ; and as we had received all the help, and got all the information we wanted from the yamen, we thought it best to resume our journey.

From Kai-fung-fu we traveled eastward to Lung-mun-Kou, where the Yellow River changed its course in 1853–'54, and, after inspecting that place and making such measurements and observations as the means at our disposal would permit, we turned northeastward along the general course of the river to Tung-ming, in the lower part of the province of Chihli, where a disastrous breach occurred in the embankment last summer.

We had no adventures on the way worthy of record, unless we except the fact that I came near being swallowed up in the quicksand, or rather the "quick mud" (for there is no sand in this part of the Yellow River), as we were leveling up from the water's edge to the bottom of the old bed of the river. I broke through the frozen crust of an exceedingly soft place and went down "by the run," but, having had some experience in that sort of thing before, struggled on to hard ground without assistance, and indeed without my danger having been discovered until it was all over.

The breach at Tung-ming had been thoroughly repaired by the construction of a new and very strong embankment, revetted with bundles of millet-stalks laid butt-ends outward, and bound into the earth by ropes fastened to cross-timbers resting against the face of the revetment. This region was further protected by the construction of a new embankment a mile or so from the river. It was noticeable not only because it was of full section and good alignment, but particularly because it was finished with the only properly planned road-crossing we saw in all our travels. The country in this region was said to have been infested by robbers, and one of our attendants told us that three had been captured, at or near Tung-ming-Chi, and executed, and that he had seen the head of one of them in a cage, hanging on a tree, outside the town. We saw nothing of the kind, and, in fact, nothing which indicated the presence of robbers, except two men, one mounted and the other on foot, both armed, and running rapidly as far as we could see them. Our mandarin assured us that they were highwaymen; and, since returning to Tientsin, we have been informed that the region in question (Tsou-Chou) is one of the most lawless in China, and that soldiers are quartered at various points in it for the purpose of suppressing the robbers and maintaining order.

Turning almost directly east toward the Grand Canal, we found both roads and inns fairly good; but the country presented the same unbroken dead level, the same mud-built villages, the same endless succession of plowed and fallow fields, broken here and there by scattered graves or by a family burying-ground, surrounded by a grove of yew or cypress trees, till we caught sight of the higher peaks of the western hills of Shantung looming up on the horizon like an island seen from the deck of a ship.

Our course toward them resembled the track of a ship beating against a head-wind; and what made the similitude still greater was that new islands were seen far away to the south, and afterward the faint outline of a distant coast rising on the horizon showed itself as we continued our western course. The first hill, or island—for it was as much an island as if it had been surrounded by water instead of by plain—which we came to was a bald, barren mass of stratified limestone two or three hundred feet high, and covered on the western side by a village built of stone, surrounded by a weather-beaten stone wall, with a crenelated parapet on top.

The wall ran straight up the hill-side and along its summit, and there was something about both wall and village which clearly betokened that some time in the lapse of ages past they had seen better days. The scene was not only picturesque, but in such noticeable contrast with the dead level of the plains we had been traveling over for so long, that we unpacked the camera and took two photographs of it. Farther on, the "coast-line" receded before us, and, sweeping around to the southward and westward, to another hill abreast of the first one, also surmounted by a village and castellated ruins, appeared to inclose a beautiful landlocked bay.

We continued our march along the foot of the hills to our left, skirting the shore, as it were, and admiring the beautiful scene in the bright sunlight, but in two or three hours the distant coast-line had resolved itself into a series of detached hills, rising sharply up from the level of the plain. Threading our way through them, we reached the Grand Canal beyond them at about two o'clock, and by four had reached Chi-ning-Chou, a city of one hundred and fifty thousand inhabitants. Like all the others, it is surrounded by a brick wall of great height and thickness, surmounted by a crenelated parapet, and furnished with sally-ports, gates, buttresses, and turrets, but all fast going to decay.

A withering blight seems to have stricken them as

THE HOME OF CONFUCIUS.

well as the business of the city they inclose. This city is situated on the Grand Canal, and was doubtless once the seat of a great commerce, which has decayed as the canal has become more and more difficult to navigate. There is an imperial telegraph-station here, the second on the line south of Tientsin, and about two hundred and forty miles from the first one. Halting here over night, and sending telegrams to Tientsin and Shanghai to apprise our friends of our safety, and to get the news, we pushed on the next day to Yen-Chou, and the day after to Chü-fu, the home of the Kung family, the descendants of Confucius, the "immortal sage and philosopher" of China. On our arrival we selected the best inn we could find, and made preparations to remain several days.

The city of Kü-fu is the seat of a district magistracy, or *hsien*, and is situated near the eastern edge of the Great Plain, in sight of the hills. Like every other Chinese town of its class, it is surrounded by a high brick wall, furnished with a crenelated parapet, buttresses, turrets, moats, and gates, which are closed every night. It contains within the walls the ducal residence and the pavilions, temples, and tablets sanctified in every Chinaman's eyes, as far as anything can be sanctified, by their association with the name and worship of Confucius, their great lawgiver and teacher.

I sent Wang-Fuyeh immediately after our arrival to the magistrate's yamen with our cards, and the information that we should call to pay our respects at such hour as would best suit his convenience. He received our messenger with great politeness, and explained that he was just starting into the country to be gone till night, but would on his return communicate further with us.

Early in the evening he sent his cards to us, with the information that he would be glad to receive us at any hour the next day which would best suit our convenience, and would arrange for us to see the Confucian temples, and also, if possible, for an interview with the young Kung, the "Ever-Sacred Duke" of the Chinese, and the seventy-sixth direct lineal male descendant of the sage. This, of course, gives him an authentic genealogy reaching further back into the past than any man living, and makes him a great curiosity on that account, if nothing more. It will be remembered that Confucius was born 551 years before Christ. Having named ten o'clock for our call upon the magistrate, he sent a mounted escort to conduct us through the streets to the yamen, so that we got there at the appointed time without delay or annoyance, and were received at once with every mark of respect and friendly consideration. We found the prefect, or magistrate, a special friend of the Viceroy Li, to be a mandarin of the crystal button, about fifty years of age. He was clad in black silk and furs, and was surrounded by his official servants. He greeted us cordially, after the usual Chinese form, and, after asking our ages and other questions, in accordance with the rules of Chinese etiquette, he sent our cards to the "Ever-Sacred Duke," with the request that he would grant us an audience.

While the messenger was gone, the magistrate informed us that the present Duke was a boy only fourteen years old, engaged in his studies under the tutorship and direction of his uncle, and would therefore probably decline to grant us an audience. During the absence of the messenger, who was gone about an hour, we conversed with the magistrate in regard to the condition of the canal and of the country in that part of the province. We were somewhat surprised to learn that no silk is grown, and no manufacturing of any kind carried on nearer than Chi-nan-fu. The people devote themselves exclusively to agriculture, the principal articles of which are wheat and cotton.

As the magistrate had intimated, the guardian of the

young Duke sent word that we could not be received by his ward; but that the temples and grounds would be opened for our visit, and that a member of the family would receive and conduct us through them. We accordingly took leave of the magistrate, and, escorted by two of his subordinate officers and a squad of mounted and dismounted soldiers, we rode to the northwest quarter of the city, which is separated from the rest of the city by a high brick wall, inclosing the Confucian temples, which occupy the site of the sage's home, academy, well, shade-trees, and favorite walks. We entered the grounds through a high gateway, and walked down an avenue of fine old cypress, fir, and yew trees to the official reception-room, into which a servant showed us, and, after serving tea, left us to await the coming of the Duke's representative. While we were waiting, a crowd of men and boys, who had entered the grounds with us, pushed up to the door and windows, eager to see the foreigners. They were quiet and respectful; but, as they could not all look through the door at one time, some of them punched holes through the paper window-panes, without reference to the fact that they were the private property of the "Ever-Sacred Duke." One big boy took particular delight, as is the custom the world over, in twigging the ears and queue of a smaller boy in front, and in otherwise annoying him. The little fellow seemed to take it all as a matter of course, and never once lost his temper, though his patience was sorely tried.

After half or three quarters of an hour, we were informed that the mandarin had come, and would receive us at the entrance to the outer pavilion of the main temple, to which place we were led by the official servants of the place, and followed by our own attendants. Our path was through a back and crooked path between houses and walls for three or four hundred feet; but it brought us out in front of a large pavilion, under which we were received by a mandarin of great dignity, elegantly dressed, and wearing on his official hat a blue or amethyst button and peacock's feather. We at first supposed him to be the uncle and guardian of the young Duke, but afterward learned that he was a more distant relative, having charge of the temple, cemetery, and grounds. He received us with urbanity and dignity, saluting us in the usual Chinese fashion, and showing us to seats near a table on which tea was served at once. After a short conversation, during which he told us we were at liberty to take photographs of whatever we pleased, he escorted us through the grounds to the Grand Pavilion, in which is an effigy of Confucius seated on a throne, raised four or five feet above the floor, and draped with beautifully embroidered lambrequins and curtains of yellow satin. A tablet surmounts the throne inscribed with Chinese characters, which are translated, "The most prescient sage, Confucius, his spirit's resting-place." In front of the throne are two tables, on which are placed several copper vases of elegant design, enameled with blue and green figures on a yellow ground, and also several bronze tripods, urns, and sacrificial vases, said to be very old, some of them, it is alleged, dating from eleven hundred to twenty-three hundred years before Christ; but their appearance does not indicate any such antiquity.

The hall contains statues of the son and grandson of Confucius, besides those of Mencius, with his principal disciples, and of twelve other worthies distinguished in Chinese story. They are arranged around the wall and across the ends of the grand hall, and look much brighter and fresher than the effigies we had seen in other temples. The hall is a hundred and sixty feet long, eighty-eight feet wide, and seventy-eight feet high, and is paneled in black marble, and brilliantly painted in bright colors and gilding, freshly laid on.

The roof is supported by stately wooden columns and ceiled with beautiful carved wood, in the center of which is a dragon holding in its mouth a gray ball some two or two and a half inches in diameter, said to represent the exact size and color of a veritable pearl presented to the temple by one of the emperors several hundred years ago.

The whole place is much cleaner and in better repair than any other temple we have seen in China; but withal it presents no striking indications that the worship of Confucius is a living cult. There is no doubt that his teachings have had a powerful influence over the Government of China, and in developing the civilization of the Chinese people, as exemplified by the educated class; but it may well be doubted if the plain people know or care much about the "most prescient sage" or his philosophical teaching.

The pavilion inclosing the grand hall has an exterior appearance quite like that of the great pavilion at the tomb of Yung-loh. It is surrounded by a veranda twelve or fifteen feet wide, supported by fifty-four monolithic pillars (the only ones I saw in China) twenty-five feet high and three feet in diameter, those in front being elaborately decorated with the imperial dragon, deeply carved into their surface, and extending from top to bottom.

A large part of the court in front is occupied by a raised platform of stone, surrounded by a marble balustrade. The roof is covered with green and yellow tiles, and the exterior of the building, the most of which is wood, is also elaborately painted and carved after the usual Chinese style. The court is flanked on the right and left by long, low pavilions divided off into stalls or shrines, each containing a tablet sacred to the memory and virtues of Confucius or of some distinguished disciple. These shrines and tablets were erected by emperors in times gone by, and indicate that reverence for the sage was formerly a more active sentiment than it is at present.

We took several photographs of the front of the main pavilion, but, owing to the darkness within, could not get a view of the interior.

The well of Confucius, walled up with rather fresh-looking brick, and curbed with an annular stone of anything but a venerable appearance, was pointed out to us. A decaying tree supported by props was shown us in another court, and is said to mark the exact place once occupied by the favorite shade-tree of the sage; and in still another court a wedge-shaped piece of brown, dingy-looking wood at the root of a growing tree was shown as the stump of a cypress, or what was left of it, which was flourishing at the time the sage was alive. We took separate photographs of the well and of the old tree, with a boy belonging to the Confucian family sitting under and against it holding a book in his hand.

The entire grounds are thickly planted with cypresses and firs, and covered with pavilions and tablets so close together that it is impossible to get a single view of them. These grounds are adjacent to those of the present Duke, but separated from them by a high brick wall.

The last pavilions we entered, our amiable conductor informed us, occupied the exact site of the house in which Confucius had his study and taught his disciples; and, after showing us through the lower story, he led us up two flights of very steep stairs to the loft, where, according to another guide, the school was actually held. Inasmuch as the building is of wood, and does not differ architecturally from other modern Chinese buildings, we concluded that we were not obliged to believe the last guide, though he was evidently honest in what he told us.

All of the buildings seem to have been recently painted,

and are, therefore, brighter looking than any other temples we have seen; but the dust and the flocks of birds which roost in and about them, aided by the habitual neglect of the Chinese, will soon deprive them of their brightness.

After again drinking tea with the amiable mandarin who showed us about, we took leave of him, he having voluntarily offered to call for us in his cart at half-past eight the next morning and go with us to the cemetery, which lies about a mile and a half outside and north of the city wall. During the afternoon the prefect returned our call in state, and showed us every polite attention. He sent us several pounds of excellent tea, and a copy of the charcoal rubbings taken from some of the most noted tablets; and we reciprocated his civility by sending him a bottle of Curaçoa and a box of cut-loaf sugar, together with a small American gold coin for the Tai-tai, his wife.

Having spent a comfortable night in a very fair inn, we were up betimes and just ready to start for the cemetery, when a messenger arrived from the magistrate with the information that the Confucian mandarin could not join us, as the house of the young Duke had caught fire, and was then burning. Sending our cards with our regrets, and offering our help if we could be of any service whatever, we rode at once to the cemetery, which is connected with the city by an avenue of noble but sadly neglected yew and cypress trees. Standing on the roadside, with no other trees near them, the northern winds have full sweep at them, and have wrenched and torn them till not one is left with its proper natural shape. Curiously enough, too, the broken trunks and limbs have not been cut off in any instance, but are left standing, to decay and disfigure the trees which might otherwise appear to great advantage. Unless they are looked after better than they have been so far, it will be but a few years till the avenue falls into complete ruin.

On the way we passed under or through a beautiful marble *pailow* spanning the road, and a short distance beyond entered the outer gate, which is connected with the inner gate of the cemetery by a continuation of the avenue, and with a high brick wall on either side. The gates are covered by the usual pavilions, and the cemetery itself is inclosed by a brick wall surmounting an earthen embankment. The area inclosed is from forty to fifty acres, thickly planted with Chinese forest-trees, beneath which "heaves the turf in many a moldering heap." This cemetery is strictly reserved for the family, and contains the graves of unnumbered descendants of the Confucian clan.

The grave of Confucius is within a separate inclosure, the entrance to which is covered by a large pavilion of the usual type, where the descendants of the sage come twice a year to offer sacrifices and worship him. A paved, sunken road, which runs between low retaining-walls on each side, leads to the tomb, which is a simple mound of earth about twenty feet high, overgrown by bushes and forest-trees, including an oak, from which we obtained a pint of acorns for propagation in America. A stone tablet, nearly as high as the mound, a stone table, and an urn or incense-burner stand in front of it. It is flanked by the burial-mounds of the mother, son, and grandson of Confucius, and the whole inclosure is heaped into mounds covering the remains of the successive heads and dignitaries of the family.

West of the sage's tomb is a small pavilion erected to the memory of Tze-Kung, a favorite disciple, on the spot where he is said to have mourned for six years, watching the tomb of his dearly beloved master.

There is no special beauty in the landscape, for, although covered with trees, it is left in an entirely uncultivated state; the ground looks broken, but this arises from the great number of mounds rather than from any natural undulations. There is a large ditch running through the southern part of the inclosure, which is generally dry, but carries water in the rainy season. It is spanned by a marble bridge of rather picturesque design.

We spent the whole morning in the grounds taking photographs of the tomb, pavilion, and the carved stone figures on either side of the avenue in front of it. These figures are preceded by a pair of stone pillars of octagonal section, after which come a pair of leopards, next a pair of fabulous animals, and, lastly, two heroic statues, supposed to represent the ministers of state, who attend upon the distinguished dead. On our way out, we took photographs of the bridge and of the *pailow* beyond the inclosure.

During our visit to the tomb, as well as to the temple, we were deeply impressed by the reverence with which Wang-Fuyeh worshiped before the various tablets of Confucius and his most famous disciples. As he came to each and read the inscription, he prostrated himself on hands and knees, face to the floor, and, murmuring a prayer, knocked his forehead against the ground with a reverent and serious air, showing that he was sincere in what he was doing.

On our return to the inn we sent him to inquire what damage had been done by the fire in the Duke's compound, and on Wang's return he informed us that it had totally destroyed the four principal buildings, together with all their contents, including family relics of great value. He also said that there was great excitement among the citizens about it, owing to the fact that the fire had started in the house occupied by the family of the young Duke's uncle, his mother's brother. It seems that, before his father died, he directed his wife and son never to permit any other persons except the family servants to live within the compound, for the reason that it would increase the risk of burning up the buildings and destroying the family relics and possessions. In spite of this request, and for reasons not explained, the widow invited her brother and family to occupy one of the houses, which he did at once. This was followed by signs and portents, and especially by the crowing of the Confucian cocks and hens after nightfall, which was looked upon as the sure precursor of some impending calamity.

After the fire had completed its work of destruction, and it had become known that the uncle's wife had gone crazy from the excitement and had jumped or fallen into the well, from which she was rescued with great difficulty, all these omens were recalled, and were thought to be proof positive that the spirit of the late Duke had set fire to the house for the purpose of punishing his wife and son for their disobedience. It was, perhaps, quite fortunate for us that the towns-people took this view of the matter, for they might just as readily have attributed the fire to the Duke's displeasure at the visitation of the temple and grave of Confucius by the foreigners.

During our stay, however, in the city, we received no incivility except that of being stared at. Indeed, the people seemed quite civil, but there was nothing in their manners, appearance, houses, or surroundings, different from those of other Chinamen, notwithstanding the fact that many, perhaps the most of them, were descendants of the great sage.

Even the servants about the reception-room, temple, and cemetery were exactly like those we had seen elsewhere. They were evidently a chance lot gathered up for the occasion, and therefore a fair sample of the whole. Their regular occupations were doubtless toiling in the fields or at the wheelbarrow, for the scanty living which constitutes the average Chinaman's inevitable portion.

Having seen all the curiosities and points of interest in and about Kü-fu, we left the same afternoon for Taian-fu about sixty miles to the northward, for the purpose of visiting the sacred mountain of China. Our route at first lay through the plains, but always in sight of the hills, which on the right were continuous, but on the left stood out in isolated knobs or peaks.

After crossing the Ta-Wen-ho, a broad, clear, swift-flowing stream, and the only one of the kind we had seen since leaving Tientsin, our road led us for about ten miles through a depression in an outlying limestone ridge, overlaid by beds of loëss, a yellow, clay-like earth, peculiar to the hill-regions of China, and, as before explained, supposed by Baron Richthofen to be a sub-aërial deposit composed of dust from the arid regions of Central Asia.

We made this part of the ride after night, and had a rough time of it. Our ponies were tired, and, being far from sure-footed, gave us several falls, but fortunately in soft places, so that no bones were endangered.

Reaching the city at about eight o'clock, we had some difficulty in finding a suitable inn, but, after looking at several, we settled down at the "Lien-Sheng-tien," which we found to be the best one we had seen in all China. It has both an outer and inner court-yard, and is unusually clean; its rooms are paved and neatly papered, and the windows have glass and curtains in them. We soon had a good fire of charcoal, and a lot of very nice boiled chestnuts, which we warmed up on the edge of the charcoal-pan, and found a most excellent substitute for supper, which we knew would come late if at all, as our carts were several hours behind, and had a bad road for night-driving before them. They, however, came at about ten o'clock. Supper and bed soon followed, and made us entirely comfortable.

Having completed all our arrangements, we made an early start the next morning (January 22d), to climb the sacred mountain. Each member of our party was provided with a chair lashed firmly to a hand-barrow, which was borne by two coolies, who travel abreast over all the steep places, both going up and coming down. As the chair faces the handle of the barrow, the passenger of course makes the trip sidewise, and this is by no means comfortable or reassuring at the start, especially if the first experience is in coming down, as it was with me. The chairmen carry most of the weight by means of straps attached to the handles of the barrow and passing over their shoulders, and, as they are very sure-footed and agile, after one has become used to the motion it is pleasant and exhilarating.

The mountain is known as "Taishan," or "Great Mount," and is the highest peak of a range trending generally east and west through the Shantug promontory. It rises sharply from the plain or broad valley, at the edge of which stands the city of Taian-fu, and is celebrated for its historical and religious associations. It is mentioned in the classics as a sanctified spot over 2,200 years B. C. It is visited by thousands of devotees of all ages and both sexes yearly, but generally of the literary or official class, and is a truly national place of worship, on the top or sides of which every sect has its temples.

The road leads up a gorge with but few windings or turnings, and is well paved with blocks of undressed granite and porphyry. It is broken into alternate reaches of gently ascending ramps and flights of granite steps, and is furnished with a stone parapet, eighteen or twenty inches high on the outside, and where required on both sides.

An avenue of beautiful fir, cypress, and yew trees shades the path for the greater distance, and after that a few scattering pines are seen still higher up the mountain-side. None of these trees are very old, however, and even the paved roads and temples are of comparatively modern construction.

At first the flights of steps are short, and the ramps long, but, as the path ascends, the ramps become shorter and the flights of steps higher and higher, till they are almost continuous. The rise is nearly as great as the tread, and hence the steps are unusually steep and hard to climb. The road, which is from twelve to fifteen feet wide, and crosses from one side of the gorge to the other several times, is exceedingly picturesque. It is carried along the face of crags, which are frequently of great height and beauty, and are everywhere indelibly marked with pious or reverential inscriptions in Chinese characters. Temples, shrines, and *pailows* occur at frequent intervals, and the view of the plain below is not only extensive and beautiful, but can be caught from almost every point, so that the ascending pilgrim or devotee, however great may be his fatigue, or however frequently he may be compelled to halt for breath, can always refresh himself with the contemplation of scenery, which of itself amply repays him for his toil.

The distance from the city to the top of the gorge and the end of the steps is about three miles, possibly four, and took me four hours to climb it. There is at this spot a pavilion, standing on a brick foundation, through which the path runs by an archway, leading into the court of a temple, the elevation of which was found to be 4,600 feet above sea-level, by one of Queen's best aneroid barometers.

From the temple to the summit of the mountain there

is a road winding to the right, along the edge of a cliff, and this road is also lined with shrines and temples, built into the face of the mountain.

The topmost peak is called Yu-wang-shang-to, and is crowned by a small stone pavilion and tablet, said to have been erected by Kien-lung, from which the whole horizon can be swept, by simply turning on one's own ground. The view is remarkable for its breadth and beauty, taking in, as it does, mountain-tops, valleys, plains, and rivers, spread out below in almost endless succession and variety. The height of this peak was found to be 5,100 feet.

A short distance away is another eminence, rising from the same mountain-mass, but not so high by about twenty feet. It is crowned by a large temple, partly in ruins, which covers it entirely, and is picturesque in the extreme.

We spent three hours examining the temples and taking photographs of the most beautiful views, including one of a remarkable inscription cut on the face of the rocks, and another of Wang-Fuyeh-Li, and one of our servants worshiping at the Lao-mu Miao, or the temple of the "Holy Mother." This temple is mostly visited by women, who go there to pray that children may be granted to them. It contains two magnificent bronze tablets, fourteen feet high, also erected by Kien-lung.

It is certain that emperors, governors, and high officials of every class, including Confucius himself, have visited this mountain from time immemorial, for the purpose of worshiping "the High God of Heaven and Earth"; but, withal, the stones of the pathway leading to it do not indicate, by their smoothness, the passage of untold millions of feet over them. It is probable, rather, that while it is the temple of all the gods, as well as of the highest, it is visited more by the rich and educated than by the masses of the Chinese people.

The devotions of our attendants were quite interesting, although not materially different from the ceremonies they went through in worshiping the river-god near Kai-fung-fu. It consisted of burning incense, and gold and silver paper-money, in presence of the image of the god, and of prostrating themselves and knocking their heads against the floor, while the *bonze*, or priest, clad in somber-colored robes, stood by and called the attention of the divinity to the presence of the worshipers by striking a large and sonorous bell with a wooden mallet.

Our descent from the mountain was made in two hours and a quarter, all of us riding down in the chairs, not only because it was much easier than walking, but more rapid.

The next morning, after visiting a celebrated temple in the north part of the city, and finding it and its grounds somewhat more extensive than temples and grounds commonly are, but quite as dirty and decaying as the worst of them, we started on our journey back to the Grand Canal by the valley of the Ta-Wen-ho to Tung-ping. Thence our route lay through An Shan and Tung Ur, skirting the canal to Shih-li-pu and the Yellow River to Chi-nan-fu. We passed through several important cities, situated on the loëss terraces, between the river and foot-hills. At one of these, called Ping Yin, we were called upon by two missionaries of the Church of England, working quietly and unobtrusively, and, it is to be feared, without any very encouraging results, among the common people of that remote region. They were, however, deeply in earnest, and seemed hopeful and courageous, although they candidly admitted that so far as they knew they had not yet made a single convert.

At Chi-nan-fu we found seven American Presbyterian missionaries—Mr. Reid, Mr. and Mrs. Burgen, Mr. and Mrs. Murray, Dr. and Mrs. Coltman, and Mr. Chalfant—

all settled and hard at work. These worthy people are encouraged by several hopeful signs that they will ultimately "get the thin edge of the wedge in," and make their mission one of great usefulness to the Chinese people. Mr. Reid and Mr. Burgen wear the Chinese dress, and, as they are good Chinese scholars besides, they are doing most excellent work. Mrs. Burgen has, however, made the greatest progress, inasmuch as she has made the acquaintance and exchanged social civilities with a number of educated Chinese ladies, who have become her fast friends, and through whom her influence is rapidly spreading. It can not yet be said that they have made many converts, but the leaven is working, and it seems certain that, if these missions are supported and re-enforced as they deserve to be, they may materially assist in opening China to a realization of the fact that Christian civilization is much ahead of their own.

If some benevolent American would send Mr. Reid an assortment of our best mechanical devices, including a sewing-machine, a band-saw, an electrical plant for light and telpherage, a small steam-engine, a turning-lathe for wood, one for iron, a magic lantern, and a competent young graduate of the Stevens Institute, or the Boston School of Technology, who could lecture upon these machines, and explain the principles of modern science as applied to the mechanic arts, and could at the same time turn his hand to surveying, mineralogy, geology, and botany, it is believed that it would prove an invaluable aid to the cause of modern progress in this far-away land.

There are only three influences which, so far as I can see, can be successfully exerted upon the Chinese people to awaken them to their real condition as compared with the people of other countries: first, war and diplomacy, which work spasmodically, but very effectively at times;

THE WORK OF THE MISSIONARIES. 283

secondly, commerce, which has done and is doing much along the sea-coast; and, thirdly, the missionaries, who push out into the interior armed with dogmatic religion and good works, are slowly making their way, though not nearly so much by the former as the latter. They are truly the advance guard of civilization; and, while they carry its highest and most abstract principles to those who are but little fitted by habit or education to receive or understand them, they are surely and steadily gaining the confidence and regard of those among whom they are laboring. The more practical and the less abstract their work becomes, the more rapidly will good results flow from it.

The city of Chi-nan-fu is beautifully situated on the edge of the plains, along the foot of the hills, and is abundantly supplied with pure water by a series of remarkable hot and cold springs which well up from the ground within the city walls, and, after supplying the people fully, fill the moats, and form a large creek, which empties into the Yellow River only a few miles away. The population of the city is estimated at four hundred thousand souls, but what it really is no one knows.

From here we turned northward, and recrossed the river at Chi-ho, where there was once a stone bridge across the Ta-ching-ho. When the Yellow River took possession of this channel to the sea, it destroyed this bridge by cutting a new channel around its southern end. The ruins remained for many years, but they are now entirely obliterated, and there is nothing left to mark their site except the half-buried *pailow*, which used to span the entrance to the bridge.

The river at the time we crossed it was frozen hard both above and below the ferry, but as no one seemed to be crossing on the ice, and as the ferry had been kept open, we embarked in two good-sized junks, and were rowed slowly across without accident or delay. Our servants, however, did not consider it necessary to propitiate the river-god as they had in crossing at Kai-fung-fu.

The elevation of the fore-shores above the surface of the water was nine and a half feet, and the top of the first embankment nineteen feet. The second embankment, about two miles farther back, seemed to be much stronger, and had not been recently broken, so far as we could learn. The site of Chi-ho, and the country between the two embankments, had been overflowed to the depth of four feet the year before, and the country on both sides of the river lower down had suffered greatly from the same cause.

The river at this place was from a thousand to twelve hundred and fifty feet wide, and, according to the testimony of the junkmen, had a navigable depth at that time of at least twelve feet to the bar outside its mouth. It could be readily navigated by good-sized steamboats, especially by such as are used on our Western rivers, certainly as far as Yüshan, and, with slight improvements for concentrating the channel, perhaps to the great bend in Southwestern Shansi ; but, up to this time, much to the detriment of the people, it has been kept exclusively for the junks, and steamboats are not permitted to enter or ply upon it. There is no large city nearer its mouth than Chi-nan-fu, the capital of Shantung, and the country between that place and the sea is not only thinly settled, but quite desolate.

It is apparent that the whole work of controlling and regulating the river is limited to the building of embankments, and the opening of side-channels to facilitate the discharge of flood-water. Those having the subject in hand seem to have no idea of the advantage to be gained by meteorological observations and reports from the country drained by the river, and make no adequate study of the downfall of rain, the volume and rapidity of discharge,

NEGLECT OF THE EMBANKMENTS. 285

the coming of floods, the cross-section and slope of the water-surface, or even of the proper location, construction, and care of the embankments. Nothing has yet been done to remove obstructions, or to increase the average capacity of the natural channel. Indeed, the whole Chinese system of river-engineering is exceedingly crude. There is no element of science in it, and, while much of their embankment is excellent, it is on the whole so neglected that nothing else except failure is possible.

In the journey back to Tientsin, which required six and a half days, the distance being not far from two hundred and forty miles, we crossed a number of depressions corresponding to lines on the maps representing rivers, but the most of which were dry, and evidently are not running streams except during the rainy season. About fifty miles north of Chi-ho we crossed the Lao-Hwang-ho, which had been occupied by the Yellow River about nine hundred years ago. It is one thousand feet wide by measurement, and contains some water, which has a perceptible current. It doubtless connects with and carries off water from the Yellow River during freshets, but its most remarkable feature is that the old embankments, built to confine the water when it was occupied by the Yellow River itself, are situated immediately on its shores, and are twenty-two feet high, or about double the height of the embankments built nowadays. They are from fifty to sixty feet wide on top, and three hundred and ninety feet at the base. Another thing worthy of observation is that this river-bed, so far as I could discover, is not silted up at all. This is conclusively shown by the fact that the surface of the water in it was at the time we crossed it about ten feet below the general surface of the country, as measured by the hand-level. At the time these embankments were built, which may have been a thousand or even fifteen hundred years ago, it was evidently the practice to locate them close to the river-front, to give them much greater height and thickness, and possibly to watch them much more carefully than is done nowadays.

It has been recently proposed to cut a canal into this old river-bed and build a series of sluices across it, so that the Yellow River can be relieved at will, by turning its surplus water into it; and the Board of Works has, according to the "Peking Gazette," approved the project.

The country from a few miles north of the Yellow River to the neighborhood of Ter-chou, on the Grand Canal, is apparently drier, better drained, and better cultivated than it is farther west, closer to the line of the canal; and this is as it should be. It is farther away from both the river and the canal, and, even if a breach occur in the embankment of either, the flood-water must spread out and get shallower as it approaches the region in question, although its real elevation above sea-level may be no greater than that of the country at the river-bank. The villages in this region are also more flourishing in appearance than they are along the canal, but they are all built of sun-dried bricks, and are otherwise like innumerable other villages in the Great Plain. It was in this portion of my travels that I saw men wheeling coal in a barrow two hundred miles from the mines! They were aided by donkeys and small sails, but the toil seemed to be of killing severity.

There is a flourishing American mission in this region, at a town called Pang-Chia-Chwang. It has an excellent hospital and school attached, and has gained much favor with the simple-minded natives by the success and kindliness of its medical and surgical ministrations, which are, of course, free to all comers.

I was naturally curious to know how a mission came to be located at such an insignificant country village, far off the highways, and with nothing particular to distinguish it from a thousand other villages just like it ; and the following is the explanation : It seems that one of the earlier missionaries made a convert among the common people of this region, who by his zeal and intelligence induced the missionary to locate in his native village, where he was head-man. Other missionaries came, then the school, and then the hospital followed. The first convert grew in a worldly way with the mission, if not in grace, and in the course of time came to look upon it as his personal appanage. He became a sort of village boss, a great man among his neighbors, and brought many of them into the fold ; but, having been the first convert, he also claimed to be first in all contracts and business for the mission, and like nearly everybody else, Christian as well as heathen, when he found he had a good thing he grew grasping and avaricious, and it is said "squeezed" the missionaries harder than they thought proper or honest. A contract for hauling brick and sand was given out, and perhaps for other work also, but, instead of the first convert's getting it, it was given to another, who had made a lower bid for it. The first convert claimed it as his "*pidgin*" (business) by right, without regard to price, and his neighbors, according to their light, sided with him and against the new man. The missionaries stood firm, however. The villagers then boycotted them and their new man, whereupon they appealed to the district magistrate, and had the first convert arrested and thrown into prison. This made matters worse ; the common people could not understand why the first convert should not have the business, which, according to all Chinese custom and precedent, was his. They looked upon his arrest as arbitrary and unjustifiable, and they stood by him to a man. The missionaries then appealed to the American consul at Tientsin ; he appealed to the Viceroy Li, and the latter sustained the missionaries. But that did not end the trouble. The first convert was released, or permitted to go home on a holiday. That night the missionary stable was burned, and, although there was no proof, suspicion fell upon him, and he was again arrested. Excitement grew apace, and, when I last heard of the case, the missionaries were calling loudly for the deportation of the first convert as the only way of restoring quiet. Both parties had become uncharitable and unreasonable. The missionaries seem to have carried the matter too far, and would have done better not to stand out so strongly against the "squeezing" of their first convert; and it is entirely clear that the latter had failed to appreciate the essence of Christianity, and, with all his protestations and apparent zeal, was still a grasping heathen at heart. It is to be feared that most of the Chinese converts experience a change of belief for business rather than spiritual reasons, and come late in life, if ever, to that perfect sincerity of faith "which passeth all understanding."

From Ter-chou north our route was almost identical with the one pursued going south. It was free from incidents of special interest, except that we lost our road in the middle of a field on the open plain, while following the imperial highway, and this was in broad daylight. It was in a region where the roads are particularly soft in the rainy season, and every one is at liberty to select a path for himself. In the dry season they all look alike, and are vague and ill-defined.

Chinese New-Year, which is the most important holiday, overtook us on February 4th, while we were journeying northward. The people were all out in their best clothes, the shops were shut, and the men and boys were afield in the early morning worshiping at the graves of their ancestors. The women and girls seem to take no part in this ceremony, and it is simple enough for the men and boys. They carry out a sheet or two of gilt and silver paper, with a few incense-sticks, and, after making a burnt-offering of them in front of the grave-mound, they prostrate themselves, knock their foreheads against the ground, and then, setting off a bunch of fire-crackers to frighten away the evil spirits, they return home to spend the day in jollification. The whole ceremony lasts but a few minutes, and seems to be gone through with in the most perfunctory manner.

On that day we made an early halt, and gave the servants the best dinner the country could furnish, with *samschu*, or millet-wine, in abundance. As soon as dinner was over, they sent out for a singing-girl, who came dressed in her best, bringing her *samisen*, a stringed instrument, something like a banjo, and, seating herself on the *kang* of Wang-Fuyeh's room, sang and played accompaniments for Wang's singing all the afternoon in a manner very acceptable to her audience. She seemed to be a modest, well-behaved, obliging girl of good family, who was simply availing herself of the opportunity granted by the custom of the country, to make a little money for her dowery by singing to travelers.

On the last night of our return journey we were met by Captain Higginson, of the United States gunboat Monocacy, about twenty miles out, with our mail for the last two months. The next morning we made an early start for Tientsin, but the north wind had risen, and was carrying clouds of dust with it. By eight o'clock it was blowing a strong gale, and was very cold. The dust soon became so dense as to obscure the sun, and render it impossible for us to see the road. Traveling became almost impracticable, and would have been entirely so but for a pocket compass, which enabled us to keep in the right general direction. Anxious to get in by noon, we pushed on, the wind blowing our fur hoods off, cutting our faces like razors, and every now and then almost lifting us from our saddles. Our calculation was to strike the Taku road east of Tientsin, and thus reach the settlement by the shortest route; but we soon lost our road entirely in the blinding clouds of dust, and then had to depend entirely upon the compass, which it was difficult to use in the high wind. Knowing that there was a large, shallow pond and marsh, several miles across, south of Tientsin, and fearing that we would strike it, we changed our direction to the westward, and at eleven o'clock found ourselves on a telegraph-road, running nearly north and south. After following it for a while we recognized it as the imperial highway from Tientsin to Ter-chou, five or six miles from the Taku road, which we had expected to strike. We knew, however, that it would take us into the suburbs of the Chinese city, and so we pushed on as rapidly as our jaded ponies could carry us; and after we had entered the postern of the outer earthworks, as we thought, turned to the right to skirt the Chinese city and go to the settlement. The next thing we knew we found ourselves inside the walled Chinese city, where none of us except the interpreter and the *mafoos* had ever been before; and, as we had already got separated in the dust-storm from the *mafoos*, and our own party had become divided, it soon dawned upon us that we were lost. The streets were crooked, and the turnings frequent, and, as none of us were conscious of having entered the city gate, our bewilderment was complete. Captain Higginson and I were separated from the rest of the party, and as neither of us could speak a word of Chinese except "Kee Chong," the Chinese designation of Russell & Co., and could find no Chinamen who could speak a word of English, or knew what we meant by "Kee Chong," we wandered about in all directions, like lost children, for an hour. Finally, we came across two *jinriksha* men, and made them understand by signs and the free use of "Kee Chong" that we wanted them to guide us to the foreign settlement. Of course, they turned us directly back from the course on which we were traveling, and in twenty minutes led us to the paved road, in the outskirts of the Chinese city, leading to the settlement. We both recognized that at once, and, paying our guides liberally, rode directly to Russell & Co.'s compound, where we found a hearty welcome from Mr. Thorburn, and an excellent *tiffin* awaiting us. Mr. Nichols and the interpreter had got there before us, but they had been lost also, although the interpreter soon got himself put on the right road.

I had been lost before for three hours with Mr. Nichols in the streets of Chinan-fu, and the experience, however natural, was by no means an agreeable one, but to be lost first on the plains, and then in the city, within three miles of the settlement, after traveling over fifteen hundred miles without guides, in a country that none of our party had ever seen before, was puzzling, not to say surprising, in the extreme. It was, of course, due entirely to the dust-storm, which prevented our seeing the roads and landmarks, and even hid the city gates and wall where we entered them.

The things which most impressed me during this trip were the vast extent and dead-level uniformity and dreariness of the Great Plain, the homogeneity of the people, and the sameness of their manners, customs, dwellings, and occupation; their healthfulness, and immunity from disease and suffering; their avid curiosity, mingled with kindness and civility to strangers; and their contented and placid disposition. I was surprised at the crookedness of the Grand Canal, the bad repair of its embankments, and the utter neglect into which they have fallen. The absence of locks for the utilization of its water-supply, and the general crudeness of their engineering works, were by no means unexpected, for nothing else could be looked for in a country entirely unacquainted with science; and I had been prepared for what I saw, in relation to those matters, by what I had read in the "Peking Gazette." Neither was I surprised at the number and size of the cities, but I must confess withal that I was not impressed as I expected to be with the density of the population. I saw no evidence whatever of overcrowding, and do not think there is any. To the contrary, I am sure that with proper drainage-works, improved methods of cultivation, varied industries, and a fair supply of railroads, a much denser population can be supported than now lives in any part of the Great Plain. This region is the very home of the Chinese, and they live now just exactly as they did a thousand years ago. Their occupations, implements, and manners are absolutely unchanged. They never see foreigners, nor do they buy anything of foreign origin except needles, thread, cotton cloth, and kerosene. Foreign arts and civilization have made no progress in their midst, and no changes in their mode of living or thinking. An occasional wandering missionary has, in a small way, familiarized them with the fact that the foreigner is not necessarily a barbarian, as is the early belief of every nation. Perhaps a dawning sentiment of toleration has begun to make itself felt, and a sense of expectation has been aroused, but it is absolutely certain that there is yet no commercial or intellectual movement anywhere discernible. Life, hope, and aspiration are absolutely stagnant, and nothing can stir them into activity but newer and better education, the building of railroads, and the establishment of new industries. As it is in the Great Plain so it is everywhere in China, except at the treaty ports, and in the country immediately about them.

But what most amazed me was the insignificance of the Hwang-ho, or Yellow River; the small volume of water it was carrying, the narrowness of its channel, and the insecure and generally neglected condition of its embankments. Of course, it presents a very different appearance at flood, during which it must carry an enormous volume of water to the sea. Having no valley or border of hills, after it enters the plain it is free to spread itself indefinitely over the neighboring country, when once it has overflowed its banks and broken through the dikes which should confine it.

There is no place of refuge in the plain except the river embankment, or here and there the site of a village or hamlet, the level of which has been raised from five or six feet for the purpose of keeping out the water. This precaution is not always taken, nor are the villages always surrounded by earthen embankments, as they might be, and it is the absence of such works which makes the far-spreading inundation so destructive to life and property, and fills the minds of the simple people with such a feeling of awe and helplessness when once it is upon them. Should it overtake them by night, which it not infrequently does, and there is no ground near by, above its reach, the first refuge is the top of the house, or the limbs of the trees, if there are any; or, better still, the boat, which is frequently kept even far inland for just such an emergency.

Withal, I have no doubt that the Yellow River can be bridged wherever it may be desirable to cross it with railroads, nor do I doubt that bridges and railroad embankments can be built and maintained anywhere in the Great Plain, just as they are in the deltas of the Mississippi and the Danube.

After my return to Tientsin I reported fully but in general terms to the Viceroy Li, and had many interesting interviews with him, the details of which, for obvious reasons, I do not feel at liberty to publish at this time.

Having completed as far as possible my business with the Viceroy, I again visited Peking, where, through the kindness of Colonel Denby, our worthy minister, I was received by the Prince and Ministers of the Tsung li Yamen, or Board of Foreign Affairs. The interview with these distinguished Manchu and Chinese dignitaries was quite interesting; many subjects were touched upon and discussed, and, so far as I could see, without prejudice or illiberality on their part. They are evidently men of great natural intelligence and of distinguished attainments in Chinese learning, however ignorant they may be in regard to foreign arts and sciences. Prince Ching, the president of the board, belongs to the imperial clan, and is a near relative of the young Emperor. He is of medium stature, and seems to be an exceedingly sensible and prudent man, not over fifty years of age. He and his associates (who were older) entertained us handsomely with sweetmeats, fruits, and hot *samshu,* and seemed to be really pleased to see and converse with us. Their manners were grave and dignified, and would have been considered polite and courtly at the most refined capital of Europe.

CHAPTER XVIII.

Visit to Formosa—Description of the island—The inhabitants—The savages—Mountain - ranges—Camphor-wood—Eastern coast—Lack of harbors—Port of Kelung—Tamsui—City of Twatutia—The governor's *yamen*—Chang-hwa, the future capital—Valleys of the Tamsui — Tea-plantations — Tea-culture — Energetic operations of Governor-General Liu Ming-Ch'uan—Foreigners in Formosa—Mats and opium-smoking—Houses in Formosa—Prevalent diseases—Domestic animals—Climate—Future value of Formosa.

AFTER completing my travels in Northern China, I returned to Shanghai and made a trip by steamer up the stately Yang-tse-kiang in company with Consul-General Smithers to the old capital of Nanking, where we were received and politely entertained by Tseng Quo-Ch'uan, brother of Tseng Quo-Fan, uncle of the Marquis Tseng, and governor-general of the province of Che-kiang. He is a venerable and able man, who has rendered great services to his country, and is now said to be a decided liberal in reference to Chinese policy. He received us with every mark of respectful consideration, and seemed to be deeply interested in what we had to say touching the important needs of the empire, as did his "deputy for foreign affairs" and his English-speaking and very intelligent secretary. Immediately after getting back to Shanghai I sailed for Japan, and traveled there for six weeks, at the end of which time I returned to China, for the purpose of making a visit to the Island of Formosa, first made famous by the French impostor, George Psalmanazar, who published a fictitious account of it in 1704, which was so cleverly written that it imposed upon all Europe.

I sailed from Shanghai by the Chinese transport steamship Way Lee, formerly the British steamship Waverley, Captain Danielsen commanding, on the 4th of June, and arrived at Tamsui, the principal port of this island, on the 6th. The next morning I proceeded by steam-launch to Twatutia, the seat of government, for the purpose of conferring with His Excellency Liu Ming-Ch'uan, the governor-general.

By reference to the map of Asia, it will be seen that Formosa, or Taiwan, as it is called by the Chinese, is about four hundred miles south of the mouth of the Yang-tse, and one hundred from the mainland of China. It lies between 25° 20' and 21° 50' north latitude, is nearly two hundred and forty miles long, by an average of seventy-five miles wide, and has an area of about twelve thousand square miles. It is remarkable for its beauty and fertility, and also for the variety of its products. It was formerly attached to the province of Fohkien, and governed by a resident commissioner; but since the Franco-Chinese War, during which the French, under Admiral Courbet, were foiled in their efforts to take possession of it, it has been erected into an independent province by imperial decree, and is now governed by Liu Ming-Ch'uan, an able and progressive man, with the title and almost unlimited authority of governor-general.

The island was once in the possession of the Spaniards, who called it Formosa (beautiful), but did not colonize it. It then passed into the hands of the Dutch, who built Fort Zealandia, and established a trading-post on the southwest coast, near the present city of Taiwan-fu, and another known as the Red Fort, at Tamsui, on the northwest coast. But the Dutch in turn abandoned the island about the year 1660, immediately after which it was occupied and colonized by the Chinese from Amoy and other points on the coast of Fohkien. The population is now estimated by the governor-general at four million Chinese and sixty thousand savages, but the first figures are doubtless much too large.

The savages are a fine race of men of the Malay or Polynesian type, who hold nearly all the east coast and the mountain-region, covering over one half the island. They live mostly by hunting and fishing, or upon the natural products of the forest, and cultivate but little land. They wear scarcely any clothing, use bows, arrows, and knives, together with a few old-fashioned matchlocks, and yet withal they have up to the present time successfully resisted all efforts to subjugate them or to take possession of their fastnesses. They are brave, fierce, and active, but have made scarcely any progress in the arts of civilization. They are naturally kind and hospitable to Europeans, but look upon the Chinese as their deadly enemies. This is due not only to the fact that the latter have been pressing them steadily back for two hundred years, but have, it is alleged, treated them at times with marked cruelty and treachery. More than one case is mentioned where the Chinese are said to have invited the savages to a friendly parley and feast, and after filling them with *samshu*, to have fallen upon and decapitated the whole lot. On the other hand, the savages seem to have a natural passion for the acquisition of skulls and scalps, or Chinese queues, and whenever they capture a Chinaman they put him to death and scalp him. Governor-General Liu has, however, adopted a more humane policy, and partly by fighting when necessary, but mostly by peaceful negotiations and trade, is making rapid progress toward the subjugation and civilization of his aboriginal neighbors. Only a short time ago over eight hundred of the latter were induced to come in and shave their heads and adopt Chinese clothing in evidence of their submission. Should this policy be continued, it is quite likely that within a few years the whole mountain-region will come under Chinese sway and be opened to settlement.

The mountain-ranges throughout this region are generally parallel with one another and with the eastern coast, and have a northeasterly trend, as do those in both China and Japan. They are covered with a dense forest-growth, including camphor-trees and a great variety of valuable hard woods. Bamboos, palms, long-leaved pines, and tree-ferns of rare species are found almost everywhere, and give the landscape a beauty which it is difficult for one to realize without seeing it.

From the abundance of camphor-trees, gum-camphor was formerly one of the principal articles of export, but of late years its production has been on the decrease, and now there is relatively but a small amount gathered or exported. This is owing to the fact that the trees have been nearly all cut off in the Chinese part of the island, and the savages make it very dangerous for Chinamen to venture into the virgin forests for them. Governor-General Liu and the later commissioners have brought over from the mountain-regions of Quang-tung and Kwei-chau a number of Hakkas, an aboriginal tribe of brave and skillful woodsmen, who are very successful in fighting and driving back the Formosan hill-men. These Hakkas are now the principal camphor-wood cutters, and really produce nearly all the gum which is offered for export.

The eastern coast of the island is unusually bold and rocky, and presents much magnificent scenery. The water immediately off shore is very deep, and there is but one good harbor, that of Kelung, of which I shall say more farther on, and only one or two good anchorages on

THE ISLAND OF FORMOSA. 299

the whole of that coast. The hills and mountains rise sheer up to a height of 6,000 or 7,000 feet above the water, and several of the peaks, although situated well toward the middle of the island—notably, Mount Morrison, 12,850 feet; Mount Sylvia, 11,300 feet; an unnamed peak in Dodd's Range, 12,800 feet; and West Peak, 9,000 feet high—can be seen in favorable weather from a great distance at sea. The west coast-land is generally low and undulating, though outlying hills from one to two thousand feet high come down to the sea in several places. The sea between the island and the mainland, like that to the northward as far as Corea, and between Corea and Japan, is remarkably shallow. It varies in depth from twenty to fifty fathoms, while that north of it varies from twenty to seventy-five fathoms.

There are no harbors of any kind on this coast except that of Tamsui, at the mouth of the Tamsui River. It has only fifteen or sixteen feet of water on the bar at high tide, and, owing to this fact, and to the extraordinary velocity of the outgoing tides during freshets and typhoons, it is by no means safe or satisfactory. The absence of good harbors and anchorages and the frequent recurrence during the summer months of violent typhoons, have been a serious drawback to the island, and must always exert a modifying influence upon its development. Both Kelung and Tamsui being at or near the northern end of the island, and it being impossible to make safe harbors and anchorages on either coast south of them, one or the other of these must become the principal port.

Kelung has by far the best entrance and anchorage. It is well marked by bold headlands, and can be entered at all times by the largest ocean-steamers. The hills about it abound in excellent bituminous coal, and it is susceptible of easy defense by properly placed fortifications and torpedoes; but its entrance is open to northeast typhoons, and the anchorage is of but limited capacity, being only a little more than a mile long. It is, however, sufficient for all possible business for many years. Its most serious disadvantages for the present are that there is but little level ground about it suitable for building-sites, and neither river nor roads connect it with the rich interior of the island. Curiously enough, Kelung River flows back of the hills (two hundred and fifty to four hundred feet high) within two miles of it, and, after joining the Tamsui River, a short distance from its mouth, enters the sea at Tamsui ; but neither of these streams is navigable for anything except flat-bottomed junks and sampans.

Thus, while Kelung has the best harbor—in fact, the only good one in the island—Tamsui has the best and only water communication with the interior, and is consequently the principal seaport, and likely to remain so until a railroad is built from Kelung to the new capital and beyond. It should be borne in mind that there are no roads and no wheeled vehicles on the island, and that all the transportation is done in boats or on the backs and shoulders of coolies. The city of Taiwan-fu, situated on the southwest coast, and estimated by the governor-general to have as many as two hundred thousand inhabitants, was formerly the capital ; but, when the French captured Kelung, and endeavored to capture Tamsui, and to take possession of the island, Governor Liu removed the seat of government to Twatutia (Twat-u-téeah), an important city situated on the right bank of the Tamsui River, ten miles from Tamsui, and twenty from Kelung. Banka, a place of equal size and importance, is situated on the same side of the river, a mile farther up.

The governor's *yamen* is nearly midway between the two, but about a third of a mile back from the river. It is surrounded by a new and well-constructed wall of excellent rubble masonry, about eighteen feet high and ten feet thick, surmounted by a crenelated parapet, with loop-holes and embrasures for small-arms, and is furnished with salients, sally-ports, iron-bound gates, and moats, all in the style of the feudal times. The wall incloses about half a square mile, and is about two miles around, but most of the land inside is under cultivation in rice. The official designation of the seat of government just described is Taipak-fu, although, as before stated, it is practically a part of Twatutia.

Notwithstanding the extent of this wall, and the large sum of money it must have cost, it is understood that Taipak-fu is only a temporary capital, and that the Imperial Government has designated Chang-hwa as the future and permanent capital. This is a large and important town (latitude 24° north), about eighty miles southwest of Twatutia, situated in the center of a fertile region, under high cultivation in sugar, rice, sweet-potatoes, oranges, hemp, tobacco, and indigo, and, with proper highways and railroads, to connect it with Kelung and other parts of the island north and south, it will certainly become a still more important city. Its present population is about one hundred thousand, and that of Twatutia, Banka, and Taipak-fu is probably as great.

I have carefully explored and examined the island between Tamsui, Twatutia, and Kelung, in boats, sedan-chairs, and on foot, crossing it from sea to sea, and going around the north end of it in a steamer, and have never seen a region possessing greater attractions and advantages in surface, soil, and productions.

The valleys of the Tamsui and its tributaries, including the lower Kelung, are broad, level plains, mostly given up to rice-fields, from which two crops a year are harvested; but the hills are everywhere in sight, and in many cases are covered to the very top with tea-plantations, producing large quantities of the Formosa oolong, or black tea, now so rapidly and deservedly gaining favor throughout the United States. It is perfectly pure, uncolored, and unadulterated, and is carefully prepared and packed, under the supervision of foreign houses. It is grown upon virgin land, and is peculiarly rich and smooth in flavor. As some would say, "There isn't a headache or a nervous tremor in a hogshead of it." It is surely replacing both Amoy and Japanese tea, and the output is said to be increasing at the rate of about twenty-five per cent per year. Its cultivation was begun only a few years ago, but since nearly all of the hill and mountain region of the island is adapted to its growth, it is evident that any quantity required by the world can be supplied.

The soil of the tea-fields is a reddish, clay-like loam, which at a distance contrasts strongly with the green covering of the unplanted hill-sides. The plantations are generally small, containing, as a rule, from a quarter of an acre to three or four acres; but Messrs. Russell & Company have one said to contain four hundred acres, and to produce a superior quality of tea.

The development of tea-culture in Northern Formosa, although accompanied by a falling off in the production of sugar, to which the soil and climate are also well adapted, has given rise to a general feeling of confidence in the future growth of this island, while the effort of the French to capture it, following, as it did, upon the landing of the Japanese on the southwestern coast for the purpose of punishing the natives for the maltreatment of some shipwrecked sailors, has directed the attention of the Imperial Chinese Government to its importance and value as a constituent portion of the empire.

As before stated, Governor-General Liu is a vigorous and progressive ruler, who seems to be determined not only to develop the commerce of his province, but to furnish it with roads and bridges, and to put it into a state of defense which will enable him to hold it against all comers. He is at present engaged in building fortifications at Kelung and Tamsui, to be armed with $600,000 worth of Armstrong breech-loading cannon, five of which are to weigh forty tons each. He has also contracted for some armed cruisers, and has on hand an abundant supply of Remington-Lee rifles and Gatling-guns. He is erecting a cartridge-factory, and is seriously considering many other improvements, both civil and military, for the various parts of the island. He is a friend and *protégé* of Li Hung-Chang, and, like him, is quite friendly to foreigners, upon whom he does not hesitate to call for advice and assistance in matters which he does not himself understand. His liberality as well as his humanity compare favorably with those of the French, at least, and this is shown by the fact that the latter are said to have shot many Chinese prisoners, and even a number of poor, defenseless women, during their occupation of Kelung, while Liu did not retaliate, but, instead, treated all French prisoners with marked kindness and consideration, giving them $100 each, and sending them back to their own lines in good condition.

This island imports American petroleum, cotton, sheetings, shirtings, and drills in increasing quantities. It also takes lamps, matches, needles, and many other articles of foreign manufacture, and will take more and more of all these things in the future. There are, perhaps, a hundred and fifty foreigners altogether in the island, employed in the customs service and in mercantile and shipping business and as missionaries. The greater number of foreigners live here and at Tamsui, but there are also a few at Kelung and Taiwan-fu. The majority are English, the Americans come next, and then the Germans, with a sprinkling of Danes, Norwegians, and other nationalities, all of whom live on excellent terms with one another, though here, as well as in other Oriental countries, there is but little, if any, intercourse between the missionaries and business or official people.

America takes nearly all the Formosan tea and sugar, which are the principal articles of export to foreign countries, but furnishes in exchange by no means a proportional part of the imported goods consumed in the islands.

The governor-general says the best thing produced in Formosa is a kind of mat used for sleeping upon in hot weather. It is made of a species of palm-leaf, and is in texture and feeling exactly like the material of a Panama hat, though not so white. It is quite fine, soft, and flexible, and it is said that a mat four by six feet, of the best quality, costs even here as much as $100. The governor adds that the worst thing in Formosa is opium-smoking, which is widely practiced, and, from my own observation, I am compelled to say, it seems to spare neither class nor condition of man. High as well as low are the victims of the habit, and they resort to it openly and without shame. I have seen high officials withdraw from the table upon social occasions for the avowed purpose of taking a whiff. Such men as the Viceroy Li and Governor-General Liu openly denounce and frown upon it; but, withal, there is reason to believe that the consumption of the drug, both foreign and native, is on the increase.

China owes this curse principally to the British Government and its subjects, who have fought for and succeeded in securing almost a monopoly of the traffic in the foreign article. Happily, under the treaty between the United States and China, the traffic in opium is unlawful for American citizens, and this fact has strengthened Americans with the Chinese authorities. Were it not for the late outrages upon Chinese subjects in America, there is little room for doubting that American experts, in all kinds of public and private business, would have the preference in China over all other foreigners.

The cities and towns, manners, customs, farming and farmsteads, buildings and architecture are much the same in Formosa as in other parts of the empire. There are no highways worthy of the name, the streets are crooked and dirty, and the houses are low, dark, and squalid, but they are generally built of red fire-burned bricks, and not of sun-dried mud or gray fire-burned bricks, as is the case in the delta country of the mainland.

Another feature peculiar to Formosa is that the houses are not thatched, but covered with tiles, and, instead of having plain fronts, are in many cases furnished with an arcade, supported by square columns of brick, inside of which passers walk and do their visiting and bargaining. This peculiarity is, doubtless, due to the frequency and heaviness of the rains, the downfall of which is said to be as much as one hundred inches, and even more, per year.

The people have all the characteristics of the Chinese of the mainland, but, on the whole, they do not seem to be either so well fed or vigorous. The climate in the lowlands is malarious, intermittent fevers are common, and the complexion of the inhabitants strikes one as being somewhat more sallow than in Northern or even Middle China. Small-pox is an every-day affair, and is lightly regarded. Consumption is not common, but blood-spitting, or bleeding from the lungs, is said to occur frequently, and to be due to the development of a sort of fluke or worm in the lungs, the germ of which is taken in with drinking-water, and developed in some way not clearly understood. Curiously enough, this parasite, according to my informant, is rarely fatal to the person in whose lungs it has formed its nidus.

The largest domestic animal is the water-buffalo (*Bos*

bubalos), which may be seen on every uncultivated hillside and river or canal bank, and always watched by boys or old men, generally one to each buffalo.

The most common animal is the black Chinese hog, the flesh of which in all forms, from roast pig to smoked sausages, constitutes the principal animal food of the average Chinaman. Duck-raising is a great industry on the rivers and ponds. Chickens are abundant, and their eggs can always be had at moderate cost. Turkeys and geese are also met with occasionally, but are less common. Pheasants, plover, snipe, and wild ducks, also several kinds of deer, and the brown bear, are found in their appropriate haunts on the plains or in the forests and jungles of the mountain-region. There are but few ponies and beef-cattle, and no sheep except such as are brought over from the mainland. Mosquitoes, house-flies, fleas, and many other kinds of insects, are plentiful and pestiferous; and yet, if this island were within one hundred miles of the American coast, and belonged to us, it would justly be looked upon as an earthly paradise.

The climate, on the whole, is salubrious and agreeable, for, although the island lies partly within the torrid zone, its temperature is never hot. It rarely if ever rises above 90° Fahrenheit. Fresh breezes blow every day, and high winds, and even tornadoes or typhoons from the surrounding seas, are not infrequent; and, however annoying the latter may be, they cool and purify the air, and render it healthy and invigorating. But little clothing, and that of the most inexpensive kind, is needed, and vegetable food can be produced in great abundance, and at as low a cost perhaps as in any other country.

Bituminous coal of good quality is mined in many parts of the island. Petroleum has been discovered, but is not yet produced in any quantity. Iron-ore, and even gold and silver, are thought to exist in the mountains.

PRODUCTIONS OF THE ISLAND. 307

The importing and exporting business of the island is in the hands of able and experienced merchants, and there is no place in it for adventurers.

A few specialists might find employment with the Government, and American manufacturers of machinery, cotton goods, thread, lamps, nails, and certain classes of hardware, after sending competent men to ascertain exactly what kinds and styles of goods were required by the people, might extend their business with the island, though it should not be forgotten that, notwithstanding the development of tea culture and export, as explained above, trade here, as everywhere else in China and Japan, is in a depressed condition, due almost entirely to the fall in the price of silver, and the disturbance of the rates of exchange with Europe and America.

But, besides the natural riches of Formosa, and its availability as a place of settlement for large numbers of Chinamen from the mainland, it has a great future value to China as the site of a naval station, for which Kelung, with its coal-mines and defensible harbor, is exceedingly well situated and adapted. The Pescadores, a group of rocky islands, which are situated in the Formosa Channel, midway between the island and mainland, also belong to China. They have several fine harbors, which are susceptible of easy defense, and therefore offer another exceedingly good base of naval operations against any maritime power threatening the Chinese coast.

CHAPTER XIX.

Chinese system of education—Confined to classics, jurisprudence, and history—Influence upon the governing class and common people—The arrest of development—How China is to be prepared for the higher civilization—Substitution of Western sciences for the dry husks of their worn-out philosophy—The earliest communication with the Chinese by the Portuguese—The Spaniards—The French—The Russians—The English—The East India Company—The Americans—The Chinese authorities have from the first sought to restrain trade—The period of small ships—The first Protestant missionaries—The attitude of the Chinese officials in reference to trade—The hong-merchants—Lord Napier's refusal to confer with them—Action of the English merchants—The discussion at Peking—The opium-traffic—The Emperor's efforts to suppress it—Captain Elliot—The destruction of the opium—The Opium War—The conclusion of peace—the Chinese concessions—The settlement of Hong-Kong—The influence of the war.

THE most noted particular in which the Chinese differ from all other people, and especially from Europeans and Americans, is in respect to education. Up to the time of the Reformation they were abreast, if not in advance, of the rest of the world, in many of the things that constitute civilization. Their towns and cities were as well walled and defended; their canal and river navigation was better; their manufactures were in many particulars of a higher order, and their general education, while developed on different lines, was perhaps as far advanced as that of any Western nation. It is not my intention to enter into a discussion of its details, nor even to give its general features, for both are set forth at large in the "Middle Kingdom" and the cyclopædias. It is sufficient for my purpose to say that it has always had but one object and aim, and that is to teach the classics, jurisprudence, and history of China. Whatever human thought that could not be brought within this realm has been counted as of little value. The range and methods of instruction have been laid down and established from time immemorial in the laws and customs of the land, and there is neither material change nor improvement in them. They are based primarily upon the teachings of Confucius, "the most prescient sage and philosopher," and upon the commentaries of his disciples. What he or they may have said is conclusive, and when quoted puts an end to all further discussion. What they do not say is not worth considering. It may be sensible and irrefutable, or it may even have the force and sanction of law, but it is neither classic nor sacred, and can be of no permanent or binding effect, as against the slightest precept or statement of Confucius, which can be arrayed against it. The result has been to arrest all intellectual development and progress in China, and to mold the Chinese mind entirely upon one model. Nothing new or spontaneous can come from it, and every individual Chinese soul is bound and circumscribed by it, and is as powerless to escape its thralldom, through any volition of its own, as are the spokes of a carriage-wheel to escape from the felloe and tire which surround them. It can not aspire to anything better, for it can not imagine or conceive that anything can be better. There is no source of doubt or light left open to the great mass of the Chinese people, bound and fettered as they are by tradition, by the isolation of their country, by the poverty and inflexibility of their literary language, and by the settled and narrow limits of their system of instruction. The absence of hereditary nobility, and the equality of condition and rights within the system, render the system itself popular, and tend to disseminate a feeling of contentment. Where all men are poor and ignorant alike, and the lot of each is unalterable, discontentment can not prevail to any great extent; and discontentment, so far as I can ascertain, does not prevail among the mass of the Chinese people. Neither the face of the country, nor the course of Nature, changes about them. The Government remains the same from generation to generation. Dynasties rise and fall from the operation of natural causes as the seasons come and go, but the laws, and the machinery for their enforcement, remain substantially unchanged from century to century. The Tartar and the Manchu emperors, no less surely than those of strictly Chinese origin, become subject to the sway of the "most prescient sage" and his teaching; and, like the common people, are bound by the custom which comes down to them sanctified by age, and based upon a system of philosophy which, so far as they know, has never been questioned.

As China and its people were at the time of Luther, or even of Christ, so they are now in all essential particulars. They have had no awakening, and have made no protest. They have had no great teacher to overthrow or to build upon the old philosophy. No great statesman has filled the throne since the days of Arkwright, Watt, Fulton, Stephenson, and Morse, and hence there has been no one in China with power enough to reach out toward or to comprehend the great movement which characterizes what we call modern progress.

There is no effective system of common schools, and the machinery of education has undergone no change whatever for two thousand years. It stands just where it did at the beginning of the Christian era. Printing by blocks has been practiced by the Chinese for over eight hundred years but there is no such thing known in the interior as a newspaper which gives all the news and comments upon or criticises it from the standpoint of an independent, questioning intelligence. Of course, it should be borne constantly in mind that I am speaking of interior China, and the countless millions inhabiting it, who are powerless to change, or to desire change, and must remain so, till they can be brought within the range of the newer thought and thus be prepared for the higher civilization. The great question is: "How is this to be done? Can it be done by missionaries, or by school-teachers, or even by newspapers and books disseminated among and acting directly upon the common people? Can any one or even all of these means be brought to bear efficiently upon the great work of education, without the concurrence of the Government?" I am compelled to answer that they can not. In China, as everywhere else in the world, the toiling millions must first be reached through the thinking few. In short, the Chinese people must be reached through the literary or official class, which governs and controls everything, and this must be done in various ways and by various means which I will point out more fully in the closing chapter of this book. It is all summed up, however, in the declaration that they must substitute the Western sciences for the dry husks of their worn-out philosophy, and adopt the Western methods of education, before they can elevate the Chinese people and put them abreast of the rest of the world. They must adopt Western arts and appliances before they can understand or appreciate at their true value the advantages of Western civilization. They must be led to adopt our ways by showing them that our ways are better than theirs, and this can be done most efficiently by giving them object-lessons on a grand scale. They must be led forward step by step from the concrete to the abstract, their needs must be pointed out to them, and they must be shown how to attain them in the shortest and best way. We must teach them how to utilize their own resources; how to build railroads and operate them; how to open mines, and to work them; how to make iron and steel, and to use them; how to find and extract the precious metals; how to establish manufactories and to conduct them profitably. The Government and some of their leading men have already learned the value of steamships for commerce, of ironclads, great guns, and torpedoes, for naval defense; of breech-loaders and Western tactics for the army; and of the telegraph for communicating rapidly with the remote parts of the empire, but the masses in the interior are almost if not entirely ignorant upon all these subjects.

It is now universally recognized that the greatest industrial movement of all time, is the one which has supplied and is still supplying the world with steamboats and railroads. It has given profitable employment to more capital and labor than ever co-operated with each other before in any period of the world's history. It has made itself felt in every branch of human industry. It has opened mines and quarries, built furnaces, rolling-mills, and machine-shops. It has improved every human appliance, increased the sum of human comfort and happiness more than any other movement in which human beings have ever participated. It has annihilated time and space. It has overcome Nature, and brought its beneficent fruits to all nations and races of men. And it is this movement which has already crossed the borders of China, and now threatens to break down the last barrier of her conservatism and isolation.

Communication at rare intervals has been had between Europe and China from the time of Marco Polo down to the present day. Friar Odoric, who landed at Canton, and lived in the country from 1286 to 1331, describes how the Chinese at that time used cormorants in fishing, wore long finger-nails, and compressed the feet of their women. He was followed by many Jesuits, who were tolerated and permitted to travel and teach throughout the country. The Portuguese Jesuit, Benedict Goës, who went overland from Europe, and died on the frontier at Sechuan, was the first person to point out that Cathay and China are the same country.

Up to the conquest of the Manchus, trade and travel in China seem to have been free to such foreigners as could reach it overland or otherwise. The Portuguese, Rafael Perestrello, was the first man who conducted a vessel to China under a European flag. This was in 1516. He was followed the next year by Ferdinand Andrade, and he by his brother Simon. They were both bad men, and, although they opened trade at Canton and along the coast, their behavior was such as to fill the timid natives with apprehension. Portuguese traders and adventurers followed in goodly numbers, and Macao was settled by them in 1560.

The Spaniards who had taken possession of the Philippines, made their first appearance on the Chinese coast in 1575. The Dutch took possession of the Pescadores in 1622, and of Formosa in 1624, built forts at Zelandia, Tamsui, and Kelung, founded colonies and trading-stations, sent missions to Peking, and carried on a desultory trade with the mainland, till they were driven out of Formosa by the great Chinese pirate Koxinga in 1662. Afterward they traded at Canton on the same footing with the representatives of other nations till 1863, when their relations with the Chinese were regulated by the Treaty of Tientsin.

The French Government has never till late years sent an embassy to Peking, nor made any effort to open trade or to establish trading-posts on the Chinese coast, but the French Jesuits gave the world more information about China prior to this century than all other travelers put together.

The Russians sent many trading expeditions from their settlements in the Amur Valley to Peking between 1567 and 1677. They established relations which were more or less intimate, and by firmness and fair dealing succeeded in making the first treaty which was ever agreed to by the court of Peking. It was signed at Nipchu, on the 27th day of August, 1689, and the ratification of it by the Russian Czar was carried to China by Ysbrandt Ides in 1692. The Czar sent Vladislavitch as minister to Peking in 1727, and he was permitted to establish there a permanent legation and college for the education of interpreters. This legation has been steadily maintained from that time to this, and, barring the friction along the frontier of the two countries, and especially in the valley of the Amur, the relations of China and Russia have been uniformly friendly. The Russians are, however, pressing steadily forward upon the Chinese border from the remotest corner of Turkistan to the coast of the Pacific Ocean, and there can be but little doubt that this presents the greatest possible danger to the integrity of the Chinese Empire. From this side it can be successfully assailed as soon as the railroad has reached the valley of the Amur, and, when the policy and interest of Russia in Asia are considered, it will be seen that the danger just alluded to must soon become an imminent if not a fatal one. It is already believed by careful observers in China that sooner or later the Russians will regard themselves as compelled to occupy the valley of the Yellow River, and thus gain access to ports on the Yellow Sea which can be reached and kept open at all seasons of the year.

The first ships bearing the English flag anchored off Macao in 1635, and, after trading awhile peaceably, got into a difficulty with the natives, and ended by fighting and beating them. They came again in 1644, and visited Amoy in 1677, but did not succeed in gaining a footing at Canton till 1684. In 1699 Catchpool was appointed consul, or king's minister, and attempted to open trade at Ningpo and other points farther north. In 1703 the East India Company farmed out all the English foreign trade at Canton to one man. In 1742 Commodore Anson arrived off the coast with the Centurion, the first English frigate which had ever sailed into Chinese waters, and made an overpowering demonstration of English strength and determination. From that day forward, for about one hundred years, the East India Company practically monopolized the Chinese trade with foreigners. In 1792 the English Government sent Earl Macartney with three ships and a brilliant staff on a special mission to Peking. They were received with every mark of respect and attention, and, although they gained no great diplomatic advantage or concession, it may be said that they opened China to foreign diplomacy. Lord Amherst was appointed embassador, and reached Peking in 1816, but he was summarily dismissed because he would not perform the *kotow*. Trade was carried on, however, for many years thereafter under greater and greater restrictions. The Chinese authorities grew more and more jealous and apprehensive, and finally resolved to put an end to all intercourse whatever with foreigners.

In 1834 the East India Company's monopoly in China came to an end, and Lord Napier was appointed chief superintendent of British trade, and sent to Canton with instructions from Lord Palmerston to protect and foster that trade, and extend it, if practicable, to other parts of the Chinese dominions, but forbidding him to conduct any diplomatic negotiations whatever with the Government at Peking.

The first American trading-ship visited China in 1784, and from that time our merchants have done business there on the same footing as those of other nations, subject to the same restrictions, and enjoying the same privileges. Our friendly relations have never been interrupted, though, according to Williams, our Government for many years "left the commerce, lives, and property of its citizens wholly unprotected and at the mercy of the Chinese laws and rulers."

The trade and intercourse of the lesser European nations have grown up and been conducted under the example and leadership of England, and, until late years, have not been characterized by any events of special importance.

From the foregoing statement it will be seen that commerce between the Chinese and foreigners began, in a small way, by sea in 1516, and was carried on by the Portuguese, Spanish, and Dutch in a desultory and predaceous manner till the English made their appearance on the scene in 1635. From that time down to the present day the English have not only taken the most prominent and active part in it, but have controlled a larger share of the business than all other nations put together. They have never hesitated to ask frankly for what they wanted, but have always been bold, outspoken, and firm in their demands. Their Government has stood ready to back them by diplomacy and, if need be, by arms, and it is but just to say that whatever they have gained for themselves has also been conceded to others, perhaps reluctantly and grudgingly at times, but always fully and fairly. It can not be denied, and the Chinese should not lose sight of the fact, that, after that from Russia, the next greatest danger to the Chinese Empire arises from

THE GROWTH OF FOREIGN TRADE. 317

the juxtaposition of its western and southwestern provinces with the Indian possessions of the British crown, and the grasping and aggressive demands of British trade. This truth is fully attested by Chinese experience, and is generally admitted by the rest of the world.

The Chinese authorities from the first sought to limit trade to Canton, and to hamper it by terms and conditions which were extremely onerous. They seem to have been apprehensive of foreign influence from the accession of the present dynasty, and to do all in their power to discourage their own people as well as the foreigners from engaging in commerce. For over two hundred years the trade of foreign merchants was strictly confined to Canton, and was conducted through Chinese or Co-hong merchants, who were specially licensed for that purpose by the Government. Foreigners were not permitted to travel in the country; "they are permitted only to eat, sleep, buy, and sell in the factories"; and even the first Protestant missionary, who reached China in 1807, was confined strictly to the hongs of the foreign merchants. Inasmuch as Chinese merchants have no social or official status, foreign merchants were put upon the same footing, and the result was that the influence of the latter reached no further than the minds of those through whom they conducted their business. They exerted no influence whatever upon the literary or governing class, and did nothing which could be measured to change either the civilization of the Chinese people or the methods of the Chinese Government.

This was the period of small ships and strictly commercial methods, during the whole of which foreigners counted for nothing with the Chinese authorities. "They constituted," says Williams,* who was himself one of the

---

* "The Middle Kingdom," vol. ii, p. 453 *et seq.*

318   CHINA.

earliest missionaries, "a community by themselves, subject chiefly to their own sense of honor in their mutual dealings, but their relations with the Chinese were like what lawyers call 'a state of nature.' The change of a governor-general, of a collector of customs, or a senior hong-merchant involved a new course of policy, according to the personal character of those functionaries. The Committee of the East India Company had considerable power over British subjects, and could deport them if it pleased; but the consuls of other nations had little or no authority over their countrymen. Trade was left at the same loose ends that politics was, and the want of an acknowledged tariff encouraged smuggling and kept up a constant spirit of resistance and dissatisfaction between the native and the foreign merchants, each party endeavoring to get along as advantageously to itself as possible. Nor was there any acknowledged medium of communication between them, for consuls, not being credited by the Chinese Government, came and went, hoisting and lowering their flags, without the slightest notice to or from the authorities. Trade could proceed, perhaps, without involving the nations in war, since, if it were unprofitable, it would cease; but, while it continued on such a precarious footing, national character suffered, and the misrepresentations produced thereby rendered explanations difficult, inasmuch as neither party understood or believed the other."

While, therefore, it is strictly true that foreigners produced no change either in the civilization of the Chinese people or in the methods of the Chinese Government, it can not be said that they did not make their presence felt by the authorities at Peking during the long period which closed in 1843. The fact is, that, owing to the centralized character of the Imperial Government, every public act of the foreigners was reported promptly to it, and had its influence in building up the policy of non-intercourse which finally came to be the ruling idea of Chinese diplomacy. So long as trade was confined to one port, and conducted through the Co-hong merchants under regulations laid down by the Peking Government, it was tolerated; embassadors and ministers were even received at Peking, but it was always understood by the Emperor and his advisers that they came as tribute-bearers from subject nations, and not as the representatives of equal sovereignties. The very moment a pretension of this sort, on the part of Lord Napier, was suspected, the governor-general directed him to remain at Macao until he obtained legal permission to go to Canton. This notification was, however, not received in time, and Lord Napier proceeded to Canton as any unofficial foreigner would have done. At that place he ignored the hong-merchants, and sent a letter to the governor-general, addressed as from an equal to an equal. When the governor-general heard of his presence at Canton, he issued a proclamation to the hong-merchants, denouncing what he styled an "infringement of the established laws," and laying down the principle that "the Celestial Empire appoints officers—civil ones to rule the people, military ones to intimidate the wicked. The petty affairs of commerce are to be directed by the merchants themselves; the officers have nothing to hear on the subject." When the letter addressed to him was presented he declined to receive it, because he feared that he would thereby admit the equality of the foreign representative. Both parties stood firm, and a dead-lock resulted. Lord Napier refused to confer with the hong-merchants, and demanded an audience, with such treatment as might be "befitting His Majesty's commission and the honor of the British nation"; while the governor-general refused to receive any communication which was not framed and addressed as a petition from an inferior to a superior. Messengers were sent from one to the other, and much parleying followed, but in the end trade was suspended, and Lord Napier retired to Macao, where he died shortly afterward. Thereupon trade was resumed, and the Chinese claimed that they had "driven him out" and "expelled his ships."

The principles on which they acted throughout this affair are apparent. They feared that if they granted official intercourse by letter they would thereby give up the whole question, that the King of England could no longer be considered as a subject prince; that both he and his people would be released from their allegiance, and, finally, that they would want to enter the borders of China and take possession of her soil. And here, after all, they had a true conception of one of their greatest dangers, which has lost nothing by the lapse of time, but is likely to increase *pari-passu* with the growth of the British Empire in Southern and Southeastern Asia.

The English merchants at Canton now took up the matter, and sent a petition to the King in Council, recommending that a commissioner be sent, with a small fleet, to one of the northern ports for the purpose of arranging the manner of conducting future intercourse; but this sensible suggestion was not adopted. Whether it would have been successful, no one can tell; but, even if it had failed, it would at least have strengthened the moral position of England. The trade of other nations was suspended, and resumed with that of England. The English Government in a measure repudiated the course of Lord Napier, and then the English pamphleteers and newspaper writers took up the question. Even the Duke of Wellington participated in its discussion. Trade went on, however, very much as it did before, and efforts were made to open new ports, but the Chinese officials did not relax their vigilance, and it was found to be impossible to penetrate the country against the will of its rulers. The opinion now became wide-spread among them that any increase of foreign trade would bring with it unmitigated evil, because it would also increase the importation and use of opium, which had been first introduced in the ninth century, and, from the impulse given it by foreign trade, had now come to be looked upon as a national misfortune. On the other hand, Sir George B. Robinson, who had succeeded Lord Napier, and established his headquarters on an opium-ship, expressed his conviction to the home Government that "there was little hope of establishing a proper understanding with the Chinese Government except by resort to force, and the occupation of an island at the mouth of the Canton River."

Sir George B. Robinson was in time succeeded by Captain Elliot, who dropped the pretension of corresponding with the governor-general as an equal, removed to Canton, and signified his willingness to "conform in all things to the imperial pleasure." Meanwhile, a discussion sprang up at Peking between members of the governing class, and spread to the provinces, as to the true policy of the Government in regard to the opium-trade. One party contended that it was impossible to suppress it, and that it should therefore be legalized and regulated, not only for the purpose of stimulating home production, but saving the money annually sent out of the country for the foreign article. Another party contended strenuously for its total suppression, and supported their views by showing that it was productive of great suffering and distress, and was surely ruining those who used the pernicious drug, in health, mind, and property.

The foreigners, nearly all of whom where engaged in the traffic, and were making large sums of money out of it, also joined in the discussion, and, I am sorry to say, most of them, and especially the English, found excuses of one kind and another for advocating the continuance of the trade ; but withal, after due deliberation, the Chinese Emperor Taukwang and his advisers decided against legalizing the admission of the drug, because it was injurious to the Chinese people. They had right on their side, but were sorely perplexed by the discussion as well as by the evident determination of the English to continue the trade, no matter what might be the amount of harm done by it. The increasing demand for the drug and the large profit realized from smuggling it into the country proved too great a temptation for the foreigners, and while the English took the lead in the business, all nationalities lent a willing hand, according to their opportunities.

The Emperor, feeling assured, however, of the support of the leading men throughout the country, redoubled his efforts to suppress the trade. More than one native trader was executed for exporting silver and importing opium ; smugglers were seized and tortured, boats were captured and destroyed, consumers were taxed and threatened with death, and every device known to the Chinese authorities was resorted to for the purpose of keeping opium out of China, but all in vain. The Chinese merchants became as much interested in the trade as the foreigners ; the customs officials connived at it, and even the son of the Governor of Canton took part in it. The coast-guard service and the native customs officers became demoralized, and in its desperation the Government finally ordered the execution of a convicted dealer in front of the foreign factories at Canton, hoping thereby to strike terror into the hearts of the foreign merchants and their employés, but the latter sallied out and drove the executioner away. A crowd gathered to see what was going on. The foreigners tried in turn to drive the crowd away ; blows followed, and the foreigners were overpowered and driven back into the factories. The district magistrate appeared upon the scene, followed by lictors and a few soldiers, and order was soon restored, but the riot impressed both the Government and the people with a feeling of hatred for the foreigners, the majority of whom were engaged in the opium-trade, and all of whom had now come to be looked upon as violators of the law.

It is impossible to even summarize the events of the five years which followed, but in all of that time the Government did not relax its efforts to suppress the trade. It appointed special commissioners, and finally succeeded in getting most of the foreign merchants to sign a paper, pledging themselves not to deal in opium nor to introduce it into China, but this pledge was soon broken by most of the parties who had signed it. The Imperial Commissioner, in despair, next called upon the foreign merchants to surrender all the opium they had in order that it might be destroyed, and shortly afterward under the advice and guarantee of Captain Elliot, who exceeded his authority in giving it, the merchants complied. They surrendered 20,291 chests of opium, worth nearly $11,000,000, and it was all effectually destroyed. Sixteen English, American, and Parsee merchants were banished, and a bond was demanded from those who remained that they would not engage in the illegal traffic. General trade was alternately suspended and resumed, but the opium-ships continued to come and go as before, and the traffic in that drug never for one moment ceased. When it could not be carried on openly it was carried on by smuggling, and always with such profit that no risk was regarded as too great to be taken in connection with it.

On December 6, 1839, the Chinese Commissioner issued an edict declaring all trade with British merchants at an end, and the close of that year saw the two nations involved in difficulties which rendered war inevitable.

The British Government regarded itself as in duty bound to pay for the opium which its subjects had surrendered under the advice of its chief superintendent of trade, and the latter recommended that the Government should compel the Chinese to refund its money-value. The question was debated in Parliament, and discussed at length in the newspapers of the day, and finally the British ministry declared war, for the pupose of obtaining "reparation for the insults and injuries offered Her Majesty's superintendent and subjects ; indemnification for the losses the merchants had sustained under threats of violence ; security that persons trading with China should in future be protected from insult and injury ; and, lastly, that trade should be maintained upon a proper footing."

A formidable expedition, consisting of five ships of war, three steamers, and twenty-one transports, made its appearance on the Chinese coast July 4, 1841. The next day a force of three thousand men landed and captured Ting-hai near Ningpo, killing many of the Chinese who endeavored to hold the place, and striking terror into the hearts of those who escaped. Two days later, Admiral Elliot and Captain Elliot, who had been appointed joint plenipotentiaries, arrived at Chusan, and demanded that the authorities at Ningpo and Amoy should forward a letter which they bore from Lord Palmerston, the British Prime Minister, to the Emperor at Peking, but this the authorities declined to do. The Island of Chusan was captured by the British, the Yang-tse and Ming Rivers were blockaded, and the Chinese coast was harried and annoyed by the British forces. The plenipotentiaries, finding that they could produce no impression on the southern coast, proceeded to the Pei-ho in Northern China, and there opened communication through the Governor of the province of Chihli, with the Peking Government, which resulted, after much argument and some delay, in the appointment of a Chinese plenipotentiary, to meet those of Great Britain at Canton. Meantime the Chinese provincial authorities were busy all along the coast in raising troops and making arrangements for defense, but, withal, trade was never entirely suspended. The British were active and persistent ; several skirmishes occurred ; several forts were taken ; and in the end the Chinese plenipotentiary became convinced that successful resistance was impossible.

On the 20th of January, 1842, the English plenipotentiaries announced that peace had been concluded on the condition that the Chinese should cede the island and harbor of Hong-Kong to the English ; pay an indemnity of six million dollars in annual installments ; permit the immediate resumption of British trade at Canton ; and finally conduct official intercourse thereafter with the British on terms of equality. All other captured points were to be restored to the Chinese, and all Chinese prisoners were to be released. It soon, however, became apparent that this treaty would not be complied with, and that the Peking Government had resolved "to destroy, wipe, clean away, to exterminate and root out the rebellious barbarians." Hostilities were renewed, the Bogue forts were all taken, many Chinese were killed, and the British were within five miles of Canton, when the prefect, under a flag of truce, met Captain Elliot, and sued for a three days' suspension of hostilities, which was granted. It, however, expired without leading to satisfactory results. The British again advanced, and after taking every fort, raft, battery, stockade, and camp, had the city at their mercy. A second truce was agreed upon, and trade was reopened, but the Chinese steadily pushed their warlike preparations. Seeing that nothing would satisfy them but absolute defeat and the capture of Canton, the British resumed their operations, and driving back the Chinese troops, took possession of their last fortifications. Negotiations were again resumed, and a new treaty was made, which provided for the payment of six million dollars as a ransom for the city, besides additional compensation for the loss of foreign property and shipping ; and, finally, that the Chinese troops should evacuate the city.

Shortly afterward, Sir Henry Pottinger and Admiral Sir William Parker, arrived from England, and assumed direction of affairs. They approved the last truce, and continued trade at Canton, but in August sailed northward with a fleet of nine men-of-war, four steamers, twenty-three transports, and a force of about thirty-five hundred men, captured Amoy, Ting-hai, Chiu-hai, and Ningpo, together with many guns, ammunition, and property, but the Chinese authorities only redoubled their efforts to drive back and destroy the barbarians. T'si-ku and Chapu were also taken, and finally the expedition entered the Yang-tse-kiang, captured the works at the mouth of the Wusung River, and took possession of Shanghai, which they ransomed for $300,000. The Emperor collected large forces at Chin-kiang, Nanking, Suchau, and at Tientsin. The British expedition, reenforced by a strong detachment under Lord Saltoun, now proceeded up the Yang-tse, for the purpose of breaking the Grand Canal. After a sanguinary engagement they captured Chin-kiang, took possession of Iching, and invested the old capital of Nanking. So vigorous were their operations, and so helpless had the Chinese showed themselves to be, that there was no longer any doubt, even in their own minds, of their entire overthrow, and the invincibility of the British land and naval forces. Negotiations were again opened, and after the exhibition of full powers by the plenipotentiaries of both sides, ac-

companied by many ceremonies and formalities, the
Opium War was concluded by a treaty which covered the
following important points : A lasting peace between the
two nations; the opening of Canton, Amoy, Fuchau,
Ningpo, and Shanghai, to British trade, under a well-un-
derstood tariff; the cession of the Island of Hong-Kong
to Her Majesty; the payment of $6,000,000 for the opium
destroyed at Canton; $3,000,000 for the debts due the
British merchants ; and $12,000,000 for the expenses of
the British expedition, the entire amount of $21,000,000
to be paid before January 1, 1846 ; the release of all prisoners held by the Chinese ; the pardon of all Chinese
subjects who had aided the invaders ; the establishment
of a regular and fair tariff and transit dues ; the conduct
of all official correspondence on terms of equality ; and
the restoration of places held by the British according to
payments agreed upon therefor.

The victory of the British was complete, but it will
be observed that the traffic in opium was not even mentioned in the treaty. It is said, curiously enough, that
the Chinese plenipotentiaries declined to discuss the subject until they were assured that it had been brought up
by Sir Henry Pottinger merely as a topic for private conversation ; but it is much more likely that the victors
would not permit it to be made a subject of negotiation.
The trade was evidently too valuable to be given up in a
treaty, every provision of which was clearly wrung from
the Chinese by the might of British arms. There is
abundant evidence for the statement that the Chinese
appealed in vain for fair treatment in regard to the importation and growth of the drug, which they justly look
upon as a curse to the human family. They asked the
British to prohibit the cultivation of the poppy, but this
they declined to do, under the plea that such action
would be inconsistent with British laws, and inefficacious

besides. They claimed that if they did not supply the demand for the drug others would, and even suggested that the Chinese should legalize the traffic, and thus limit the facilities for smuggling.

It is not my purpose to point out the immorality of the course adopted by the British in regard to this matter, for, whatever may be the facts of the case, or the consequences flowing therefrom, it is certain that all other nationalities were equally guilty with the British, according to their opportunities, in engaging in the trade, and that so far no power has made it unlawful by treaty except the United States, and even they have failed to pass laws for the punishment of such as violate the treaty.

My purpose in summarizing the events of the Opium War is to call attention to the fact that two hundred years of peaceful commerce at Canton had produced no direct effect whatever upon the Chinese people or their Government, except to convince them that the foreigners were all alike, greedy and turbulent. It brought with it no benefit, except the little that flowed from the sale of tea and silk, and the purchase of a few articles of foreign manufacture, and this was offset ten thousand-fold by the opium scourge, which has become a source of never-ending misery to the Chinese people. Indeed, it is apparent that commerce alone, conducted, as it was, through factories, trade superintendents, and hong-merchants, could never have in any way changed the manners and customs of the Chinese, much less could it have modified the polity of the Chinese Government, or brought it to realize that the Chinese Emperor was not sovereign lord over all the nations of the earth. Throughout the whole period, from the beginning of foreign trade with the Chinese down to the Treaty of Nanking, it is evident that the Chinese *literati*, as well as the Chinese Government, regarded all outside nations not only as barbarians but as

EFFECTS OF THE OPIUM WAR. 329

subjects of their Emperor. They considered all ambassadors and ministers as tribute-bearers, and all presents to their Emperor as an acknowledgment of his sovereignty.

The Opium War dispelled this illusion forever, and opened the eyes of the Chinese to the terrible efficiency of modern military enginery. It showed them that their vast numbers were powerless against foreigners in warfare, and that their Government could not protect them for a moment against the cupidity of the latter, when once it had been aroused. But what is still more important is, that it resulted not only in the exaction of an enormous indemnity for the alleged injuries inflicted, but opened many new ports to foreign trade and settlement, in each of which the Chinese absolutely, though unwittingly, yielded the right of the British Government to control the persons and property of its subjects residing therein. The other foreign powers claimed for themselves and their merchants all the privileges granted to the British, although they had taken no part in the Opium War, and the Chinese yielded without dispute, perhaps without even knowing, at first, that there was any difference whatever between the outside barbarians. Thus the exercise of exterritorial jurisdiction, and the custom of co-operation between foreign nations in China, had their origin, and thus the isolation and pretended supremacy of the Chinese Government were ended forever. Commerce alone had done nothing, but commerce and war together had shown themselves to be invincible. They had secured a firm foothold for foreigners and foreign civilization upon Chinese soil. Tariff and commercial regulations were now adopted and carried into effect, for the government of Chinese trade " with all countries as well as of England. Henceforth, then," says the edict of Kı-ying, the Imperial Commissioner, " the weapons of war shall be forever laid aside, and joy and profit shall be the perpetual lot of all." Trade acquired a new impetus at Canton, and was speedily opened at all the other ports. The Americans and French made treaties without delay ; and the former, negotiated in 1844, by the late Caleb Cushing, was so clear and distinct in its terms and provisions that it served as a model for all others up to 1860. The Chinese paid the indemnity of $21,000,000, and, notwithstanding the terrible lesson they had received, and the continued activity and baleful effects of the opium-trade, the country seemed to be fairly prosperous and peaceful. There was still some hostility to foreigners, and especially at Canton, where the British had to again resort to force in 1847. They once more battered down the Bogue forts, and compelled the Chinese, by force rather than by argument, to grant a larger space for residences and warehouses on the south side of Pearl River, and also to consent that the city gates should be opened to foreigners after two years. When the time came around, this agreement was repudiated, and the British wisely forbore to insist upon its enforcement. Activity prevailed in the settlement, and the gates of Canton were not freely opened to the foreigners till 1858.

CHAPTER XX.

History of the Taiping rebellion again adverted to—The operation of the treaties—The rapid increase of trade—The establishment of the maritime customs under foreign management—The influence of Canton and the Cantonese—The affair of the Chinese lorcha Arrow—The first and only difficulty with Americans—Demands of England, Russia, France, and the United States upon the Peking Government—The Emperor and court greatly alarmed—The practice and doctrine of co-operation—The allied fleets proceed to the Pei-ho—Negotiation—Signature of the treaties—Principal concessions—The affairs of the Taku forts—The British repulse—Return of the allies—Capture of the forts and the advance to Peking—Treaties ratified and exchanged—Death of the Emperor Hien-fung—The regency—The influences surrounding the present Emperor—The necessity for Western education.

As before stated, the detailed history of the Taiping rebellion, which started as a sort of Christian uprising, and became, in some degree, a national revolt against the Manchu power, ravaged the country for seventeen years, and cost the lives of from ten to twenty million Chinamen, does not come within the scope of this work. I have briefly adverted to its influence in educating the Chinese Government and the leading Chinese statesmen, and have specially pointed out how it brought Li Hung-Chang, Tseng Quo-Fan, Tseng Quo-Chu'an, and Tso Tsung-Tang, as well as the thousands of nameless soldiers who took part in it, into daily contact with foreigners, and gave them a better understanding than they could otherwise have obtained of the superiority of foreign arms, organization, and discipline. It is now almost certain that if Hung Tse-Chuen, the rebel leader, had adopted true instead of spurious Christianity, and called capable foreign advisers to his assistance, he would most probably have secured the countenance of the foreign powers, and ultimately overthrown the Imperial Government. But his head was turned by his early successes; he grew insolent and careless; his pretentions were exposed; foreign sympathy was withdrawn from his cause, and finally foreign skill, courage, and arms were combined by the imperial leaders to bring about his overthrow and destruction. The rebellion had an inglorious ending; but its influences and lessons were yet to be disseminated broadcast throughout the empire. Everywhere the story was told of the "foreign devils" who led the "Ever-Victorious Army." Their courage was extolled, the power and destructiveness of their arms were exaggerated, and their marvelous achievements were loudly praised even within the sacred precincts of the Throne. But, what is still more significant, is the fact that the Emperor, in acknowledgment of their extraordinary services, bestowed posthumous honors upon Ward, and granted money, titles, and, above all, the "Yellow-Jacket" to Gordon, by edicts which were officially promulgated in every province. This put the seal of authenticity upon the story which had already penetrated to the remotest corners of the empire. The interest and curiosity of all classes had been profoundly moved; and although, in a country where there is no public press, and intercommunication is necessarily so imperfect, the effect of all this was more or less evanescent, it is certain that a large part of it was radical and permanent, and that, even to a greater extent than ever before in China, War had shown herself to be the most efficient servant of Progress.

Under its influence commerce was greatly stimulated at the five open ports, and especially at Shanghai. The foreign population increased threefold, steamship companies were organized, steamboats were introduced, foreign settlements grew up, and all the appliances of foreign civilization were brought into the country.

Under the operation of the treaties, the relations of the Chinese and foreigners gradually adjusted themselves on a fairly satisfactory basis. The foreigners claimed the right to mark off and occupy a separate tract of land adjoining the native city at each treaty port, and to govern themselves according to their own customs and laws. The Chinese authorities unwittingly conceded this right, and thus grew up what has come to be known as the "foreign concessions," which are governed by the consuls of the treaty powers, or by local city authorities, deriving their power from the consuls. The English and French carried this right so far that they even claimed absolute jurisdiction over Chinese subjects who were found within the limits of their allotted districts.

The rapid increase of trade, and the great influx of foreigners, all of whom were entirely ignorant of the Chinese language, gave rise to the necessity for many interpreters, and experienced Chinese traders or *compradores*, and these were naturally looked for at Canton, where business had been carried on with foreigners for over two hundred years. This accounts for the fact that the Cantonese hold most of the higher places in the foreign hongs at all the treaty ports. Many of them speak "pidgin English" (business English), and are shrewd, capable servants of their employers, but withal they do not fail to take care of their own interests at the same time. It is worthy of note that the British and other powers have always been able to employ as many Cantonese as they wanted to-assist them in their hostile operations against China, and that for that reason, if for no other, the people of North and Central China are not overfond of the Cantonese, but are disposed to look upon them rather as foreigners than natives of their common country.

Owing to the disturbed condition of affairs which the rebellion brought about at Shanghai in 1853, it became necessary for the native collector of customs to remove the custom-house to the foreign settlement. He had formerly been a hong-merchant at Canton, and as such had acquired confidence in the ability and honesty of the foreign merchants, and therefore willingly entered into an arrangement for putting the collection of foreign duties into the hands of three commissioners, to be selected by the English, American, and French consuls respectively. The chief duty of organizing the service fell upon Mr. Wade (afterward Sir Thomas Wade), who spoke Chinese fluently. He was succeeded by Mr. Lay, of the English consulate, and he in turn by Mr. (now Sir Robert) Hart. This was a wise measure; it has been carried into effect at all the treaty ports, and has led to far-reaching consequences. The service was ably organized and honestly administered; it has now over a thousand foreign employés, representing nearly every nationality, and is an ever-present proof to the Imperial Government of the superiority of foreign over native methods of conducting public business. The amount of revenue collected has advanced from about five million to nearly twenty million dollars per year, without any increase of the fixed tariff rate of five per cent *ad valorem;* but what is more important is the fact that the money is all honestly collected and paid over to the imperial treasury, and this is the only branch of the Chinese revenue service of which as much can be said. In addition to collecting and accounting for the maritime customs, the department has established lighthouses and buoys at the entrances to the treaty ports, and at many other points along the Chinese coast. It has, in later years, established an efficient revenue-cutter service, and has begun the work of sounding and surveying the places most dangerous to steam navigation. Moreover, nothing which the Chinese Government has ever done has gone so far toward breaking up the smuggling of opium, and it is safe to say that if it is ever broken up altogether it must be done through the agency of this effective organization.

Notwithstanding the large number of Cantonese employed by foreign merchants, and the great amount of business done at the port of Canton, there has always been more friction between the natives and foreigners at that place than at any other in China. As the Taiping rebellion approached that city, the foreign merchants who sympathized with them at first made unusual exertions to sell them arms and military supplies. Civil war broke out in the city, and several hundred thousands of lives and many houses were destroyed. The consuls at the settlement and at Hong-Kong were powerless to restrain the cupidity of their countrymen, and, to make matters worse, the Chinese governor-general obstinately refused to see any foreign minister. In his blind efforts to suppress smuggling, he was arbitrary and unreasonable toward the foreigners. The British availed themselves of the opportunity to build up and develop the trade of Hong-Kong. They made it a free port, reduced the charges upon shipping to almost nothing, and did all in their power to induce Chinese vessels to carry on trade under the British flag. An enormous smuggling trade was developed in opium, in spite of the Chinese revenue service to suppress it. Coolies were kidnapped and sold to the Portuguese barracoons at Macao, and piracy became common. The Chinese *lorcha* * Arrow, sailing under a British register which had expired, was suspected of being engaged in contraband trade, and was seized, and the British ensign was hauled down. The British consul, Mr. Parkes, and the British governor-general of Hong-Kong, Sir John Bowring, immediately demanded redress; but the Chinese governor-general was obdurate, and could not see that any reparation was due.

During the complications with the British (in 1856), the Americans for the first and only time became involved in difficulty with the Chinese. An American man-of-war's boat had been fired into by design or mistake at the Barrier forts, and one man had been killed. Commodore Armstrong, who was lying near by with the San Jacinto, Portsmouth, and Levant, at once attacked and captured the forts, killing several hundred of their defenders, and with that the matter was allowed to drop. Not so with the British. They sent at once to India for re-enforcements and to England for instructions. The condition of affairs at Canton was discussed in Parliament, and the British Government resolved to follow up the Treaty of Nanking by demanding the reception and residence of a British minister at Peking. France, Russia, and the United States were invited to co-operate, for the common benefit of Christendom. Special plenipotentiaries of great skill and ability were appointed by the European powers, as well as by the United States, and by the end of the year 1856 they had arrived at Canton in great ships of war, and, after their ultimatum had been delivered, they landed an allied force of about six thousand men and captured the city. The governor-general and all the high officials were taken prisoners, and a new government, composed of high Chinese officials under the protection of the

---

* A foreign-built hull with Chinese rig.

allies, was at once set up. Order was promptly restored, and the Cantonese were shown for the first time how just and reasonable the foreigners could be toward them, and yet how firmly they could deal with their rulers.

The allied ministers now proposed to the American and Russian plenipotentiaries, who had taken no part in the hostile operations, but had satisfied themselves with playing the part of deeply interested spectators, to join them in laying their demands before the Imperial Government at Peking. Letters were written by all and duly forwarded; but the Chinese Emperor and his court were greatly alarmed, and could not bring themselves to consent to receive the representatives of the hated foreigners at the capital. Such a thing had never been done, and so evasive answers were returned. The powerful fleet of the allies, accompanied by the American and Russian men-of-war, proceeded at once to the Pei-ho, forced the batteries at its mouth, and sent the ministers forward to Tientsin. Here they were received by two high Chinese commissioners, and negotiations were at once opened. The British minister, Lord Elgin, took the lead in the discussions. The Chinese were overawed, and, "ignorant beyond conception of the gravity of their situation," they granted almost everything that was asked of them; and the treaties thus negotiated, or, perhaps, I should say forced upon the Chinese, became bound into one mass by the favored-nation clause, which they all contained, and by the doctrine of co-operation, which then for the first time was practically carried into effect by the four great powers of the world, although it must not be forgotten that the representatives of the United States and Russia had been specially instructed not to resort to force, and had not been consulted by Lord Elgin. The situation was tersely summed up in the declaration made by him that he "was compelled to treat with persons who yield nothing to reason and everything to fear, and who are at the same time profoundly ignorant of the subjects under discussion and of their own real interests." Another British officer still more pithily expressed it by saying, "Two powers had China by the throat, while the other two stood by to egg them on, so that all could share the spoil." And, arbitrary as all this was, the obstinacy, exclusiveness, and folly of the Imperial Government left the foreigners no other course to pursue.

By the first week of July, 1858, the four treaties had been signed and ratified by the Emperor Hienfung, and the fleet had left the Pei-ho. The tariff was revised shortly afterward, and through the persistence of the British was made a part of the treaties, the opium-trade was legalized at a low rate of duty, which removed from it alike the necessity for smuggling, and the stigma of immorality which had hitherto been attached to it. Hang-kow, on the banks of the Yang-tse, a thousand miles from the sea, was declared a treaty port, and opened to foreign residence and business; missionaries were granted the right to travel throughout the land and preach the gospel; and foreign ministers were authorized to reside at Peking; but the four envoys returned home without visiting that far-famed city.

The Chinese authorities at once began reconstructing the fortifications at the mouth of the Pei-ho, on what they considered to be foreign plans, and every effort was made to prevent the return of the allies. Peking had been designated as the place for the exchange of the treaties, but the Chinese sent commissioners to Shanghai, and exerted all their arts of diplomacy to get the French and English envoys to go through with the ceremony at that place, but in vain.

The British endeavored to force their way again (June

29, 1859) into the Pei-ho, but they were repulsed, with the loss of eighty-nine killed and three hundred and forty-five wounded. It was during this action that Commodore Tatnall lowered his gig, and, with the declaration that "blood is thicker than water," towed boat-loads of British marines into action.

The American minister and his suite landed at Pehtang and made their way overland to Peking, but, owing to the difficulty of arriving at a satisfactory agreement in regard to the ceremonies to be observed, did not have audience with the Emperor. The latter waved the requirement of the *kotow*, or prostration in his presence, and suggested the bending of one knee, but as there had been some inadvertent suggestion of a religious significance to the ceremony, even after it had been shorn of its more objectionable features, Mr. Ward determined to return to Pehtang and exchange the ratifications of the treaty at that place. There was no special violation of right in this, for the American treaty was silent in reference to the place at which the ratification should be exchanged; but it must be confessed that, having gone to Peking by invitation, his retirement without accomplishing the object for which he had gone was justly regarded by the representatives of the other powers as a sacrifice of dignity more or less injurious and embarrassing to them.

The British, smarting under their repulse from the Pei-ho, opened negotiations at once with their allies the French, and the two powers agreed to send back the plenipotentiaries who had negotiated the treaties, at the head of a powerful fleet and a strong land-force. The united fleet and transports contained over two hundred vessels, carrying about twenty thousand men, and presented by far the most formidable array of power that had ever been brought to bear against the Chinese Empire.

The plenipotentiaries arrived at Chee-fu in July, 1860,

and at once made known their demands in no uncertain terms. They required an apology for the repulse of the English at the Pei-ho, the ratification and exchange of the treaties at Peking, and that they should be carried into effect without further delay, and finally that the Chinese should pay the expenses incurred by the allies. The Chinese replied as usual with indirect and evasive language, so there was nothing left for the allies but to make sail for the coast of Chihli, land their troops, and force their way to Peking, and this they proceeded to do. They disembarked at the mouth of the Pehtang, about ten miles north of the Pei-ho, turned the forts at Taku, took them in the rear and captured them. They then marched at once for Tientsin, which, although strongly fortified, was surrendered without a battle.

The Chinese now offered to treat, but, finding that they were trifling and trying to gain time rather than to comply with what was asked of them, the foreign plenipotentiaries broke up the conference and resumed their march toward the capital. They had not gone far, however, before they found themselves confronted by a large army; hence they advanced with circumspection and always in readiness for battle. The Chinese redoubled their efforts to stay the approach of the foreigners, and sent out great dignitaries with fair protestations and urgent offers to exchange and ratify the treaties. The allies paused again, and sent forward Mr. (afterward Sir) Harry Parkes, to select a camp and arrange terms. He was received with all external marks of courtesy, but soon discovered that the Chinese generalissimo, Prince Sankolinsin, was preparing an ambush for the allied army. On endeavoring to make his way back to the latter, he and most of his companions were taken prisoners, hurried off to Peking, and treated with great cruelty. The allied commanders discovered the perfidy of the Chinese, and,

THE ALLIED ARMIES AT PEKING. 341

advancing to the attack, drove them in confusion from the field, captured eighty cannon and burned their camps. Several minor engagements followed, in which the allies were easily victorious. The Emperor and court fled hastily to Jehol, on the borders of Manchuria, and left Prince Kung, the second brother of the Emperor, to make the best peace he could. Meanwhile the allies advanced with deliberation to the immediate vicinity of Peking, burned and pillaged the Summer Palace and all the neighboring villas as an act of retribution upon the Chinese for their violation of the flag of truce carried by Mr. Parkes, and for the savage treatment inflicted upon him and his companions during their imprisonment. The Chinese Government was powerless to resist the demands contained in the ultimatum of the allies. The treaties were ratified and exchanged with great pomp inside the imperial city, an additional sum of £100,000 was exacted for the benefit of the prisoners and their families, and another of 8,000,000 taels to defray the expenses of the victors. Kowlung, on the mainland opposite to Hong-Kong, was ceded to the British; permission was given for the emigration of Chinese, coolies either voluntarily or under contract; and the question of the residence of foreign ministers at Peking on terms of equality, and their reception by the Emperor, without the *kotow* or any other form of humiliation, was settled forever. The French as well as the English received a money indemnity, but, instead of asking for a concession of land, they demanded and received payment at Peking for all the churches, schools, cemeteries, lands, and buildings wrested from the persecuted native Christians throughout the empire in years gone by.

War and diplomacy were again signally triumphant; they secured for the foreigners all that the plenipotentiaries asked for, and they asked for all they thought of;

and yet their victory was not complete. The walls of exclusion were broken down in a measure, but the huge, lumbering machinery of the Chinese government was not exposed or interfered with. The Emperor and most of the court had fled, and the latter did not return till the allied army had departed. They never saw its terrible enginery, nor obtained any adequate conception of its organization, discipline, and power. It is true that the Emperor had signified his willingness to receive the foreign diplomatists, but death intervened at his place of retreat to spare him that humiliation. The allied armies hurried to get out of the country. Peking by some strange oversight was not opened to trade or foreign settlement, and as soon as the Government, which had now passed into the hands of a regency, composed of Prince Kung and the two Empresses-Dowager, returned to the capital, it shut itself up within the walls of the Forbidden City, and would have nothing to do with the resident diplomatists that they could avoid. As far as possible they ignored the occurrences of the last year, and resumed their usual sway over their distressed and impoverished country. Had the successful plenipotentiaries and the allied army remained long enough to hale the Government from the Forbidden City and compel it to conduct its operations in the light of day, and to treat with foreign ministers, without unnecessary or vexatious restrictions, through the members of the regency, they would have greatly facilitated the progress of modern ideas and that enlightenment of the governing class without which it is impossible to secure an intelligent administration of the government.

The Emperor Hienfung died August 17, 1861, leaving the throne to his son, then only six years old. The latter assumed the direction of affairs in 1872, at the real age of sixteen, though the Chinese called him seventeen.

RECEPTION OF FOREIGN MINISTERS.

The country had been pacified throughout its extent, and a fair degree of prosperity had returned to it. The question of the reception of the foreign ministers now came up again, and after a long and careful discussion was settled to their satisfaction. The *kotow* was dispensed with, and the ceremony, as finally carried into effect, was not accompanied by any extraordinary circumstance to mark its significance. The young Emperor was a puppet in the hands of his family, and fortunately for himself, if not for his country, he died on January 9, 1875. The Government again passed under the control of the regency, and remained there down to February 7th of the present year. As stated in a previous chapter, the Empress of the Eastern Palace, the senior co-regent, died on the 4th of April, 1881, and left the Government to the sole control of her sister. During the two regencies, a period of over twenty years, the dowagers and their surroundings have remained in absolute seclusion. No foreign minister or official, and no foreigner of any rank, has ever had audience with either of them; so that although the foreign ministers are comfortably settled in Peking, and are in no way molested by the people or the Government, they are practically ignored, and exert little or no influence for good. Most of the questions which they might consider with the Chinese Government are referred to the First Grand Secretary, Li Hung-Chang, for settlement, or to some consul, for investigation and report. They can not reach any member or department of the Government which has power to act. The walls of the Forbidden City, within which the court and most of the great dignitaries reside, are completely shut to them. They may go to the Tsung li Yamen, or Board of Foreign Affairs, but, as before explained, that board, like all the others, has advisory powers only, and can not act except by command of the Emperor.

Now that the young Emperor has taken personal charge of the government, the foreign ministers will again claim audience, and it must be granted; but it is safe to say that little can come of it. The foreign ministers have quite recently been received by his father, the Seventh Prince, and the latter has shown himself to be a courteous gentleman; and many believe him to be an able and progressive statesman. It is supposed by some that he, or his elder brother Prince Kung, will have a potential influence in shaping the policy of the Emperor, and that, owing to the youth and inexperience of the latter, one or the other, instead of the Empress-Dowager, will become the power behind the Throne. But this is all conjecture. In any other country it might readily be as suggested, but in China tradition, old custom, and the code determine everything; and those who hold the reins of power are the judges. It is hardly to be supposed that a regent who has had supreme control of the country for nearly a quarter of a century, and is still in the full vigor of life, will lay down all her influence even if she does go into absolute retirement, and no longer seek to control the conduct of the Emperor whom she had selected, or to direct the Government over which she has so long been an absolute Empress. There is no doubt that she is a strong, vigorous woman, and altogether the wisest and best ruler the country has had since the death of Kienlung; and whether she retain the substance or only the semblance of power, will probably depend altogether upon herself. The most natural solution of the difficulty is that she and the Seventh Prince will remain for many years the principal advisers of the Emperor, notwithstanding the absurd customs in the way of their free intercourse. And hence the great question with foreigners, which still remains to be solved, is how to reach and influence those two great personalities? So far only one of them has come within the reach of foreign ideas, and that only to a limited degree. During the recent visit of the Seventh Prince to Tientsin, Taku, Port Arthur, and Chee-fu, he saw foreign-built ships and heavy guns, and met foreign consuls, for the first time. He is said to be the intimate friend of Li Hung-Chang, and it is certain that he will hereafter see much of that astute statesman, if he takes an active interest in the Admiralty Board, of which they are both members. It is also said that he is on most excellent terms with the Empress-Dowager, and that both have expressed themselves in favor of railroads, as well as of steamboats and telegraphs. What little is known of the two, favors this statement; but, after all, they, like the rest of mankind, are likely to be controlled by their surroundings, their servants, friends, and intimates, first, and their official advisers afterward; and there is too much reason for believing that they are in nowise different from the classes to which they respectively belong. The Chinese are wonderfully alike, without respect to station, in their ignorance of what constitutes progress, and in believing that their own wisdom is superior to that of any other people. Education can alone change all this, and education, in a broad and comprehensive sense, whether it be by war, diplomacy, commerce, missionaries, or the school-teacher, or by all combined, must prove to be a slow process, in a country of such wide extent and so completely isolated, and with a people of so many millions, speaking a language so utterly unlike the modern scientific languages used by the rest of the world.

CHAPTER XXI.

The rights of missionaries in China — The Tientsin massacre — The French and Russians indemnified—The influence of the missionaries generally minimized—Ancestral worship and superstition—The practice of fung-shuy—The conversatism of the governing class—The censors—Chinese statesmen are progressing—The establishment of the Tung-wen College—The Burlingame mission—The Chinese students in America—Their recall—The Emperor all-powerful—Railways wanted by leading statesmen—Difficulties to be overcome— Probable solution of the question—The duty of our own Government—Impossible to predict when China will move—Surrounded by great perils—Russia's menacing position—The British Indian Empire—Their permanent interests—But little danger from Germany and France—The Chinese may perceive their real danger—Not a warlike people—Their true policy—The victories of peace.

AMONG the results of war, secured by the demands of diplomacy, there are none more important than the right to the missionaries of all nations to travel and preach in China. This right was finally accorded by the treaties of Tientsin, but it was not generally used till 1861, nor clearly defined till later. From that time men and women of every Christian denomination have traveled and resided in every province of that widely-extended empire. They have generally been received with nothing worse than indifference, although occasional instances of rudeness and even of outrage upon them have been reported in the far-away districts. The Jesuits have reclaimed their old churches and property, in many cases where it had been out of their possession for nearly two hundred years, and the

Protestant denominations have established permanent missions, schools, and hospitals, at all the treaty ports, Peking, and many of the provincial capitals.

The outbreak against the Jesuits and Sisters of Charity at Tientsin, which occurred on the 21st of June, 1870, resulted in the massacre of twenty French and Russians, the destruction of the French consulate, cathedral, and orphanage. It was instigated by ignorance and superstition, and was attended by circumstances of great atrocity.* It was investigated somewhat tardily by the Peking Government. Foreign men-of-war were assembled in a few weeks; the guilty, so far as they could be found, were punished; the sum of four hundred thousand taels was paid to the French; indemnity was also given to the Russians; the premises destroyed were rebuilt; and generally the Chinese authorities did as much as could reasonably be expected of them in restoring order, repairing the damage done, and in taking precautions for the prevention of similar outbreaks elsewhere. The incident, unfortunate as it was, has not been without its benefits to the missionaries of all denominations. It has made them more circumspect, and the natives everywhere more tolerant and unsuspicious. The authorities were fearful that all the foreign powers would become aroused, and would unite in demanding further guarantees, and hence they voluntarily laid down a set of rules for the government of officials everywhere, and for the promotion of the safety of all foreigners traveling under passport beyond the limits of the settlements; and it may be said—whether through the effect of these rules, or the natural mildness of the natives, is immaterial—that missionaries of both sexes now penetrate into the remotest districts of the empire in almost perfect safety. The people are full of curiosity,

---

* " Middle Kingdom," vol. ii, p. 700, *et seq.*

and sometimes annoy travelers by exhibiting an excess of that very excusable quality, but it hardly ever happens that they wantonly misuse anybody, even in the remoter and more unfrequented regions. The missionaries are nominally required to have passports, but it is claimed by the Chinese that this is rather for keeping track of and protecting them, than for the purpose of putting any restrictions upon their right to come and go without let or hindrance.

It is quite the custom of merchants and secular people generally to minimize the services and utility of the missionaries in China, and, so far as the making of intelligent· and genuine converts to Christianity is concerned, it must be admitted that the results are discouraging ; but when it is considered that the brave men and women of all denominations, who are carrying the gospel to every town and district in the empire, are the advance-guard of a higher and better civilization, and are gradually teaching the Chinese that the foreigners are not "devils" but intelligent and kindly people, striving to do them good and not evil, and that many of them not only understand the precepts of "the sages and philosophers," but teach even a higher form of humanity, it will be seen that their labors are far from wasted. If, in addition to the hospitals and primary schools, which constitute so large a part of the working machinery of the missionaries, they could have a system of technological schools, or at least a series of lectures upon science and mechanics, with apparatus and machinery established in the larger cities, and made free for all to attend, the aim being to show that the arts and sciences of foreigners are better than those known to the Chinese, I do not doubt that in the end Christian truth and morals would find a much more ready lodgment than they now find in the native mind. As it is at present, no Chinaman belonging to the literary class will attend a Christian meeting or listen to a Christian teacher. Serene in the conviction that there never was a greater sage and philosopher than Confucius, with the writings of whom he is well acquainted, he thinks it absurd to waste time with any one who claims to bring him "good tidings of great joy," whether they come from Christ or Buddha. Nominally the religion of the latter is adopted and practiced by many people in China, but so far as I could see it is not a living cult, nor are the Chinese a religious people in any sense whatever. Ancestral worship is perhaps the most vital form of religion among them, and that, although based upon immemorial custom, needs the strong hand of the Imperial Government to keep it alive. Superstition, or the science of good and bad luck, if I may coin a phrase, the meaning of which neither the words geomancy nor fortune-telling properly conveys, and which the Chinese comprehend under the words "*fung shuy*," literally, "wind and water," constitutes by far the most potential factor in the daily conduct of the average Chinaman's life. It regulates all his important transactions, and the *fung-shuy* man is his counselor and guide in youth, manhood, and old age. He tells what day is lucky for starting on a journey, or marrying, or for beginning business ; what place is lucky ; and how the house or the grave should face in order to insure the happiness of its occupant. He finds lost or hidden property, tells fortunes, and directs in all difficult matters. He is paid according to the importance of the occasion and the wealth of the man or the family he is serving ; and if he is not formally employed, he makes himself disagreeable by commenting unfavorably, by predicting misfortune and disaster, or even by stirring up the prejudices of the vicious and ignorant against those who think they can get on without him. The practice of *fung shuy* is an occult trade, in which humbug is the principal art, and of which credulity and ignorance are the surest support. The practitioners are of course venal, and if properly approached can be retained for or against any given measure or on any side of any possible question. In all great or novel undertakings, where the common people can exert any influence, or make any trouble, and especially where foreigners are concerned, it would be well for the person having the matter in hand to bear this statement in mind, and take timely measures to get the *fung-shuy* men on his side. Liberality in compensating them may lead to great saving in the end. Of course, an ignorant or unaided foreigner could not manage such a guild, but would be compelled to rely upon good interpreters and skillful assistants who understood the Chinese character perfectly. I may remark here that foreign influence, and the progress which has already been developed in China, have given the death-blow to "the fung-shuy pidgin," at the treaty ports, and there is reason for believing that it is sensibly on the wane even in the interior of the country, and especially at Peking.

By far the greatest difficulty in moving the Chinese Government arises from the conservatism of the literary or governing class, and this conservatism finds its most efficient agent in the Board of Censors, and the system of espionage of which it is at the head, throughout the empire. The censors, as before indicated, supervise the business of the Great Boards, and are at liberty to memorialize the Throne upon all subjects and at all times. They are the guardians of the law and of the customs of the people, and it is their special duty to speak before the public or the empire has been injured. It is true that they must write decorously, temperately, and without prejudice, and may be rebuked for ignorance or willful falsehood, but the "all-examining court" of which they are members is above all other courts and boards, next to the Throne, and can reach it in much less time and with much less trouble than any other court or person. From its position and functions its members may always know what business is likely to come before the Throne, and hence it is easy for them to assail any measure which does not receive their approbation. They are specially on the alert against innovations and foreign schemes, more than one of which—good as well as bad—they have killed or indefinitely postponed before it had received imperial consideration.

The censors, and almost all other great functionaries of the empire, are old men, who have reached their high positions by a lifetime of laborious study, devoted exclusively to Chinese classics and jurisprudence, and so great has been the competition through which they have been compelled to gain their honors, that it would have been impossible for them to devote much time to the study of foreign sciences or history, even if they had desired to do so. Having overcome and surpassed the rest of mankind in China at least, they naturally look with contempt upon the world beyond. They can see no good in anything which Confucius did not teach, and a system which produced them must be perfect, and needs no amendment. Having attained their great altitude, "nothing remains for them but to walk in the footsteps of the immortal sages who have gone before them."

And yet the Chinese statesmen are learning. With them the day of bows and arrows, bamboo-spears, matchlocks and gingals, war-junks and wooden ships, has passed away. Lee-Remington rifles, ironclads, and Krupp guns have been adopted. Arsenals and machinery, dock-yards and heavy fortifications, abound; naval and military academies have been established; schools for the study of Western languages and sciences have been opened at several of the treaty ports, and what is of still greater importance is the fact that the Imperial Government itself has founded and opened the Tung-wen College at the capital, for the instruction of the official class in the Western sciences. The memorial which brought the project to the Emperor's attention, and constitutes its charter, was drawn up by Prince Kung, and was concurred in by four ministers of the Board of Foreign Affairs. It sets forth that its object is "to teach mathematics and astronomy, as indispensable to the understanding of machinery and the manufacture of fire-arms," that only the scholars of high grade should be admitted, and that "men from the West shall be invited to give instruction." They declare that the scheme "did not originate in a fondness for novelties, or in admiration for the abstract subtilties of Western sciences; but solely from the consideration that the mechanical arts of the West all have their source in the science of mathematics." It points out that if China undertakes to build steamships and machinery, and yet declines to borrow instruction from the men of the West, there is danger that, following their own ideas, they "will squander money to no purpose." The writer of this remarkable document, knowing the prejudices of the class to which he belongs, then says:

"But, among persons who are unacquainted with this subject, there are some who will censure us as wrong in abandoning the methods of China for those of the West; and some who will even denounce the proposal that Chinese should submit to be instructed by the people of the West as shameful in the extreme. Those who urge such objections are ignorant of the demands of the times.

"In the first place, it is high time that some plan should be devised for infusing new elements of strength into the Government of China. Those who understand the times are of opinion that the only way of effecting this is to introduce the learning and the mechanical arts of Western nations. Provincial governors, such as Tso Tsung-Tang and Li Hung-Chang, are firm in this conviction, and constantly presenting it in their addresses to the Throne. . . . Should it be said that the purchase of fire-arms and steamers has been tried and found to be both cheap and convenient, so that we may spare ourselves the trouble and expense of home-production, we reply that it is not merely the manufacture of arms and the construction of ships that China needs to learn. But in respect to these two objects, which is the wiser course in view of the future, to content ourselves with purchase and leave the source of supply in the hands of others, or to render ourselves independent by making ourselves master of their arts, it is hardly necessary to inquire.

"As to the imputation that we hereby abandon the methods of China, is it not altogether a fictitious charge? For, on inquiry, it will be found that Western science had its root in the astronomy of China, which Western scholars confess themselves to have derived from Eastern lands. They have minds adapted to reasoning and abstruse study, so that they were able to deduce from it new arts which shed a luster on those nations; but in reality the original belonged to China, and Europeans learned them from us. If, therefore, we apply ourselves to those studies, our future progress will be built on our own foundation. Having the root in our possession, we shall not need to look to others for assistance, an advantage which it is impossible to overestimate."

After pointing out that the Emperor Kanghe gave his hearty approbation to the science of the West, promoted its teachers, and that "in the olden times yeomen and common soldiers were all acquainted with astronomy," that "mathematics were studied with the classics," and that, according to a Chinese proverb, "A thing unknown is a scholar's shame," he adds: "As to the allegation that it is a shame to learn from the people of the West, this is the absurdest charge of all. For under the whole heaven the deepest disgrace is that of being content to lag in the rear of others. For some tens of years the nations of the West have applied themselves to the study of steam navigation, each imitating the others, and daily producing some new improvement. . . . Of the jealous rivalry among the nations of the Western Ocean it is unnecessary to speak ; but, when so small a country as Japan is putting forth all its energies, if China alone continues to tread indolently in the beaten track, without a single effort in the way of improvement, what can be more disgraceful than this ? Now, not to be ashamed of our inferiority, but, when a measure is proposed by which we may equal or even surpass our neighbors, to object to the shame of learning from them, and forever refusing to learn—to be content with our inferiority—is not such meanness of spirit itself an indelible reproach ?

"If it be said that machinery belongs to artisans, and that scholars should not engage in such employments, in answer to this we have a word to say. Why is it that the book in the *Chau-li* on the structure of chariots has some thousands of years been a recognized text-book in all the schools ? Is it not because, while mechanics do the work, scholars ought to understand the principles ? When principles are understood, their application will be extended. The object which we propose for study to-day is the principles of things. To invite educated men to enlarge the sphere of their knowledge, by investigating the laws of Nature, is a very different thing from compelling them to take hold of the tools of the workingman. . . . In conclusion, we would say that the object of study is utility, and its value must be judged by its adaptation to the wants of the times. Outsiders may vent their doubt and criticism, but the measure is one that calls for decisive action. Your servants have considered it maturely. As the enterprise is a new one, its principles ought to be carefully examined. To stimulate scholars to enter in earnest on the proposed curriculum, they ought to have a liberal allowance from the public treasury to defray their current expenses, and have the door of promotion set wide open before them. We have accordingly agreed on six regulations, which we herewith submit to the eye of Your Majesty, and wait reverently for the imperial sanction."*

Without quoting those regulations, it is enough for my present purpose to say that the Tung-wen College was duly organized under the presidency of Dr. W. A. P. Martin, a distinguished American scholar and divine, and that, assisted by an able corps of professors, he has succeeded in making a permanent place for it, even against the prejudice and covert opposition of the conservatives. I am glad to add that, for the current year, it has more pupils than ever before, and all it can accommodate.

Dr. Martin, its efficient and vigorous head, has been many years a resident in China, and is perhaps more profoundly learned in Chinese history, literature, and methods of thought, and by his position comes more closely in contact with the leading men of the Chinese Government, than any foreigner. In speaking of the intellectual movement and the renovation of China, he said, in 1880, what, notwithstanding the retirement of Prince Kung, for his progressive ideas, is true now : "The present is a minority reign ; and the influential men who surround the Throne are leaders in the movement to 'infuse new

* "Hanlin Papers," by W. A. P. Martin, D. D., LL. D., President of the Tung-wen College, Peking. London, Trübner & Co., 1880.

elements of strength into the Government of China.' The Emperor, a lad of thirteen [now nearly seventeen], may imbibe their spirit and shape his policy on theirs; and in a few years he will receive in person, as by treaty bound, the ambassadors of foreign powers. He will thus have an opportunity for acquiring new ideas such as his forefathers never enjoyed." *

What will be the outcome of it all, or just what the course of events will be, it is impossible for any one to predict with certainty; but while it is true that no adviser of the Throne has been willing to assume beforehand the duty of marking out or forestalling a policy of innovation and progress for the young Emperor, it is nearly certain that such a policy must be adopted at no distant day. With trade, the missionaries, diplomacy, and science, all working to the same end, and all having been greatly helped at various times, as we have seen by war the most potential agency that has ever made itself felt in the advancement of civilization and progress, the end can be neither uncertain nor long delayed. Every consul and envoy sent out by the Chinese Government, every scholar educated abroad, and indeed every coolie who seeks his fortune in America, becomes a liberal and a teacher of progress on his return home.

One of the most significant and promising measures ever adopted by the Imperial Government was that of sending the Hon. Anson Burlingame, upon his retirement as United States minister at Peking, in November, 1867, on a general mission to the principal governments of America and Europe. He was accompanied by three imperial envoys, and a large suite of *attachés*, clerks, and servants. Just what arguments were used to induce the Government to take this unheard-of step, or what were

---

* "Hanlin Papers," p. 329.

its secret purposes in doing so, is not clearly known, but partly from Mr. Burlingame's enthusiastic representations, and partly through the hopes of the world at large, his mission was everywhere hailed as the sure precursor of an era of progress and prosperity for China. It was thought that it betokened a new and liberal policy toward foreigners and foreign enterprises, and especially toward railroads and telegraphs, on the part of the Imperial Government; and, while this was denied, with much unfriendly comment by the foreign merchants, and especially by the English residing in China, the mission made the most satisfactory progress till brought to an untimely end by the death of Mr. Burlingame, at St. Petersburg, in February, 1870. It negotiated and enlarged a number of treaties, but it lost its momentum in losing its head, and speedily returned home, to be dissolved and forgotten. Whatever good effects in the direction of progress might have otherwise resulted from it, were suppressed by the disgrace and retirement of Prince Kung, whose approval and advocacy certainly had much to do in causing it to be sent forth.

Shortly after the return of this mission a number of Chinese boys, perhaps a hundred and fifty, were sent (early in 1872) to America to be educated; many of them developed talents of a high order, and all made rapid progress in learning our language and receiving our education. After they had been with us from six to nine years, some one reported to the home Government that the boys were forgetting their own language, and were growing up in ignorance of their own country, its laws, literature, and customs, and should be recalled at once. A censor was sent out to examine and report, and in a short time this promising measure was reconsidered, and all the boys were called home. To make matters worse, they were roughly treated and assigned to uncongenial employments. Some of them had found homes in refined and well-to-do American families, where they had been kindly nurtured and cared for; nearly all had adopted American clothing and customs, and the lot of the least fortunate had been far happier in America than was possible for the richest of them at home, and, of course, they were all more or less distressed by the unexpected change in their lot. I met quite a number of these young men during my travels. They are now from twenty to twenty-eight years old, and are all employed either as teachers of English or the sciences, or are connected with the Government service in the provinces as interpreters, telegraph operators, and writers, but the most of them, judging from what I saw, are unhappy and discouraged. They say that there is no chance for them so long as Western learning is looked down upon in China, and the customs of that country remain unchanged. All high offices are given to old men, and they look upon that class as all alike—conservative, ignorant, and intolerant—and that no true progress can be made so long as they remain in power. This is in some degree true, but that class can not always remain in power. Such men as Li Hung-Chang and Tso-Tsung Tang, who never were out of their country, became liberals, and have gained the highest rank and influence ever enjoyed by a Chinese subject. It is now an open secret that Prince Kung, the uncle, and Prince Chun (the Seventh Prince), the father of the Emperor, are liberals, and favor the policy of progress. The Marquis Tseng and others, who have traveled and held diplomatic office abroad, are said to be still more pronounced in their liberal sentiments, and so even the young men who were partly educated in America may hope that some of their number will yet reach high rank and wield great influence in the affairs of their country. If ever one of them should

NECESSITY OF EDUCATION. 359

attract the attention of the Emperor, and gain his confidence, or that of any one closely connected with him, the consequences might not only be immediate but far-reaching. Neither is it impossible that some foreigner connected with the Tung-wen College, the maritime customs, the navy, the army, or even with the foreign legations, or with one of the great foreign trading-houses in China, may attract the Emperor's attention or the attention of those around him, as did Mr. Burlingame, and thus secure the opportunity, directly or indirectly, to favorably influence his action, and start the Government upon a course which will end in making China one of the most progressive nations of the world. The Emperor is all-powerful when he chooses to assert himself. He can control the official class by a simple exercise of the will, and the official class can control the people almost as easily. The inaccessibility of the one, and the small number of the other, are circumstances which encourage the observer to believe that the movement when once determined can be maintained until it is entirely successful. In other words, it is necessary to educate but comparatively few men up to the conviction that Western arts and sciences are better than those of Eastern countries, and that the appliances of Western civilization are superior to those of China, in order to control and direct the common people, in making China one of the richest and most powerful nations of the earth, instead of, as she is now, the poorest and weakest. She is rich beyond any other power in labor, while her mineral resources are entirely undeveloped, and yet there are good grounds for supposing them to be second to those of no other country under the sun. With intelligence enough on the part of the Government and the official class to control and direct the people in utilizing the resources within their reach, there can be but one result.

And this brings us to the question which has been asked me so many times since my return home, "Are the Chinese going to build railroads, open mines, and erect furnaces and rolling-mills?" I answer, unhesitatingly, "Yes—whenever they can be shown that this can be done with their own money, obtained, at first, by private subscription, and by their own labor, under the direction of foreign experts, who will treat them fairly and honestly." They will not for the present borrow money on the credit of their Government or a pledge of its revenues for the purpose of paying for such works, nor will they grant concessions or subsidies to foreigners. So far as I can see, they will not even take money from any power or syndicate, and agree to secure the repayment of the same by a mortgage upon the works to be created thereby. As has been shown in a previous chapter, their leading statesmen want railroads, and have an intelligent understanding of how they are to be utilized for the benefit of the country; but they are not willing to have them upon any terms which will increase European influence in China, or give European powers the slightest pretext for intermeddling with the internal affairs of the country or its government. They have no surplus in the public treasury with which to establish and pay for a system of state railroads, and nothing but a great emergency could induce them to raise the money by taxation or to borrow it, even upon the simple pledge of the Imperial Government's faith to repay it; for, while they know they can pay interest on a hundred million dollars, if necessary, they look with doubt upon their capacity to repay the principal, and therefore dread to assume any such obligation. They are, without knowing it, strong protectionists, and look upon it as a national calamity to be compelled to send money out of the country for the purpose of paying interest. If they could build railroads with Chinese money, Chinese skilled labor, and Chinese materials, including steel rails and machinery, there is good reason for believing that they would start at once, notwithstanding the opposition of the censors and the Board of Revenue, which have been strong enough heretofore to kill off or to postpone indefinitely every proposition which has been submitted. Under proper Government protection there is also good reason for believing that the necessary money for the initial lines can be raised from the native merchants at the treaty ports, and of course common labor can be had in any quantity and at the lowest prices; but, inasmuch as there are no iron-mines opened, and no furnaces or rolling-mills built, it would greatly delay the construction of the first railroads if it were necessary to wait till steel rails and machinery could be manufactured therefor at home. They know this, and that the first roads built in this way would cost much more than they would if imported materials were used, but they do not care. They argue, with great cogency, that the money would all be spent at home, and that even if the roads cost ten times as much per mile, built of native materials, with native labor, and the least possible number of foreign experts, it will be better for the country in the end; and at all events, that is the way they would like to have it.

The best practical solution of the present difficulty will probably be for them to lay out and construct the initial lines, using capital subscribed by Chinese subjects, and materials bought wherever they can get them cheapest. They should, of course, employ American experts and adopt the American system of construction, for the reasons that they are more practical, economical, and efficient, and better adapted to the requirement of the case in hand. Besides, the Americans are their nearest neighbors, and, having no desire to establish colonies or to acquire foreign possessions, are less liable to quarrel with China, or to interfere under any pretext with her internal affairs.

On the other hand, our Government should do all in its power to foster friendly relations with the Chinese. It should establish its legation at Peking, and its consulates throughout the empire, on the most liberal scale. Its diplomatic and consular agents should be habitually selected with great care, and should be paid as much as any other power pays for similar service ; they should be housed at the public expense, and surrounded with every appliance likely to increase the respect or attract the admiration of the Chinese people and authorities. Whatever may become the policy of our Government in reference to the continuance of diplomatic relations with Europe, it is certain that for many years, perhaps for centuries, we must maintain a minister at Peking, and he should in rank, state, and consideration be a fitting representative of the power, wealth, and intelligence of the Great Republic. The Chinese, like all Oriental people, are more or less impressed by the external evidences of strength and greatness ; and, purely as a matter of business, our Government could not do better than to buy the land offered it by the Chinese Government, erect suitable buildings thereon, furnish them handsomely, advance the pay of the minister, secretaries, and *attachés* to the highest rates and allowances that anybody has ever suggested in their behalf, surround them with servants, and even give them a platoon of cavalry, splendidly equipped and mounted, to act as escort upon all visits and occasions of ceremony. This would not be in accordance with our ideas of republican simplicity, but it would pay, and that is a sufficient argument; besides, the Chinese authorities do not care for, or understand, simplicity in official matters.

OUR COMMERCE WITH CHINA.

Our commerce with the Chinese is in its infancy,* and as commerce is not only profitable in a pecuniary sense, but is primarily the origin of all progress, we should lose no time in putting our diplomatic and consular service

---

* The following extract from an able and interesting speech delivered by the Hon. Richard W. Townshend, of Illinois, in the House of Representatives, on February 3, 1887, will give a fair idea of the importance of the China trade:

"Owing to our superior advantage over Europe in distance, and other respects, we should control most of the foreign trade in China, but statistics reveal to us the fact that England has outstripped us in that trade, and that France is fast overtaking us. Indeed, it is said that to-day three fourths of the trade of China is with England and her colonies.

"There are twenty-two 'treaty ports' in China open to foreign commerce.

The imports at treaty ports in 1885 were.......	$168,000,000
Exports at treaty ports in 1885 were..........	105,625,000
Total trade........................	$273,625,000
In 1886 United States imports from China......	$18,972,963
In 1886 United States exports to China........	7,520,581
Total	$26,493,544

"This does not include Hong-Kong, which, although a British island, yet, as it is only a few miles off the coast of China, and its trade is actually as much a part of the trade of China as if it was under the Chinese dominion, it being merely a point of transshipment of products destined for China or brought from China, our trade with Hong-Kong, therefore, should be added to that of our trade with China. In 1886 it was:

United States imports from Hong-Kong	$1,072,459
United States exports to Hong-Kong	4,056,236
Total	$5,128,695

"Which, added to our trade with China already mentioned, aggregates for 1886 the total of $31,632,239, which is about eight per cent of the trade of that country, as against seventy-five per cent with Great Britain, and the balance, with other countries. What a humiliation to our national pride when we see a rival situated so far away from China outstrip us when our western border is on the same ocean with China, with far superior natural advantages in our favor over those of England or any European country!"

on such a basis as will enable it to promote commerce to the fullest extent. There is a foolish law in our Revised Statutes which prohibits American ministers from recommending any one for office or employment at home or abroad. This should be repealed at once, and both diplomatic and consular agents should be instructed that the more reputable and capable Americans they can find employment for in China as experts in the arts and sciences, or as contractors for public works, or as instructors in the army and navy, or as advisers to the provincial and Imperial Governments, the better they will please the State Department. It is obvious that the greater the number of American citizens thus employed in China the greater will be our influence, and the more extended and valuable will become our commerce with the Chinese people.

Congress has passed the Chinese indemnity bill, and this has given great satisfaction to the Chinese Government and statesmen. It should as soon as possible authorize the President to lend army and naval officers; and should in addition open the Naval and Military Academies for a limited number of students to both the Chinese and Japanese Governments, who would no doubt be thankful for the favors accorded, and would in addition regard it as a gracious and kindly act. Again, I am certain that it would pay, no matter from what point of view it is considered.

Manifestly, whatever our Government and people would do they should do promptly and cheerfully, not with a niggardly or a grudging hand; for, while the Chinese are a poor people and must needs go slowly in all that constitutes the material elements of progress, they are also a self-respecting people. Their governing class is in addition sensitive as well as conceited, and do not consider themselves in any moral or intellectual sense as fit objects of charity or condescension on the part of any other people or nation.

Of course, it is impossible to predict with certainty when China will move in specific enterprises, what will be her direction and policy, or what men and nation will become her guide. That she will move, and, in fact, is moving in a general way, I think I have shown in the preceding pages ; and, when the reader considers the facts set forth, and especially the vast territory, the innumerable population, and the boundless natural resources waiting for development in that far-away country, he will find ample subjects for speculation and prophecy. That she is surrounded by great perils, and confronted by many complicated problems offering themselves to her statesmen for solution, is obvious to the most casual observer. Whether she will escape the former, and satisfactorily solve the latter, no human being can possibly know in advance. But with Russia pressing upon her northern and western and the British Indian Empire upon her western and southwestern borders, both moving in accordance with the requirements of their "permanent interests," and both carrying with them all the appliances of modern progress, it would be more than a miracle that she should escape war and spoliation, and it is not impossible that she should ultimately suffer subjugation and dismemberment, as have so many other countries and nations of Asia. The movement of Russia into the vast region between the Aral Sea and the Issyk-Kul, near the western borders of Thibet, the capture and annexation of Khiva, Tashkend, Merv, Samarcand, Khokand, and Bokhara, and the building of a railroad from the Caspian Sea, in the same general direction, has been looked upon by England as a special menace to Herat and her Indian Empire ; and it certainly is a menace of the most portentous character. But it should not be forgotten by England, and still less by China, that

Russia has for two hundred years held all of Northern Asia, from the Ural Mountains to the Pacific Ocean; that her Eastern possessions in that almost illimitable region are conterminous with those of China; that she has been for the last century engaged in subjugating the wild tribes and planting civilized colonies; that of late years her settlements in the Amur Valley have been growing with amazing rapidity; and, finally, that it can not be a great while in the world's time till they are connected with Europe by a railroad or railroads, which will bring all the resources of the empire for conquest to the very gates of China. When it is remembered that the latter is in a far worse condition for defense than is the Indian Empire, backed by all the intelligence, wealth, and military power of Great Britain and her flourishing colonies, it may well be admitted that Russia is merely protecting her flank and her lines of communication in Southern Asia, while she is really aiming at the rich plains, the open seaports, and the boundless resources of her sleeping and unconscious neighbor of Eastern Asia. Admitting, however, that her primary object is, as commonly believed, the conquest of Persia, Afghanistan, and British India, and that, if she really sets about its accomplishment with the earnestness that is attributed to her, she will succeed, it is obvious that, *pari passu*, the danger to China, although deferred for a quarter of a century, or even longer, will then be increased a hundred-fold.

In all of this I take no account of France or Germany for the present; for, although the former has twice gone to war with China, and has recently made good her lodgment on the southeastern border of the empire, and both have shown themselves anxious to push their commercial interests by all the means in their power, it can not be contended that either of them can seriously endanger the Chinese Government or its territorial possessions.

Finally, it is always possible that the Imperial Chinese Government may perceive its danger in time, rearrange and perfect its civil administration, organize its army and navy in accordance with modern methods, build railroads, and develop its natural resources, and thus, as well as by its isolation and remoteness and by the aid of its innumerable population, render its position practically secure against all hostile encroachment. It can not be claimed that the Chinese are a warlike people, and hence I, for one, do not regard it as at all likely that they will ever become aggressive toward their neighbors, or dangerous to foreign powers; but in the walks of peace, to which they are impelled by their true policy—in agriculture, the arts, and manufactures—it is almost impossible to set a limit upon their progress, or to the influence thereof upon the trade, the prosperity, and the happiness of themselves and of the world at large.

NOTE.—I have not deemed it necessary or desirable to burden this book with copies of the treaties between the United States and the Chinese or Ta Tsing Empire, as they call it, nor with statistical tables of the trade between the two countries, for they are not only cumbersome but dry, and, besides, they can be readily got at in other publications pertaining more especially to such subjects.

J. H. W

INDEX.

ADMINISTRATION, minor branches of, 186.
Allied demands on the Imperial Government in 1856, 336, 337, 340.
Americans in China, 316.
Ancestral worship, 349.
Anglo-Chinese complications in 1856, 336.
Aristocracy, nature of the, 181.
Armstrong, the American commodore, Canton forts attacked by, 336.
Avenue of Statuary, the, 225.

Banca, city of, 300.
Barkul, 52.
Boards, the Six Great, 184–193.
Boulger's "China," ix.
Bowring, Sir John, 336.
Brick-tea, 54.
British trade, aggressive nature of, 318.
Buddhism, a decadent religion, 349.
Buffalo, the water-, 74, 305.
Burgevine, 122, 123.
Burial customs, 97–100.
Burlingame, Hon. A. P., his mission to foreign governments, 356, 357.

Cambaluc, Mecca of Eastern Asia, 218.
Camel transportation, 54.
Camphor-gum, 298.
Canton, freely opened to foreigners, 330.
  seized by the allied fleet, 336.
Cantonese, the, hatred of, by other Chinese, 334.
Caravans, Mongolian, 216.
Censorate, the, 192, 193.
  its force as a foe of progress, 193.
  most powerful of all the governmental boards, 350, 351.
Central Flowery Kingdom, 56.
Chang-Chin-Chun, 243.
Chang-hwa, city of, 301.
Chee-foo, 86, 88, 89.
Cheshire, Mr., Chinese secretary, 215.
Chihli, v.
Chi-ho, 283, 284.
China and Japan, reasons for a new book on, vii.
China, area of, 26, 27.
  author's object in visiting, iv.
  canal system of, 43.
  ceremonial visits in, 107.

INDEX.

China, climate of, 31, 32.
contraction of, in historic times, 27.
first made aware of superior power of foreign nations by the Opium War, 329.
immense possibilities of, 359.
isolation of, 28-31.
lack of railroads in, iii.
Merchants' Steamship Company, 86.
mental conservatism of, 81.
military music in, 101, 116.
military weakness of, 96.
mineral wealth of, 52.
navy of, 90.
provinces of, 31.
topography of, 32.
Chin-Chiang-pu, 240.
Chi-nan-fu, v, 281, 283.
Chinese authorities refuse to sign treaties at Peking, 338.
burial-customs, 97-100.
civilization, 20-22.
civilization, future of, 83, 84.
classics, the knowledge of, sole ground of official appointment, 196.
Engineering and Mining Company, 227.
attitude toward railway improvement, iii.
indemnity bill, passed by Congress, 364.
navy, difficulties in organizing, 92, 93.
New Year, 288, 289.
non-intercourse of foreign merchants with, 102.
race, strength and health of the, 71.

Chinese revenues compared with —those of India, 209.
rulers, paucity of ability in, viii.
stagnation, remedies for, 311, 312.
Tartary, or Ili, 52.
troops partly foreign drilled, 95.
written language, 125.
Ching, Prince, President of the Board of Foreign Affairs, 294.
coadjutor in naval control, 91.
Chi-ning-Chou, 266.
Chinkiang, vi.
Chow, Duke, 174.
Chü-fu, home and burial-place of Confucius, 267-273 (see Kü-fu).
Chu-kiang, or Pearl River, 44.
Chun, Prince (see Seventh Prince), administrator of navy and coast-defenses, 91.
Ciang-ho, 227.
Civil Office, Board of, 188.
Climate of China, 31, 32.
Clothing, 76, 77.
Coal, 57-62.
Colliery of Kaiping, 57-59.
Colonial Office, 192.
Compradores, 333.
Compression of the female foot, origin of, 69, 71.
Commercial morals, 287, 288.
Confucius, v.
and his descendants, 268.
and his disciples, teachings of, the whole of Chinese education, 309, 310.
temples of, 269-273.
tombs of his family, 274, 275.
Corea, 52.
Cotton, 77.
Council, General, 182.
Curiosity of Chinese mobs, 258-264.

INDEX. 371

Denby, Colonel Charles, 294.
Dinner-party in Japanese style, 6–12.
Diplomatic corps, the, 165.
Domestic animals, their scarcity, 73.

East India Company, 315, 318.
Education, 308, 311.
 absolute need of a change in its system, 345.
Elliot, Admiral, 324.
 Captain, 321, 324.
Emperor of Japan, reception of the author by, 2; palace of, 3; description of, 4, 5.
English Government, its immorality in the Opium War, 328.
English in China, 315.
Enouye, Count, Japanese Minister of Foreign Affairs, 3.
Ethnography, 67, 68.
European communication with China, history of, 311, 321.
Examination, public, for office, 195, 196.
Expenditures, governmental, 210, 211.
 summary of, 212.

Famines, 65, 66.
Financial system, 200–214.
Food resources, 71, 74.
Foreigners in China, 21.
Foreign loans, dread of, 213.
Foreign merchants, agreement of, not to deal in opium, 323.
 influence of, in suppressing the Taipings, 23, 24.
Foreign powers, alert to control trade and internal improvements, 175 176.

Formosa, animals of, 305, 306.
 beautiful scenery in, 298.
 description of, 295–307.
 its commerce, present and future, 303, 304, 307.
 lack of harbors in, 299.
 mineral resources of, 306.
 savage tribes of, 297.
 tea-culture in, 302.
Funded debt, 212.
Fung-shuy, 349.

Gaishas, dancing and singing girls of Japan, 8–12.
"Gazette," Peking, 170, 183, 184.
Gordon, 120–124.
 award of the "Yellow Jacket" and other honors to, 332.
 Wilson's life of, author indebted to, ix.
Government, absolute character of the, 179, 180.
 formalism in the, 181.
 organization of, 182–199.
Governor-general, authority and duties of, 194, 195.
Grand Canal, v, 43, 78.
 a visit to, 233–246.
 Chinese estimate of its importance, 242.
 Li Hung-Chang's memorial on, 244.
 regulation of the waters of, 240, 241.
 solution of, possible by scientific engineering, 244.
Great Plain, the, 54–56.
 appearance of the, 96.
 character of its inhabitants, 291, 292.
Great Wall, v, 52, 78, 215–228.

372 INDEX.

Hang-kow, 338.
Hang-Chow, 54.
Hart, Sir Robert, head of imperial maritime customs, 93.
 remarkable administrative power of, 208.
 revenue collected by, 334.
"Herald," the North China, 183, 184.
Hienfung, Emperor, 167.
 death of, 342.
Hien-tsu, founder of the present dynasty, 166.
Hwang-ho, devastating spring freshets of the (see Yellow River), 36.
 embankments on the (see Yellow River), 36–38.
 its course and character (see Yellow River), 33–36.
Honan, v.
Hong-Kong, cession of, to the English, 325, 327.
 made a free port by the British, 335.
Hostility to foreigners, reasons for, 320, 321.
Houses and house-building, 75, 76.
Hubbard, Governor, American minister to Japan, 2.
Huc, Abbé, his theory of inundations of the Yellow River, 250.
Hung-tse-Chuen, Taiping leader, 28.
 possible achievements of, 332.

Ignorance of the masses, 81.
Ili, or Chinese Tartary, 52.
Imperial treasury, property of the, 360, 361.
Industrial development, the future of, 360.

Inland Sea, beauty of, 1.
Inns, a description of, 237, 238.
Intellectual development arrested, 309–311.
International relations with Japan, changes in the, 16, 17.
Iron, 57–62.
Ito, Count, Japanese prime-minister, 3.

Japan, vi.
 duck-hunting in, 7, 8.
 fascination of, for the traveler, 17, 18.
 genuine progress of, 13, 15.
 government of, 13, 14.
 railroads of, 14, 15.
 spring in, 2.
Japanese ministers, accomplishments of, 3.
Japanese wrestling, 8–10.
Jinrikishas, man-power, carriages, vi.
Jehol, 341.

Kai-fung-fu, capital of Honan, v. 246.
 visit to, 257–264.
Kaiping, v.
 coal-mines of, 226–232.
 railway, 229, 230.
Kashgar, 52.
Kelung, city of, 299.
Khoten, 52.
Kienlung, 37, 168.
Kioto, Japan, vi.
Kirin, 52.
Kirrea, 52.
Ki-ying, imperial commissioner, proclamation of, 329.
Kobe, Japan, vi.

INDEX.

Kowlung, ceded to the British, 341.
Kü-fu, burial-place of Confucius, v.
Kuldja, 52. [267, 273.
   expedition, 54.
Kung, Prince, 173.
   his memorial on Western arts and sciences, 352, 355.
   negotiator of peace with the allies, 341.
Kwang Hsu, the new Emperor, 166-168, 171-176.
Kwan-lun Mountains, 52.
Kyan-Chan, harbor of, 90.

Land-tax, 202.
Lang, Captain, naval assistant to Viceroy Li, 91, 92.
Language, written, 82, 125.
Lao-Hwang-ho, the river, 285.
Lao-mu-Miaio, temple of the Holy Mother, 280.
Lay, Mr., 334.
Liautung, 52.
Lien-Sheng-tien, a model Chinese inn, 277.
Li Hung-Chang, v, 90.
   author's report of his investigations to, 293.
   director of naval affairs, 91.
   discussion of railroads by, 113, 114.
   his relation to foreign powers, 197.
   interview with, by the author, 106-116.
   invitation to visit, vi.
   most progressive and powerful of Chinese statesmen, 24.
   sketch of, 105, 109, 110, 118, 119.
Likin, the, or tax on internal commerce, 205, 206.

Lin-ching, 240, 241.
Literary language, the, a distinct tongue, 82.
Literati, the, or office-holders, 181.
Liu Ming-Ch'uan, 152, 296.
   Viceroy of Formosa, invitation to visit, vi.
Locomotive, first, in China, 58, 227-229.
Loëss terraces, fertility of, 49.
   nature and theories about their origin, 49, 50.
Lung-mun-Kou, 248, 264.
Lung-Wang Miao, 240.

Macao, 313.
Manchu caste, distinction from the subject race, 68.
Manchuria, 52, 63, 124.
Marco Polo, story of, edited by Colonel Yule, viii.
Maritime customs duties, 208.
   organization of, 334.
Martin, Dr. W. A. P., President of Tung-wen College, 355.
Metallurgy, difficulties of Chinese progress in, 61, 62.
Military helplessness, 176-178.
Military weakness, 96.
Min, an important river, 44.
Mineral wealth, 52.
Ming tombs, 223.
Missionaries, English and American, 281, 282, 286, 287.
Missionary progress, 346, 347.
Mongolia, Inner and Outer, 52, 53.
   gold mines in, 53.
Mountain system, 48, 49, 51, 52.

Nagahama, Japan, vi.

INDEX.

Nagasaki, Japan, vi.
Nakasendo, Japan, vi.
Nanking, vi, 295.
Napier, Lord, first to protest against official non-intercourse, 319, 320.
Navy of China, 90.
Navy-yard and docks, 89.

Opium, smuggling in, 335.
  trade in, 321-323.
  war, the, 324-327.
  treaty which followed it, 327.
Osaka, Japan, vi.
Otsu, Japan, vi.

Pa-li Miao, 243.
Pang-Chia-Chwang, 286, 287.
Pan-ting-fu, 104.
Parker, Admiral Sir William, 326.
Parker, W. H., American minister to Corea, 2.
Parkes, Sir Harry, 340.
Peh-tang, the anxiety of the government about, 46.
  town and river, 227.
Pei-ho batteries, attacked by allied fleet, 337, 340.
Pei-ho River, vi.
  strategic value of the, 45, 46.
  importance of the, to Chinese commerce, 45.
Peking, v.
  description of, 160, 165.
  treaties of peace signed at, 341, 342.
Pescadores, the, 307.
Ping Yin, 281.
Population, 63, 64.
Port Arthur, 89.

Portuguese in China, 313.
Pottinger, Sir Henry, 326.
Poverty, universal, 78.
Provinces of China, 31.
Provincial governments, the nineteen, 193.
Psalmanazar, George, 295.
Punishments, Board of, 190.

Railroads, pressing need of, 53.
  obstacles to the establishment of, 99.
  a memorial concerning, by Liu Ming Ch'uan, 126-135.
  only practicable method of building, 361.
  supported by Li Hung-Chang and Lin-K'un-Yi, 135-153.
Revenue, Board of, 186, 187.
Revenues, summary of, 208.
  different estimates of, 210.
Rites, Board of, 188.
River engineering, crudity of the Chinese system of, 284, 285.
Rivers, most of the Chinese, dry in the rainless season, 47.
Robinson, Sir George B., 321.
Rockhill, Mr., First Secretary of American Legation, 215.
Russell and Company, first steamboat proprietors, 86.
Russia, danger threatening from, 314, 365, 366.
Russians in China, 314.

Sakimoto, Japan, vi.
Salt monopoly, 204, 205.
Sankolinsin's Folly, 104.
Sankolinsin, Prince, 340.
Secretariat, the Grand, 182.
Sekigahara, Japan, vi.

INDEX. 375

Seventh Prince, the, father of the Emperor (see Prince Chun).
Sha-ho, 217.
Shamo, or Gobi, sandy desert of, 52.
Shanghai, vi.
  description of, 20–25.
Shanghai, Navigation Company, 86.
Shan-hai-Quan, 54.
Shantung, v.
Shih-li pu, 243.
Shinking, 52.
Siebelin, Captain, naval assistant to Viceroy Li, 91.
Simonoseki, Japan, vi.
Spaniards in China, 313.
Summer Palace burned by the allies, 341.
Superstition, universal, 349.

Taian-fu, 277.
Taipak-fu, 301.
Taiping rebellion, v.
  at first encouraged by foreign merchants, 335.
  commerce stimulated by, 333.
  former misapprehension of, 331.
  its influence in educating Chinese statesmen, 331.
Taishan, v.
  inscriptions on the rocks of, 279, 280.
  sacred mountain, 278–280.
  temples on, 279, 280.
Taiwan-fu, city of, 296, 300.
Taku forts, 93, 94.
  capture of, by the allies, 94.
Tamsui, 296.
Tao-chung-fu, 246.
Tashkend, 52.
Tatnall Commodore, 94.
  co-operates with the allies, 339.

Taukwang, the Emperor, first to make the opium-trade illegal, 322.
Ta-Wen-ho, 240.
  the river, 277.
Taxes, how collected, 203.
  inefficiency of method, 203, 204.
  miscellaneous, 207.
Telegraph system, 124, 125.
Ter-chou, 239, 288.
Thibet, probable mineral wealth of, 52, 53.
Throne, difficulties of approaching the, 169, 170.
  present powers behind the, 344.
Tien-Shan Peh-lu, 52.
Tien-Shan or Celestial Mountains, 52.
Tien-Shan Nan-Lu, 52.
Tientsin, v.
  center of all progressive movements, 105.
  description of, 103, 104.
  destruction of French mission at, 104, 347.
  races at, 101.
  residence of Viceroy Li, 103.
Tokio, vi.
Tombs of the Ming dynasty, 222–224.
Topography of China, 32.
Townshend, Congressman, his speech on the China trade, 363.
Tseng Quo-chu'an, Viceroy, vi, 120, 295.
Tseng Quo-fan, 120.
Tsin Chi-Hwangti, builder of the Great Wall, 219.
Tsitsihar, 52.
Tso Tsung-tang, 120, 154–157.

Tsung-li Yamen, Board of Foreign Affairs, 165.
   author's report of his investigations to, 294.
   composition of, 185.
Tung Chi, late Emperor, 167.
Tung-wen College, 352-355.
Turkistan, Eastern, 52.
Twatutia, seat of Formosan government, 296.
Tycoon, decadence of the power of the, 5.
Tz'-u Hsi, Empress-Dowager, 167-169, 171, 172.

United States, the, its true Chinese policy, 362-364.
Urum-tsi, 52.

Wade, Sir Thomas, 122, 334.
Walled cities, 78, 79.
War, Board of, 189.
Ward, American minister, embarrasses other plenipotentiaries, 339.
Ward, General, organizer of the "Ever-Victorious Army," 33, 120, 121.

Ward, Gen., receives divine honors after death, 332.
Wei-hai-wei, 90.
Wheelbarrow carriages, 278.
Williams, S. Wells, missionary and diplomat, "Middle Kingdom" by, vii.
Women in Japan, 8-12.
Woosung River, 20.
Works, Board of, 191, 192.

Yang-tse-kiang, vi, 19.
   affluents of, 42.
   description of, 40-42.
Yellow River (see Hwang-ho), v.
   causes of its floods (see Hwang-ho), 236.
   inundations of (see Hwang-ho), 248, 255.
   embankments of, irregularly built (see Hwang-ho), 245, 246.
Yokohama, vi.
Yokogawa, Japan, vi.
Yungloh, Ming Emperor, 222.
Yu-wang-shang-to, 280.

THE END.

D. APPLETON & CO.'S PUBLICATIONS.

CLIMBING IN THE HIMALAYAS. By WILLIAM MARTIN CONWAY, M. A., F. R. G. S., Vice-President of the Alpine Club; formerly Professor of Art in University College, Liverpool. With 300 Illustrations by A. D. MCCORMICK, and a Map. 8vo. Cloth, $10.00.

This work contains a minute record of one of the most important and thrilling geographical enterprises of the century—an expedition made in 1892, under the auspices of the Royal Geographical Society, the Royal Society, the British Association, and the Government of India. It included an exploration of the glaciers at the head of the Bagrot Valley and the great peaks in the neighborhood of Rakipushi (25,500 feet); an expedition to Hispar, at the foot of the longest glacier in the world outside the polar regions; the first definitely recorded passage of the Hispar Pass, the longest known pass in the world; and the ascent of Pioneer Peak (about 23,000 feet), the highest ascent yet authentically made. No better man could have been chosen for this important expedition than Mr. Conway, who has spent over twenty years in mountaineering work in the Alps. Already the author of nine published books, he has recorded his discoveries in this volume in the clear, incisive, and thrilling language of an expert.

"It would be hard to say too much in praise of this superb work. As a record of mountaineering it is almost, if not quite, unique. Among records of Himalayan exploration it certainly stands alone. . . . The farther Himalayas . . . have never been so faithfully—in other words, so poetically—presented as in the masterly delicate sketches with which Mr. McCormick has adorned this book."—*London Daily News.*

"This stately volume is a worthy record of a splendid journey. . . . The book is not merely the narrative of the best organized and most successful mountaineering expedition as yet made; it is a most valuable and minute account, based on first-hand evidence, of a most fascinating region of the heaven-soaring Himalayas."—*Pall Mall Gazette.*

"Mr. Conway's volume is a splendid record of a daring and adventurous scientific expedition. . . . What Mr. Whymper did for the Northern Andes, Mr. Conway has done for the Karakorum Himalayas."—*London Times.*

"It would be difficult to say which of the many classes of readers who will welcome the work will find most enjoyment in its fascinating pages. Mr. Conway's pen and Mr. McCormick's pencil have made their countrymen partners in their pleasure."—*London Standard.*

". . . In addition to this, Mr. Conway is a man of letters, a student (and a teacher, too) of art, a scholar in several languages; one, too, who knows the Latin names of plants, and the use of theodolite and plane table. From him, therefore, if from any one, the world had a right to expect a book that should combine accurate observation and intelligible reporting with an original and acute record of impressions; nor will the world have any reason to be disappointed."—*London Athenæum.*

"With its three hundred illustrations we have seldom seen a volume which speaks to the eye and understanding so pleasantly and expressively on every page. . . . We have an exhaustive panorama of the Himalayan scenery, of the manner in which the rough marching was conducted, of ascents achieved under the most dangerous conditions, and of the troubles and humors of the shifting camps where the coolies rested from their labors."—*London Saturday Review.*

"Perhaps no book of recent date gives a simpler or at the same time more effective picture of the truly wonderful mountain regions lying behind the northern barrier of India than Mr. Conway's striking volume."—*London Telegraph.*

New York: D. APPLETON & CO., 72 Fifth Avenue.

D. APPLETON & CO.'S PUBLICATIONS.

IN THE TRACK OF THE SUN: Readings from the Diary of a Globe Trotter. By FREDERICK DIODATI THOMPSON. Profusely illustrated with Engravings from Photographs and from Drawings by Harry Fenn. Large 8vo. Cloth, gilt top, $6.00.

"In very gorgeous holiday attire comes this large octavo volume, with its sumptuous full-page illustrations and its profusion of head and tail pieces. . . . The author's style is pleasant and easy, occasionally almost conversational, and it is impossible to follow him through the intricacies of his tour without acquiring a deal of information by the way."—*Philadelphia Bulletin.*

"One of the handsomest of this year's Christmas books. . . . The author has practically abandoned the grand tour in favor of regions less known. There is not much of Europe in the volume, but a great deal about China, Japan, and the East. In this good judgment is shown. . . . A truly elegant piece of bookmaking."—*Philadelphia Telegraph.*

"Mr. Thompson is an intelligent observer, who describes what he has seen with humor and point. . . . We know of no equally convenient and handsome publication illustrating a journey round the world."—*The Outlook.*

"Few 'globe trotters' have given their impressions of travel so comely a form as Mr. Thompson in this handsome illustrated volume."—*London Saturday Review.*

"As a piece of fine printing, binding, and illustration, Mr. Thompson's volume deserves very high praise. The Appleton press has never done finer work. . . . The portrait of the Mohammedan sheik is one of the finest illustrations in recent books of travel. But the whole volume is a picture gallery which will especially commend itself to the large family of globe trotters, among whom Mr. Thompson deserves good standing for his sensible comments and his excellent taste."—*Literary World.*

POEMS OF NATURE. By WILLIAM CULLEN BRYANT. Profusely illustrated by Paul de Longpré. 8vo. Cloth, gilt, $4.00.

"A very rich volume embellished with exquisite designs. . . . The publishers have been at great pains to make this volume what it is—one of the handsomest of the year."—*Philadelphia Press.*

"The poems included in the collection are some of the choicest of Bryant's inspirations, the illustrations are lovely and sympathetic, and the entire make-up of the volume is eminently artistic."—*Philadelphia Telegraph.*

"There has probably been no more beautiful, and certainly no more fitting, presentation of Bryant's selected work than is offered in this volume. . . . Each poem is accompanied by special designs arranged with picturesque irregularity, and the volume is admirably printed. An excellent effect is secured by the use of a little lighter ink for the text."—*The Outlook.*

"The artist is primarily a painter of flowers, and under his faithful and very pretty reproductions of these the poems are delicately wreathed."—*New York Times.*

"The poetry of William Cullen Bryant is distinguished beyond that of any other American poet by the fidelity with which Nature is depicted therein. . . . No one has caught the picturesque spirit of his text so successfully as Paul de Longpré in these poems of Nature."—RICHARD HENRY STODDARD, in *the Book Buyer.*

"In beauty of print and binding and in its artistic illustrations the book is among the best specimens of the printer's art. The illustrations by Paul de Longpré tell the story of green fields and woods and mountains and singing birds without the aid of words. The book is artistically beautiful upon every page."—*Chicago Inter-Ocean.*

New York: D. APPLETON & CO., 72 Fifth Avenue.

D. APPLETON & CO.'S PUBLICATIONS.

MEMOIRS ILLUSTRATING THE HISTORY OF NAPOLEON I, from 1802 to 1815. By Baron CLAUDE-FRANÇOIS DE MÉNEVAL, Private Secretary to Napoleon. Edited by his Grandson, Baron NAPOLEON JOSEPH DE MÉNEVAL. With Portraits and Autograph Letters. In three volumes. 8vo. Cloth, $6.00.

These volumes furnish a picture of Napoleon's daily life which is believed to be unexcelled in point of closeness of observation and graphic detail by any other narrative. That Méneval was not the man to neglect his opportunities is shown abundantly by the glimpses of character revealed in his diaries and notes. Yet, for personal and other reasons, his invaluable recollections were not given to the world. They have been treasured by his family until the present time of profound interest in Napoleonic history. Of Napoleon's relations with Josephine and Marie Louise—of all the features of his domestic and social existence—Méneval had abundant knowledge, for he shared Napoleon's private life; and since he was sitting at the fountain-head of information, he is able to shed new light on many features of the Napoleonic campaigns. His narrative is most interesting; its historical importance need not be emphasized.

"The Baron de Méneval knew Napoleon as few knew him. He was his confidential secretary and intimate friend. . . . Students and historians who wish to form a trustworthy estimate of Napoleon can not afford to neglect this testimony by one of his most intimate associates."—*London News.*

"These memoirs, by the private secretary of Napoleon, are a valuable and important contribution to the history of the Napoleonic period, and necessarily they throw new and interesting light on the personality and real sentiments of the emperor. If Napoleon anywhere took off the mask, it was in the seclusion of his private cabinet. The memoirs have been republished almost as they were written, by Baron de Méneval's grandson, with the addition of some supplementary documents."—*London Times.*

"Méneval has brought the living Napoleon clearly before us in a portrait, flattering, no doubt, but essentially true to nature; and he has shown us what the emperor really was—at the head of his armies, in his Council of State, as the ruler of France, as the lord of the continent—above all, in the round of his daily life, and in the circle of family and home."—*London Academy.*

"Neither the editor nor translator of Méneval's memoirs has miscalculated his deep interest —an interest which does not depend on literary style but on the substance of what is related   Whoever reads this volume will wait with impatience for the remainder."—*N. Y. Tribune.*

"The work will take rank with the most important of memoirs relating to the period. Its great value arises largely from its author's transparent veracity. Méneval was one of those men who could not consciously tell anything but the truth. He was constitutionally unfitted for lying. . . . The book is extremely interesting, and it is as important as it is interesting."—*N. Y. Times.*

"Few memoirists have given us a more minute account of Napoleon. . . . No lover of Napoleon, no admirer of his wonderful genius, can fail to read these interesting and important volumes which have been waited for for years."—*N. Y. World.*

"The book will be hailed with delight by the collectors of Napoleonic literature, as it covers much ground wholly unexplored by the great majority of the biographers of Napoleon."—*Providence Journal.*

New York: D. APPLETON & CO., 72 Fifth Avenue.

D. APPLETON & CO.'S PUBLICATIONS.

IDLE DAYS IN PATAGONIA. By W. H. HUDSON, C. M. Z. S., author of "The Naturalist in La Plata," etc. With 27 Illustrations. 8vo. Cloth, $4.00.

"Of all modern books of travel it is certainly one of the most original, and many, we are sure, will also find it one of the most interesting and suggestive."—*New York Tribune.*

"Mr. Hudson's remarks on color and expression of eyes in man and animals are reserved for a second chapter, 'Concerning Eyes.' He is eloquent upon the pleasures afforded by 'Bird Music in South America,' and relates some romantic tales of white men in captivity to savages. But it makes very little difference what is the topic when Mr. Hudson writes. He calls up bright images of things unseen, and is a thoroughly agreeable companion."—*Philadelphia Ledger.*

THE NATURALIST IN LA PLATA. By W. H. HUDSON, C. M. Z. S., author of "Idle Days in Patagonia," and joint author of "Argentine Ornithology." With 27 Illustrations. 8vo. Cloth, $4.00.

"Mr. Hudson is not only a clever naturalist, but he possesses the rare gift of interesting his readers in whatever attracts him, and of being dissatisfied with mere observation unless it enables him to philosophize as well. With his lucid accounts of bird, beast, and insect, no one will fail to be delighted."—*London Academy.*

"A notably clear and interesting account of scientific observation and research. Mr. Hudson has a keen eye for the phenomena with which the naturalist is concerned, and a lucid and delightful way of writing about them, so that any reader may be charmed by the narrative and the reflections here set forth. It is easy to follow him, and we get our information agreeably as he conducts us over the desert pampas, and makes us acquainted with the results of his studies of animals, insects, and birds."—*New York Sun.*

THE NATURALIST ON THE RIVER AMAZONS. By HENRY WALTER BATES, F. R. S., late Assistant Secretary of the Royal Geographical Society. With a Memoir of the Author, by EDWARD CLODD. With Map and numerous Illustrations. 8vo. Cloth, $5.00.

"This famous work is a natural history classic."—*London Literary World.*

"More than thirty years have passed since the first appearance of 'The Naturalist on the River Amazons,' which Darwin unhesitatingly pronounced the best book on natural history which ever appeared in England. The work still retains its prime interest, and in rereading it one can not but be impressed by the way in which the prophetic theories, disputed and ridiculed at the time, have since been accepted. Such is the common experience of those who keep a few paces in advance of their generation. Bates was a 'born' naturalist."—*Philadelphia Ledger.*

"No man was better prepared or gave himself up more thoroughly to the task of studying an almost unknown fauna, or showed a zeal more indefatigable in prosecuting his researches, than Bates. As a collector alone his reputation would be second to none, but there is a great deal more than sheer industry to be cited. The naturalist of the Amazons is, *par excellence*, possessed of a happy literary style. He is always clear and distinct. He tells of the wonders of tropical growth so that you can understand them all."—*New York Times.*

New York: D. APPLETON & CO., 72 Fifth Avenue.

D. APPLETON & CO.'S PUBLICATIONS.

LIFE IN ANCIENT EGYPT AND ASSYRIA. By G. MASPÉRO, late Director of Archæology in Egypt, and Member of the Institute of France. Translated by ALICE MORTON. With 188 Illustrations. 12mo. Cloth, $1.50.

"A lucid sketch, at once popular and learned, of daily life in Egypt in the time of Rameses II, and of Assyria in that of Assurbanipal. . . . As an Orientalist, M. Maspéro stands in the front rank, and his learning is so well digested and so admirably subdued to the service of popular exposition, that it nowhere overwhelms and always interests the reader."—*London Times.*

"Only a writer who had distinguished himself as a student of Egyptian and Assyrian antiquities could have produced this work, which has none of the features of a modern book of travels in the East, but is an attempt to deal with ancient life as if one had been a contemporary with the people whose civilization and social usages are very largely restored."—*Boston Herald.*

A most interesting and instructive book. Excellent and most impressive ideas, also, of the architecture of the two countries and of the other rude but powerful art of the Assyrians, are to be got from it."—*Brooklyn Eagle.*

"The ancient artists are copied with the utmost fidelity, and verify the narrative so attractively presented."—*Cincinnati Times-Star.*

THE THREE PROPHETS: Chinese Gordon; Mohammed-Ahmed; Araby Pasha. Events before, during, and after the Bombardment of Alexandria. By Colonel CHAILLE-LONG, ex-Chief of Staff to Gordon in Africa, ex-United States Consular Agent in Alexandria, etc., etc. With Portraits. 16mo. Paper, 50 cents.

"Comprises the observations of a man who, by reason of his own military experience in Egypt, ought to know whereof he speaks."—*Washington Post.*

"The book contains a vivid account of the massacres and the bombardment of Alexandria. As throwing light upon the darkened problem of Egypt, this American contribution is both a useful reminder of recent facts and an estimate of present situations."—*Philadelphia Public Ledger.*

"Throws an entirely new light upon the troubles which have so long agitated Egypt, and upon their real significance."—*Chicago Times.*

THE MEMOIRS OF AN ARABIAN PRINCESS. By EMILY RUETE, *née* Princess of Oman and Zanzibar. Translated from the German. 12mo, Cloth, 75 cents.

The author of this amusing autobiography is half-sister to the late Sultan of Zanzibar, who some years ago married a German merchant and settled at Hamburg.

"A remarkably interesting little volume. . . . As a picture of Oriental court life, and manners and customs in the Orient, by one who is to the manner born, the book is prolific in entertainment and edification."—*Boston Gazette.*

"The interest of the book centers chiefly in its minute description of the daily life of the household from the time of rising until the time of retiring, giving the most complete details of dress, meals, ceremonies, feasts, weddings, funerals, education, slave service, amusements, in fact everything connected with the daily and yearly routine of life."—*Utica (N. Y.) Herald.*

New York: D. APPLETON & CO., 72 Fifth Avenue.

D. APPLETON & CO.'S PUBLICATIONS.

APPLETONS' GUIDE-BOOKS.

APPLETONS' GENERAL GUIDE TO THE UNITED STATES. With numerous Maps and Illustrations. Revised annually. 12mo. Flexible morocco, with tuck, complete, $2.50.

PART I, separately, NEW ENGLAND AND MIDDLE STATES AND CANADA, cloth, $1.25. PART II, separately, SOUTHERN AND WESTERN STATES, cloth, $1.25.

"Bears every evidence of the amount of care bestowed upon each edition."—*Baltimore American.*

"Without an equal in its special field."—*New York Herald.*

APPLETONS' CANADIAN GUIDE-BOOK. With Maps, numerous Illustrations, and an Appendix giving Fish and Game Laws, and Lessees of Trout and Salmon Rivers. By CHARLES G. D. ROBERTS. 12mo. Flexible cloth, $1.25.

"The author has the skill of a good literary craftsman in collecting and arranging the material demanded of those who aspire to write guide-books that are capable of guiding."—*New York Times.*

"The dignity of the American continent as a place of visitation among the tourists' routes becomes infinitely increased when one looks over this guide-book and finds what a wealth of scenery and historic ground lies at our own threshold."—*Philadelphia Bulletin.*

APPLETONS' GUIDE-BOOK TO ALASKA. By Miss E. R. SCIDMORE. With Maps and Illustrations. 12mo. Flexible cloth, $1.25.

"A charming little volume by an expert traveler, who sees everything that is to be seen and knows a good deal more than she can tell in half a dozen books."—*New York Herald.*

"Crowded with statistical, historical, ethnological, and purely itinerary information, and so handy in form, that it can be heartily recommended to all intending travelers to this great and noble Territory."—*The Critic.*

"As valuable as a complete work of reference for the library as to the tourist who visits the region."—*Washington Post.*

APPLETONS' HAND-BOOK OF AMERICAN SUMMER RESORTS. With Maps, Illustrations, Table of Railroad Fares, etc. Revised annually. 12mo. Paper, 50 cents.

"An enticing pamphlet of mingled pictures and descriptions, which contains about everything which it is at all desirable for the summer wayfarer to know."—*Philadelphia Evening Bulletin.*

APPLETONS' HAND-BOOK OF AMERICAN WINTER RESORTS. FOR TOURISTS AND INVALIDS. Giving complete information as to winter sanitariums, and places of resort in the United States, the West Indies, and Mexico. With Maps, Illustrations, Table of Railroad Fares, etc. Revised annually. 12mo. Paper, 50 cents.

"Unquestionably the best and fullest hand-book of American winter resorts in existence."—*Brooklyn Standard Union.*

D. APPLETON & CO.'S PUBLICATIONS.

APPLETONS' GUIDE-BOOKS.—(*Continued.*)

APPLETONS' DICTIONARY OF NEW YORK AND ITS VICINITY. An Alphabetically Arranged Index to all Places, Societies, Institutions, Amusements, etc. With Maps. Revised annually. 16mo. Paper, 30 cents; flexible cloth, 60 cents.

"A slight examination of the articles makes good the claim to semiannual revision upon the title-page. The Dictionary needs no fresh praise."—*The Nation.*

APPLETONS' EUROPEAN GUIDE-BOOK. A Complete Guide for English-Speaking Travelers to the Continent of Europe, Egypt, Algeria, and the Holy Land. With a Vocabulary of Travel-Talk in English, German, French, and Italian; a Hotel List, and "Specialties of European Cities"; Maps and Plans of Principal Cities; Information about Steamers, Passports, Expenses, Baggage, Custom-Houses, Couriers, Railway Traveling, Valets de Place, Languages, Funds, Best Seasons for Visiting Europe, Table of Coins, etc. Two vols., 12mo. Morocco, flexible, gilt edges, $5.00.

NEW YORK ILLUSTRATED. Containing One Hundred and Forty-three Illustrations of Street Scenes, Buildings, River Views, and other Picturesque Features of the Great Metropolis. With Maps. Large 8vo. Paper, 50 cents.

APPLETONS' GUIDE TO MEXICO, including a Chapter on Guatemala, and an English-Spanish Vocabulary. By ALFRED R. CONKLING, formerly United States Geologist. With a Railway Map and numerous Illustrations. New revised edition. 12mo. Cloth, $2.00.

THE FLORIDA OF TO-DAY. A Guide for Tourists and Settlers. By JAMES WOOD DAVIDSON, M. A. With Railway and County Map printed in colors, and Illustrations. 12mo. Cloth, $1.25.

CONTENTS.—History; Geography; Climate; Divisions; Health; Geology; Travel; Population; Education; Productions; Sporting; Pests; Appendix, containing Railroad Routes, River Routes, List of Hotels.

CALIFORNIA OF THE SOUTH: Its Physical Geography, Climate, Resources, Routes of Travel, and Health Resorts. Being a Complete Guide to Southern California. By WALTER LINDLEY, M. D., and J. P. WIDNEY, A. M., M. D. With Maps and numerous Illustrations. 12mo. Cloth, $2.00.

For sale by all booksellers, or sent by mail on receipt of price by the publishers.

New York: D. APPLETON & CO., 72 Fifth Avenue.

D. APPLETON & CO.'S PUBLICATIONS.

THE UNITED STATES OF AMERICA. A Study of the American Commonwealth, its Natural Resources, People, Industries, Manufactures, Commerce, and its Work in Literature, Science, Education, and Self-Government. Edited by NATHANIEL S. SHALER, S. D., Professor of Geology in Harvard University. In two volumes, royal 8vo. With Maps, and 150 full-page Illustrations. Cloth, $10.00.

In this work the publishers offer something which is not furnished by histories or encyclopædias, namely, a succinct but comprehensive expert account of our country at the present day. The very extent of America and American industries renders it difficult to appreciate the true meaning of the United States of America. In this work the American citizen can survey the land upon which he lives, and the industrial, social, political, and other environments of himself and his fellow-citizens. The best knowledge and the best efforts of experts, editor, and publishers have gone to the preparation of a standard book dedicated to the America of the present day; and the publishers believe that these efforts will be appreciated by those who desire to inform themselves regarding the America of the end of the century.

LIST OF CONTRIBUTORS.

HON. WILLIAM L. WILSON, Chairman of the Ways and Means Committee, Fifty-third Congress.
HON. J. R. SOLEY, formerly Assistant Secretary of the Navy.
EDWARD ATKINSON, LL. D., PH. D.
COL. T. A. DODGE, U. S. A.
COL. GEORGE E. WARING, JR.
J. B. McMASTER, Professor of History in the University of Pennsylvania.
CHARLES DUDLEY WARNER, LL. D.
MAJOR J. W. POWELL, Director of the U. S. Geological Survey and the Bureau of Ethnology.
WILLIAM T. HARRIS, LL. D., U. S. Commissioner of Education.
LYMAN ABBOTT, D. D.
H. H. BANCROFT, author of "Native Races of the Pacific Coast."
HARRY PRATT JUDSON, Head Dean of the Colleges, University of Chicago.
JUDGE THOMAS M. COOLEY, formerly Chairman of the Interstate Commerce Commission.
CHARLES FRANCIS ADAMS.
D. A. SARGENT, M. D., Director of the Hemenway Gymnasium, Harvard University.
CHARLES HORTON COOLEY.
A. E. KENNELLY, Assistant to Thomas A. Edison.
D. C. GILMAN, LL. D , President of Johns Hopkins University.
H. G. PROUT, Editor of the Railroad Gazette.
F. D. MILLET, formerly Vice-President of the National Academy of Design.
F. W. TAUSSIG, Professor of Political Economy in Harvard University.
HENRY VAN BRUNT.
H. P. FAIRFIELD.
SAMUEL W. ABBOTT, M. D., Secretary of the State Board of Health, Massachusetts.
N. S. SHALER.

Sold only by subscription. Prospectus, giving detailed chapter-titles and specimen illustrations, mailed free on request.

New York: D. APPLETON & CO., 72 Fifth Avenue.

www.ingramcontent.com/pod-product-compliance
Lightning Source LLC
Chambersburg PA
CBHW022110290426
44112CB00008B/622